Adopting Artificial Intelligence Tools in Higher Education

This edited volume explores the adoption of artificial intelligence (AI) tools in higher education, specifically focusing on student assessment. It examines the integration of various AI tools within higher education, discussing the challenges and opportunities they present and the innovative solutions they offer.

The chapters explore various issues surrounding the use of AI in higher education and propose potential solutions. The book begins with a systematic exploration of AI's potential, presenting innovative ways to ensure fair and accurate assessments that enhance the overall quality of education. It highlights the benefits of AI-powered grading systems that streamline assessment processes, provide timely feedback, and promote fair evaluations. The text discusses how machine learning algorithms can revolutionize assessment methods, allowing individualized, adaptive testing tailored to each student's unique needs. Furthermore, it examines natural language processing (NLP) techniques for evaluating student essays by analyzing linguistic features such as grammar and semantic coherence. Moreover, it highlights AI-powered virtual assistants offering personalized feedback and learning recommendations. Case studies illustrate successful AI assessment implementations and methods for improving AI-based evaluations. The book also addresses engagement and success in the post-COVID-19 context. It raises concerns about plagiarism and academic integrity, comparing AI solutions to traditional methods while exploring the challenges associated with adopting AI in education.

Educators, administrators, academics, and technology experts working in institutes of higher learning will find this volume compelling. It is also suitable for students taking courses in educational technology, e-learning, and digital learning.

Thangavel Murugan is Assistant Professor in the Department of Information Systems and Security, College of Information Technology, and a Faculty Fellow of the Center for Excellence in Teaching and Learning at United Arab Emirates University. He holds a Doctorate from Madras Institute of

Technology, Anna University, Chennai, and has over 11 years of teaching and research experience. His research specialization includes information security, high-performance computing, blockchain, and educational technology.

Karthikeyan Periasamy is Associate Professor at Thiagarajar College of Engineering (TCE), Madurai, since 2007. He completed his Ph.D. program in Information and Communication Engineering at Anna University in 2015. His research interests include computational intelligence algorithms and educational technology (ET). He has published over 55 papers in international journals, conferences, and book chapters.

A.M. Abirami is Associate Professor at Thiagarajar College of Engineering. She holds a Ph.D. in Text Analytics and Semantic Web. Her interests include data analytics, natural language processing, and engineering education. She has several publications in these areas and has received awards for her work in engineering education.

Adopting Artificial Intelligence Tools in Higher Education

Student Assessment

Edited by Thangavel Murugan,
Karthikeyan Periasamy, and A.M. Abirami

CRC Press
Taylor & Francis Group
Boca Raton London New York

CRC Press is an imprint of the
Taylor & Francis Group, an **informa** business

Designed cover image: Technology For Business Strategy With Robotic And Chess King High-Res Stock Photo - Getty Images

The first edition was published [2025]
by CRC Press
2385 NW Executive Center Drive, Suite 320, Boca Raton, FL 33431

and by CRC Press
4 Park Square, Milton Park, Abingdon, Oxon, OX14 4RN

CRC Press is an imprint of Taylor & Francis Group, LLC

ISBN: 9781032746685 (hbk)
ISBN: 9781032746654 (pbk)
ISBN: 9781003470304 (ebk)

DOI: 10.1201/9781003470304

Typeset in Sabon
by Newgen Publishing UK

Contents

Preface

In the rapidly evolving landscape of higher education, integrating artificial intelligence (AI) tools has emerged as a transformative force, reshaping how we approach student assessments. This edited volume, *Adopting Artificial Intelligence Tools in Higher Education – Student Assessment*, brings together a collection of insightful chapters that explore the multifaceted impact of AI on educational practices, with a particular focus on assessment methodologies. This book aims to provide educators, administrators, researchers, and policymakers with a comprehensive overview of how AI-driven evaluation techniques reshape student practices in higher education. By examining the potential of AI in student assessments, this book aims to inspire readers to explore innovative approaches and technologies that can elevate the quality and effectiveness of teaching and learning in diverse educational settings. The scope of this book is broad, covering key topics such as inclusive learning and assessment, automated grading systems, the potential and drawbacks of machine learning, natural language processing (NLP) in automated essay grading, personalized assessment models, and tools for plagiarism detection and academic integrity. Each chapter offers valuable insights, practical examples, and critical discussions that shed light on the opportunities and challenges of integrating AI tools into higher education assessments.

The potential issues that this book can aid in resolving include

- Lack of consistency and objectivity in grading practices
- Limited accessibility and inclusivity for students with diverse learning needs
- Time-consuming and labor-intensive assessment processes
- Difficulty in providing personalized feedback to students
- Challenges in detecting plagiarism and ensuring academic integrity

By addressing these issues and presenting innovative solutions, this book is a valuable resource for educators, administrators, and policymakers looking to enhance student assessments' quality through AI. Whether you are a seasoned professional looking to stay informed about the latest trends in educational technology or a newcomer seeking a foundational understanding of AI in student assessments, this book provides a valuable resource for engaging with cutting-edge technologies and approaches in the field.

Chapter 1 – AI-Driven Evaluation Techniques: Revolutionizing Student Practices explores the transformative impact of AI on educational assessments, highlighting how AI enhances accuracy, efficiency, and personalized learning experiences. It discusses the benefits of timely feedback, which supports individualized learning pathways, and emphasizes AI's ability to reduce bias through standardized evaluation procedures. Additionally, the chapter addresses ethical and privacy challenges, advocating for responsible AI usage in education. Looking to the future, it suggests that advancements in adaptive learning technologies and innovative assessment methods will further enhance teaching and learning environments, ultimately fostering a more equitable and effective educational landscape.

Chapter 2 – Inclusive Learning and Assessment in the Era of AI delves into the potential of AI to enhance inclusive learning and assessment in higher education. It examines the limitations of traditional assessment methods, which often overlook diverse learning styles and perpetuate biases. The chapter highlights how AI can facilitate personalized learning paths, adaptive assessments, and multimodal interactions, promoting fairness and accuracy in evaluations. It also addresses the importance of mitigating biases in AI algorithms and introduces the sensory learning framework for engaging diverse learners. Additionally, ethical considerations in AI implementation and future research directions are discussed, emphasizing AI's role in empowering educators rather than replacing them.

Chapter 3 – Automated Grading Systems: Enhancing Efficiency and Consistency in Student Assessments investigates the transformative potential of automated grading systems in education, highlighting their mechanisms, benefits, and challenges. It discusses how machine learning algorithms and natural language processing enhance the efficiency and consistency of student assessments, ensuring fair and objective evaluation across various formats. Key advantages include time savings for educators, immediate student feedback, and actionable data insights for tailored instruction. However, the chapter also addresses significant challenges, such as ensuring grading accuracy for complex responses and the risk of bias in algorithms. Finally, it examines future directions for enhancing these systems through advanced technologies and hybrid models.

Chapter 4 – The Potential and Drawbacks of Machine Learning for Student Assessment discusses the transformative role of machine learning (ML) in education, highlighting its potential to create customized learning paths that adapt to individual student proficiency levels. It discusses the benefits of real-time performance insights, enabling immediate adjustments to teaching strategies. By using aggregated performance data, educators can improve curriculum and better meet the requirements of their students. Identifying learning gaps and encouraging focused growth are also stressed in this chapter. Furthermore, it underscores the significance of personalized assessments in boosting student engagement and advocates for accountability and transparency in ML-driven educational decisions through explainable AI (XAI).

Chapter 5 – NLP-Driven Approaches to Automated Essay Grading and Feedback studies the role of natural language processing (NLP) in automating essay grading and feedback. It highlights NLP's ability to provide consistent and rapid evaluations, enhancing large-scale assessments while allowing educators to focus more on instruction. The chapter discusses key NLP techniques and machine learning models for analyzing various essay components, presenting empirical results showcasing model performance. It contrasts human and NLP assessments, emphasizing a hybrid approach to leverage efficiency and contextual understanding. Ethical considerations and future directions for improving NLP's capabilities and ensuring equitable assessment are also examined.

Chapter 6 – Enhancing Learning Outcomes for the Dyslexic Students Using AI-Powered Assistants explains the integration of AI-powered approaches in educational assessments to monitor and enhance the learning progress of dyslexic students. It begins with a comprehensive diagnosis of dyslexia, delving into the unique challenges these students face. The chapter outlines adaptive learning strategies and highlights the role of digital tools and AI-based virtual assistants in fostering effective learning environments. Furthermore, it discusses various assessment types – diagnostic, formative, and summative – utilizing techniques such as classification, association mining, and clustering to improve learning outcomes. Overall, the chapter emphasizes the potential of AI to transform educational experiences for students with dyslexia.

Chapter 7 – Transforming Education through AI-Powered Personalized Assessment Models explores the transformative impact of AI-powered personalized assessment models in education. It highlights how AI-driven assessments provide tailored feedback, enabling students to learn independently while addressing their unique strengths and weaknesses. The chapter discusses the role of personalized AI tools in enhancing student engagement and bridging communication gaps. It introduces the DFDLOF framework, emphasizing continuous formative assessment over traditional exams. Additionally, it examines how AI grading systems alleviate teacher workloads while ensuring fairness, and it delves into innovative feedback mechanisms that boost student motivation and promote a deeper understanding of learning material.

Chapter 8 – Enhancing Student Engagement and Success in Post-COVID-19 through AI Technologies delves into the transformative effects of COVID-19 on education, emphasizing the accelerated integration of AI technologies in teaching and learning. It highlights the role of AI-driven applications in enhancing remote and hybrid learning experiences and promoting adaptive and personalized education. Methodological insights reveal how these tools can be effectively incorporated into educational frameworks to boost engagement and outcomes. Empirical findings showcase improved student engagement, academic performance, and retention rates linked to AI initiatives. Finally, the chapter addresses future directions for AI in education alongside ethical considerations surrounding data privacy and the need for equitable learning environments.

Chapter 9 – AI Tools for Plagiarism Detection and Academic Integrity discusses the transformative role of AI in education, emphasizing the importance of safe and collaborative approaches that enhance learning while maintaining academic integrity. It addresses practical concerns, including academic honesty and the ethical use of AI tools, alongside advocating for digital equity to ensure all students benefit from AI technologies. The discussion extends to the impact of AI on teaching practices, including personalized learning and curriculum development. Finally, the chapter highlights future challenges, such as potential biases, job implications, and the ongoing research needed to optimize AI's role in fostering an inclusive and effective educational environment.

Chapter 10 – Unlocking Potential: Personalizing Learning and Assessment with Cutting-Edge Technologies examines how AI, ML, and big data analytics transform education through personalized learning. These advancements allow tailored content and assessments, real-time feedback, and dynamic adaptation to student needs. Gamification further boosts engagement with interactive rewards and challenges. However, concerns about data privacy, digital equity, and AI bias present challenges that must be addressed. The chapter highlights the importance of ethical frameworks, scalable solutions, and teacher training to ensure successful implementation, forecasting a future of inclusive and effective technology-enhanced education.

The chapters in this book are organized to provide a comprehensive exploration of the impact of AI tools on student assessments in higher education. From revolutionizing student practices with AI-driven evaluation techniques to enhancing efficiency and consistency with automated grading systems, each chapter offers unique perspectives and insights into the transformative power of AI in education. The key features of the book are as follows:

- *Cutting-edge insights*: This book offers the latest research and practical examples of how AI tools revolutionize student assessments in higher education.
- *Diverse perspectives*: Each chapter is authored by experts in the field, offering a diverse range of viewpoints and experiences on the topic.
- *Practical applications*: Readers will find real-world examples and case studies that showcase the practical applications of AI tools in student assessments.
- *Future-oriented discussions*: The chapters explore emerging trends and technologies, providing readers with a forward-looking perspective on the future of AI in education.

The book includes contributions from professionals, practitioners, and researchers from various fields related to higher education and AI. It might provide a well-rounded grasp of the difficulties and opportunities by incorporating several points of view. This might make it more pertinent and worthwhile for people looking for modern perspectives.

Editor Biographies

Thangavel Murugan is Assistant Professor in the Department of Information Systems and Security, College of Information Technology, and a Faculty Fellow of the Center for Excellence in Teaching and Learning, United Arab Emirates University, Abu Dhabi, United Arab Emirates. He received a doctorate from Madras Institute of Technology (MIT) Campus, Anna University, Chennai. He received M.E. in Computer Science and Engineering from J.J. College of Engineering and Technology, Trichy, under Anna University, Chennai (university first rank holder and gold medalist) and B.E. in Computer Science and Engineering from M.A.M College of Engineering, Trichy, under Anna University, Chennai (college first rank holder and gold medalist). He presently holds 11+ years of teaching and research experience from various academic institutions. He has published 10+ articles in international journals, 15+ book chapters with international publishers, 25+ in the proceedings of international conferences, and 3 in national conferences/seminars. He has been actively participating as a reviewer in international journals and conferences. He has attended 100+ workshops/FDPs/conferences at higher learning institutes like IIT and Anna University. He has organized 50+ workshops/FDPs/contests/industry-based courses over the past years. He has been a technical speaker in various workshops/FDPs/conferences. His research specialization is information security, high-performance computing, ethical hacking, cyberforensics, blockchain, cybersecurity intelligence, and educational technology.

Karthikeyan Periasamy has been working as Professor in the Department of IT, Thiagarajar College of Engineering (TCE), Madurai, from 2007 onwards. TCE aims to create quality professionals to meet emerging industrial and societal needs through innovative teaching, applied research, and industrial interaction. He is very proud to be a part of TCE. He completed his Ph.D. in Information and Communication Engineering at Anna University, Chennai, Tamilnadu, India, in 2015. He received his M.E. in Computer Science and Engineering from Anna University, Chennai, Tamilnadu, India, in 2004. He also received B.E. in Computer Science and Engineering from

Madurai Kamaraj University, Madurai, Tamilnadu, India, in 2002. He has published 55+ papers in refereed international journals, conferences, and book chapters. His research interests include computational intelligence algorithms and educational technology (ET).

A.M. Abirami is Professor in the Department of Information Technology, Thiagarajar College of Engineering, Madurai. She is a computer science engineer from Bharathiyar University, Coimbatore, where she was awarded the B.E. degree with first-class distinction in 1999. She then served as a software engineer at Tata Consultancy Services Ltd. from 1999 to 2006, where she worked as a QA member. She earned her M.E. degree from Anna University Tirunelveli with first-class distinction in 2010. Since 2010, she has been working at Thiagarajar College of Engineering, Madurai. She received her PhD in Text Analytics and Semantic Web from Anna University Chennai in 2018. She is interested in improving the teaching and learning methodologies of engineering education. She has earned a "Cambridge International Certificate for Teachers and Trainers" and was trained by Wipro's Mission10x program. She has been one of the top performers in the ICT Tools for Blended and Online Learning FDP conducted by IIT Bombay. She has implemented many active learning strategies for UG students' data structures, programming, and software engineering courses. She is a recognized supervisor/guide for Ph.D. scholars at Anna University, Chennai. She is a professional member of ACM, IEEE, and IET Professional Societies. She is a trained auditor for ISO 9001:2015 by TUV SUD South Asia Ltd., Chennai. She is a member of TCE's Internal Quality Assurance Cell (IQAC). She is a mentor and guide for in-house web applications, data analytics projects, and hackathons. Her research interests include data analytics, natural language processing, text analytics, semantic web technologies, and education technology. She has nearly 25 national/international conference publications, 10 national/international journal publications, and 5 book chapters in text analytics and engineering education. She received the IGIP International Engineering Educator Award and Best Paper Awards from ICTIEE conferences.

Contributor Biographies

V. Aanandaram is a research scholar in the Department of Computer Applications, Kalasalingam Academy of Research and Education, Anand Nagar, Krishnankoil, India.

Ramya Ambikapathi is a postdoctoral researcher in Environmental Ecology Research Group, Department of Environmental and Biological Sciences, University of Eastern Finland, Kuopio, Finland.

R. Annamalai is Associate Professor at the Department of Computer Science and Engineering, Amrita School of Engineering, Amrita Vishwa Vidyapeetham, Chennai. He has 20 years of experience in teaching and industry. His areas of interest include machine learning, programming languages, and optimization algorithms.

A. Arul Edwin Raj is a research fellow at University Tun Hussein Onn Malaysis, Persiaran Tun Dr. Ismail, Johor, Malaysia.

V. P. Arun is Assistant Professor at JKKN College of Engineering and Technology, Namakkal, Tamilnadu, India.

S. Baghavathi Priya is Associate Professor at Department of Computer Science Engineering, Amrita School of Computing, Amrita Vishwa Vidyapeetham, Chennai, Tamilnadu, India. She has an M.Tech. degree (gold medal) and a Ph.D. earned at Jawaharlal Nehru Technological University, Hyderabad. With 25 years of teaching and 14 years of research experience, she has supervised nine scholars and written a book on operating systems. Recognized with awards and publications, she holds memberships in CSI and IAENG.

Maridu Bhargavi is Assistant Professor in the Department of Computer Science and Engineering at Vignan's Foundation for Science, Technology and Research, Vadlamudi, Andhra Pradesh, India.

Shaik Abdul Afzal Biyabani completed his Bachelors from Jawaharlal Nehru Technological University, Kakinada and is currently pursuing his Master's in Coventry University, London, UK.

Dhananjaya G. M. holds a Bachelor's, Master's, and Ph.D. in Computer Science and Engineering from Visvesvaraya Technological University, Belagavi, Karnataka, India. He is currently serving as an Associate Professor in the Department of Artificial Intelligence and Machine Learning (AIML) at Canara Engineering College, Mangalore. With six years of teaching experience and three years of research expertise in engineering education, his research primarily focuses on Personalized recommendation system for Online Educational Environments. His areas of specialization include Data Mining, Data Warehousing, Big Data, Cloud Computing, Agile Technology, Information Retrieval, Research Methodology, and Personalized Learning Recommendation Systems. Dr. Dhananjaya is an active lifetime member of IFERP (Membership ID: PM14396728) and a member of the International Association of Engineers (Membership ID: 314882).

Sivaraman Eswaran is Senior Lecturer with the Electrical and Computer Engineering Department at Curtin University, Malaysia. He holds the position of Program Coordinator for the Bachelor of Computing (Cybersecurity) program since January 2023. In addition to his academic role, he serves as the leader of the Sarawak Digital Economy Corporation (SDEC) Cybersecurity Keylabs Working Group. In this capacity, he actively contributes to driving cybersecurity advancements in the state of Sarawak, Malaysia.

R. H. Goudar received the B.E. degree in computer science and engineering, the M.Tech. degree in Computer Network Engineering, and the Ph.D. degree in computer science and engineering. He is currently working as an Associate Professor in the Department of Computer Science and Engineering, at Visvesvaraya Technological University, Belagavi. He has 19 years of teaching experience at professional institutes across India. He was a Faculty Member of the International Institute of Information Technology, Pune, for four years, and the Indian National Satellite Master Control Facility, Hassan, India. He has published more than 150 papers in international journals, book chapters, and conferences of high reputation. His research interests include the semantic web, cloud computing, big data, machine learning, and deep learning and its applications. He has received various awards, such as the Outstanding Faculty Award, the Research Performance Award, the Young Research Scientist Award from VGST Karnataka, and the Eminent Engineer Award from the Honorable Chief Minister of Karnataka.

Senthil Jayapal is Lecturer in College of Computing and Information Sciences, at University of Technology and Applied Sciences, Ibra. He obtained his Master of Technology in Information Technology at SRM University Chennai, India, and his Bachelor of Engineering in Computer Science and Engineering at Annamalai University, Chidambaram, India.

A. Judith Arockiya Gladies is Assistant Professor in SACS M.A.V.M.M. Engineering College, Madurai, India. She has eight years of experience in teaching computer science and engineering with many technical articles published in prestigious national and international publications. Her current research interests include network and cyber security.

D. Kabalishwaran is Assistant System Engineer at Tamilnadu Egovernance Agency, Anna Salai, Chennai, India.

G. Kalaiarasi is Assistant Professor in the Department of Advanced Computer Science and Engineering at Vignan's Foundation for Science, Technology and Research, Vadlamudi, Andhra Pradesh, India.

S. Kanthimathi is Assistant Professor at Vellore Institute of Technology, Chennai, Tamil Nadu, India. She earned her Ph.D. in Computer Science and Engineering from Visveswaraya Technological University, Karnataka. She specializes in the research areas of cloud computing, network security, and machine learning.

K. Kartheeban is Associate Professor in the Department of Computer Science and Engineering, Kalasalingam Academy of Research and Education, Anand Nagar, Krishnankoil, India.

B. Kavya Sai is a second-year B.Tech. student in the Department of Computer Science and Engineering, Amrita Viswa Vidyapeetham, Chennai. She has a deep passion for mathematics which drives her interest in AI, machine learning, and quantum computing. She is dedicated to contributing to technological advancements. Her research focuses on innovative AI applications and computational biology.

D. Lakshminarasimman is Manager at IoT and Hardware Engineering, Tekion India Pvt Ltd., Pallavaram, Chennai, India.

Tamil Selvi Madeswaran is Professor at Department of Information Technology, University of Technology and Applied Sciences, Nizwa, Oman. She obtained her Ph.D. from Anna University, with 24 years of teaching and 17 years of research experience, and specializes in fuzzy logic, semantic web, machine learning, data analytics, and networks. She's a Computer Society of India member and reviewer for national and international journals.

Anjali Mathur is Associate Professor at VIT Bhopal University, Bhopal, Madhya Pradesh, India.

V. Murugananthan is a researcher at School of Computing, Asia Pacific University of Technology & Innovation (APU), Technology Park, Kuala Lumpur, Malaysia. He completed his Ph.D. in Computer Science, major in Data Mining and Data Warehousing from Bharathiar University, Coimbatore, India. He has 20+ years of IT experience, both in academic and industry in India, Nigeria, and Malaysia. He has published more than 20 research papers in reputed international and national journals which are indexed in Scopus, Web of Science, and peer-reviewed journals. He has presented nearly 15+ research papers in international and national conference proceedings and has published three monographs.

Prayasha Nanda is a second-year undergraduate student pursuing computer science (specialization in AIML) at Vellore Institute of Technology, Chennai. She is passionate about understanding how computers perceive the world through the logical frameworks developed by the brilliant minds of the past. She is also an avid writer.

Anand Nayyar received Ph.D (Computer Science) from Desh Bhagat University in 2017 in the area of Wireless Sensor Networks, Swarm Intelligence and Network Simulation. He is currently working in School of Computer Science-Duy Tan University, Da Nang, Vietnam as Professor, Scientist, Vice-Chairman (Research) and Director-IoT and Intelligent Systems Lab. A Certified Professional with 125+ Professional certificates. Published more than 160+ Research Papers in various High-Quality ISI-SCI/SCIE/ SSCI Impact Factor Journals cum Scopus/ESCI indexed Journals, 70+ Papers in International Conferences indexed with Springer, IEEE and ACM Digital Library, 50+ Book Chapters with Citations: 10000+, H-Index: 55 and I-Index: 190. He has 18 Australian Patents, 6 German Patents, 4 Japanese Patents, 33 Indian Design cum Utility Patents, 1 USA Patent, 3 Indian Copyrights and 2 Canadian Copyrights to his credit. Awarded 44 Awards for Teaching and Research. He is listed in Top 2% Scientists as per Stanford University (2020, 2021, 2022). He is Listed on Research.com (No:2 in Viet Nam; D-INDEX: 31). He is acting as Editor-in-Chief of IGI-Global, USA Journal titled "International Journal of Smart Vehicles and Smart Transportation (IJSVST)", and Managing Editor "IJKSS"-Scopus Q3 Indexed.

V. Nikhil is currently pursuing a B.Tech. degree in Computer Science Engineering with a specialization in AI at Amrita Vishwa Vidyapeetham,

Chennai, India. His research interests encompass medical image analysis, AI-based classification systems, and natural language processing (NLP). He has published and co-authored research papers on topics such as medical image classification and object detection.

Minal Patil holds MCA degree from Visvesvaraya Technological University, Belagavi. Currently, she is pursuing a Ph.D. in Computer Science and Engineering at Visvesvaraya Technological University. With 12 years of teaching experience in engineering education, her research interests include machine learning, artificial intelligence.

A. Peter Soosai Anandaraj is Assistant Professor in Veltech Rangarajan Dr. Sagunthala R&D Institute of Science and Technology, Chennai, India. He holds a Ph.D. in Information Communication Engineering from Anna University, Chennai. He has 8 years of experience in teaching computer science and engineering, with many technical articles published in prestigious national and international publications, as well as four national patents. His current research interests include network and cyber security.

R. Renugadevi is Assistant Professor in the Department of Computer Science and Engineering at Vignan's Foundation for Science, Technology and Research, Vadlamudi, Andhra Pradesh, India.

P. Ranjith Kumar is Assistant Professor in the Department of Electronics and Communication Engineering at PSR Engineering College, Sivakasi, Tamilnadu, India.

Vijayalaxmi N. Rathod received the B.E. degree in information science and engineering and the M.Tech. degree in computer science and engineering from Visvesvaraya Technological University, Belagavi. She is currently a Research Scholar with the Department of Computer Science and Engineering, Visvesvaraya Technological University. Her research interests include image processing and big data, cloud computing, pattern recognition, information retrieval, and machine learning.

Varsana Renganayagan is a second-year undergraduate student pursuing Computer Science at Vellore Institute of Technology, Chennai. She is passionate about leveraging innovative tools and algorithms to create impactful solutions that enhance everyday life and drive technological progress.

S. K. Sajida Sultana is an Assistant Professor in the Department of Computer Science and Engineering at Vignan's Foundation for Science, Technology and Research, Vadlamudi, Andhra Pradesh, India. She is passionate about technology and research. Her primary interests lie in Natural Language

Processing (NLP) and Deep Learning. She actively mentors students and contributes to academic research, shaping the future of AI-driven solutions.

T. P. Saravanan is Assistant Professor at Kongu Engineering College, Perundurai, Erode, Tamilnadu, India.

B. Saritha is Associate Professor at the Department of Bio Medical Engineering, Erode Sengunthar College of Engineering, Tamilnadu, India.

B. Senthilkumaran is Assistant Professor at the Department of Computer Science and Engineering, School of Computing, VelTech Rangarajan Dr. Sagunthala R&D Institute of Science and Technology (deemed to be a university), Chennai, India. He has published 15 research articles and filed two patents.

S. Sridevi is Professor in the Department of Computer Science and Engineering, Vel Tech Rangarajan Dr. Sagunthala R&D Institute of Science and Technology, Chennai. She completed her B.E. in Computer Science and Engineering from Thiagarajar College of Engineering, her M.E. in Computer Science and Engineering from R.V.S. College of Engineering and Technology, and her Ph.D. in Medical Image Processing from Anna University, Chennai, in the year 2015. She has 19 years of teaching experience and 8 years of industry experience.

Shravan Venkatraman is a final-year undergraduate student pursuing computer science at Vellore Institute of Technology, Chennai. With over two years of research experience in deep learning and computer vision, he is passionate about streamlining innovative solutions for real-world challenges.

S. C. Vetrivel is Associate Professor at Kongu Engineering College, Perundurai, Erode, Tamilnadu, India.

V. Vijayalakshmi is Assistant Professor in CSE, Vel Tech Rangarajan Dr. Sagunthala R&D Institute of Science and Technology, Chennai. She is pursuing her Ph.D. in computer science and engineering at Dr. M. G. R. Educational and Research Institute, Maduravoyal, Chennai. She has published papers in various international seminars and conferences. Her area of interest includes network security, IoT, cyber-security, VANET communication, and data analytics, and mobile computing. She has 10 years of teaching experience.

1 AI-Driven Evaluation Techniques
Revolutionizing Student Practices

S. K. Sajida Sultana, R. Renugadevi,
Maridu Bhargavi, and Shaik Abdul Afzal Biyabani

1.1 Introduction

In the rapidly evolving landscape of education, artificial intelligence (AI) has emerged as a transformative force, reshaping traditional student evaluation methods. As educational institutions adopt digital platforms, AI-driven evaluation techniques are becoming increasingly prevalent, enabling more personalized, efficient, and comprehensive assessments. This chapter explores the revolutionary impact of AI on student evaluation, examining how it addresses traditional limitations and presents new possibilities for enhancing student learning practices.

1.2 Comprehensive Overview of AI in Student Evaluation

It provides a detailed examination of how AI-driven techniques are currently being utilized in educational settings, offering insights into various tools such as automated grading, adaptive testing, and learning analytics. This comprehensive overview helps educators, administrators, and policymakers understand the potential applications and benefits of AI in student assessment.

1.2.1 Identification of Benefits and Challenges

By analyzing the advantages of AI-driven evaluation—such as personalized feedback, bias reduction, scalability, and timeliness—the chapter highlights how these techniques address the limitations of traditional evaluation methods. Additionally, it underscores the ethical concerns and challenges of AI implementation, such as data privacy and algorithmic bias, emphasizing the importance of responsible and equitable AI use in education.

1.2.2 Ethical Concerns of AI-Based Learning Systems

Data Privacy: Because the data that AI-based systems have to collect involves many ethical concerns about accessing data without permission, misuse of

DOI: 10.1201/9781003470304-1

the same, and leakage, some of the solution that is proposed includes data encryption, access control, anonymizing data, and transparency in policies for collecting and using data.

Bias in Algorithms: There will be a possibility of algorithmic bias if the train data isn't representative enough. Solution proposed includes use of diverse datasets, regularly auditing the model, collaborating with educators to ensure a fair outcome.

1.2.3 Ethical Frameworks in AI-Driven Education: Informed Consent

Communication should be transparent with the student and the guardians about data collection and usage. The "Letter to the Teacher" has a suggestion of AI assisting the teachers but not replacing the teacher. It makes the suggestion based on the fact that, though the teacher must be absent, his sympathy worth is not available through an AI to the student.

Audit Trails: Periodical reviews and audits of algorithms from AI are necessary so as to ensure that no groups face negative impacts either implicit or explicit.

Data Sensing and Transparency Best Practices: Privacy by design: Safety and privacy should be made present within an AI architecture of a system.

Educational Collaboration: Tools need to be designed by collaboration between educators, students, and AI developers so that educational needs and ethical standards are met. **Audits and Fairness Constraints:** Regular checks for the presence of biases and privacy issues in AI models to correct these.

1.2.4 AI Algorithms Used in Evaluation Techniques

- **NLP Scoring of Written Response:** It analyzes grammar, coherence, and the strength of arguments. While efficient, NLP models are easily flummoxed by subtle meanings.
- **Machine Learning (ML) for Adaptive Testing and Predictive Analytics:** This determines trends in student performance to change the difficulty of questions to predict outcomes. However, without diverse training data, the ML model may bias.
- Deep learning (DL) models in this aspect include CNN and transformers; they give you 360-degree view of any student performance through the text and other data types besides the image. DL has requirements like large amounts of labeled data as well as high processing capacity.

Furthermore, the chapter can be related to data requirements for all these algorithms, such that proper results could be ensured without bias in large, quality data, which is representative to the topic. Data-related and relevant ethical concerns include privacy during data acquisition and mitigations against biases in AI deployments in educational environments.

1.2.5 Exploration of Future Trends

The chapter presents an informed discussion on the potential future developments of AI in education, including more sophisticated adaptive learning systems and holistic assessment methods.

Adaptive learning systems are AI-powered platforms that customize course materials according to each student's needs, pace, and abilities. Such systems take into account student interactions to adjust the level of content difficulty and offer targeted support in the form of more practice or different explanations that fill in gaps in understanding. This method ensures real-time adjustments to ensure efficient, engaging, and individualized learning paths to help the students achieve their full potential.

Holistic assessment methods: A more holistic method of assessment approaches the capabilities and skills a student may develop in relation to a much broader outlook than relying merely on testing or examination results. A holistic assessment may include diverse aspects, including critical thinking, creativity, collaboration, and emotional intelligence, which will be addressed when using AI. In assessments, different data sources could be merged, including project-based assessments, peer assessments, and behavioral measures. Not just what a student knows is to be understood but the application of knowledge in several contexts. Therefore, such holistic assessments support a holistic view of student growth as well as preparation for a real-world challenge. Therefore, adaptive learning systems as well as holistic assessment methodologies are a new step of AI systems which do not just evaluate but actually help make pathways for personalized and lifelong learning for students.

Holistic assessment methods involve many qualities that include critical thinking, creativity, collaboration, and emotional intelligence to determine a student's skills instead of results from the test. Utilizing AI, different types of data sources such as project-based and peer assessments are combined in order to assess not only what the students know but how they apply knowledge in various contexts. This approach provides an overall view of student development and prepares them for the complexity of the real world. Together, adaptive learning systems and holistic assessments form a step in AI-driven education that supports personalized lifelong learning pathways.

1.2.6 Promotion of Informed Decision-Making

By compiling current research and including key references, the chapter serves as a valuable resource for educators and researchers looking to integrate AI-driven evaluation methods into their practices. The provided references and

DOI links facilitate access to original research, supporting informed decision-making regarding the adoption and ethical use of AI in education.

1.2.7 Advocacy for Enhanced Student Learning Practices

The chapter advocates for the use of AI to foster more dynamic, responsive, and equitable learning environments. By highlighting how AI-driven evaluation can provide immediate, personalized feedback and support diverse learning needs, it positions AI as a tool to revolutionize traditional educational practices and improve student outcomes.

Overall, this work contributes to the ongoing conversation around the role of AI in transforming educational evaluation techniques, providing a foundation for future research, policy development, and practical implementation in diverse educational contexts.

1.3 Background Work

Azevedo et al. (2021) uses both qualitative and quantitative data sources in modeling the effect of school closures, such as those from the World Bank's Human Capital Index and the PISA scores from the OECD. It considers three different scenarios: optimistic, intermediate, and pessimistic. For each of these, the study provides estimates for losses in learning-adjusted years of schooling, increases in dropout rates, and projected future income losses, reflecting how the economic impact of COVID-19 might further exacerbate school dropout rates due to household income shocks.

Ahmad et al. (2023) also highlights the predominance of grading and assessment applications, noting that they are widely explored and implemented with considerable success. However, it points out that AI alone has limitations, particularly in areas that require nuanced understanding, such as emotional and social aspects of learning, which current AI tools struggle to address effectively. Furthermore, the article includes a bibliometric analysis that identifies major research trends and geographic contributions in AI and education research from 2014 to 2022, with the United States leading in output. This analysis serves as a baseline for future research aimed at overcoming the challenges AI faces in educational settings.

Baral et al. (2021) on the automatic scoring improvement of open-ended math responses investigates AI ways that increase the accuracy grade in more complex, multimodal answers with mathematical expressions and images. Using the model SBERT-Canberra for text-mode grading as well as CLIP analysis on both text and images in one space, this error analysis shows that it depends on the complexity as well as inconsistency in the grading done by teachers. The Math Term Frequency (MTF) model monitors the frequency of the common math terms with specific scores that refine the math-specific language interpretation for enhancing the system accuracy. Using this ensemble approach would deliver more accurate, fairer scoring for the diverse responses from the students.

In Dawson et al. (2017), the authors discuss the design and impact of learning analytics in an initiative aimed at improving student retention in higher education. The research that would be emphasized is how predictive analytics can identify at-risk students through analysis of data points like academic performance and engagement metrics. From the assessment, it is apparent that ensuring timely interventions paid off for the program, hence increasing retention rates. The challenges identified include data privacy issues, integration with existing systems, and faculty buy-in. Accordingly, despite learning analytics potentially having a revolutionary effect on student success, further research might be needed in order to address some of the ethical questions and to scale appropriately in other learning environments.

Fahmy (2024) explores how students view AI-enhanced assessment tools in terms of their motivation, engagement, and feedback capabilities. The findings are that, overall, students are more fascinated with AI-driven assessments as they are personalized and adaptive, thus responding to a student's learning style and pace. According to many students, such instruments increase their desire to study because they provide instant feedback, thereby enabling them to know what they are excellent at and where they need improvement. Some issues associated with the accuracy of assessments by AI and a general lack of human contact with the learners are also noted in such discussions, where it is argued that although AI could help supplement the learning process, it should not replace human effort. Overall, findings suggest that AI-based assessments, if properly implemented, will significantly improve the motivation and engagement of the students while providing timely and constructive feedback.

Holstein et al. (2019), deals with the co-designing of a classroom orchestration tool aimed at supporting the interaction between teachers and AI systems in real-time educational settings. The article is crucial in underlining the role of teacher–AI complementarity in improving teaching practice through a well-designed tool that offers immediate feedback on student engagement and learning behavior. The co-design process engages educators and technologists to ensure that the tool will be aligned with classroom dynamics and support pedagogical goals. The findings of this research suggest that such orchestration tools may empower teachers to use AI capabilities while retaining their central role in guiding student learning, thereby creating a more interactive and responsive learning environment.

Hooda et al. (2022) explore how AI has transformed higher education assessment and how it gives students customized feedback, thus ensuring improved student learning outcomes. The article also identifies such tools as automated grading and intelligent tutoring systems through which student engagement can be fostered and weaknesses improved. Acknowledging that the possible biases and inefficiency AI holds can be lowered and diminished, there remains another major challenge of dealing with issues of data privacy. Education practitioners need training regarding use in the classroom setting and working appropriately with these types of machines. To summarize, the article calls upon making intelligent use of available tools based on AI for aiding success to students and personalize their experience within education.

1.4 The Need for AI in Student Evaluation

Traditional student evaluation practices, such as standardized testing and periodic assessments, have long been criticized for their limited scope, lack of personalization, and potential biases (Sutton, 2019). These conventional methods often fail to provide a holistic view of a student's knowledge, skills, and competencies.

- **Student Data Collection:** Collects student performance data.
- **Data Preprocessing:** Prepares and anonymizes the data.
- **AI Assessment Model:** AI analyzes data and provides initial feedback.
- **AI Feedback to Students:** Delivers personalized feedback to students.
- **Student Engagement and Response:** Students act on feedback to improve.
- **Teacher's Final Review:** Teachers adjust and validate AI feedback.
- **Continuous Learning and Improvement:** Refines AI model based on feedback loops.

As education systems seek to accommodate diverse learning styles and individualized student needs, the integration of AI offers a promising solution. AI-driven evaluation can analyze vast amounts of data in real time, providing insights that enable educators to tailor their teaching methods to each student.

1.4.1 Challenges and Solutions of "The Need for AI in Student Evaluation"

Incorporating AI into student evaluation presents unique challenges, particularly related to data privacy, algorithmic bias, accessibility, and the adaptability of educational systems.

Here is an exploration of these challenges and potential solutions, supported by references.

- **Challenge: Data Privacy and Security**
  AI-driven student evaluation systems rely on the collection and analysis of large volumes of sensitive data, including students' academic performance, personal details, and behavior patterns. This data dependency raises concerns about privacy and security. Students' data must be protected from unauthorized access, misuse, or breaches, in compliance with regulations like the General Data Protection Regulation (GDPR).

Solution: To mitigate privacy risks, educational institutions should implement robust data encryption, access control mechanisms, and anonymize techniques to protect student data. Furthermore, transparency in how data is collected, stored, and used is vital. Institutions should obtain informed consent from students or their guardians, clearly communicating data usage policies (Williamson & Eynon, 2020). Adopting privacy-by-design principles in AI systems, where privacy safeguards are integrated into the system's architecture, can enhance trust and compliance with data protection regulations.

- **Challenge: Algorithmic Bias**
  AI systems used in student evaluation may inherit biases present in their training data, potentially leading to unfair assessments. For instance, automated grading systems trained on a specific demographic's responses might not accurately evaluate students from different cultural, linguistic, or socioeconomic backgrounds (Holstein et al., 2019). This bias can perpetuate inequalities and result in biased outcomes that do not reflect the true capabilities of all students.

  Solution: Addressing algorithmic bias requires a multi-faceted approach. First, diverse and representative datasets should be used to train AI models to ensure inclusivity across different student populations. Second, ongoing monitoring and auditing of AI systems can help identify and mitigate biases as they arise. Engaging educators, students, and AI developers in collaborative discussions about the design and evaluation of these systems can provide feedback that enhances fairness (Holstein et al., 2019). Moreover, adopting explainable AI (XAI) techniques can make the decision-making process of AI systems more transparent, allowing educators to understand and challenge assessment outcomes when necessary.

- **Challenge: Integration into Existing Educational Systems**
  Many educational institutions have established traditional evaluation systems, and integrating AI-driven assessment methods may require significant changes in curriculum, teacher training, and infrastructure. Resistance to change, lack of technical expertise, and resource constraints can pose additional barriers to AI adoption in student evaluation.

  Solution: A gradual, phased approach to AI integration can help ease the transition for educators and students. Institutions should start by implementing AI tools in specific aspects of evaluation, such as automated grading of assignments, before expanding their use (Zawacki-Richter et al., 2019). Professional development and training programs for educators are essential to build familiarity with AI tools and encourage adoption. Partnerships with technology providers can also offer support and resources during the implementation process. Furthermore, involving educators in the development and customization of AI-driven evaluation systems can foster a sense of ownership and alignment with educational objectives.

While AI-driven evaluation offers numerous benefits, addressing challenges related to data privacy, bias, accessibility, and integration is essential to ensure its effective implementation. By adopting ethical practices, enhancing inclusivity, and providing adequate support to educators, AI can be harnessed to revolutionize student evaluation in a way that is fair, secure, and accessible to all.

1.4.2 AI-Based Assessment Tools

Several AI-based assessment tools have gained popularity for their ability to offer more nuanced evaluations. These tools utilize machine learning algorithms, natural language processing (NLP), and data analytics to assess student performance in various ways:

Automated Grading Systems: AI-powered automated grading systems can evaluate open-ended responses, essays, and assignments. NLP algorithms can assess written content for coherence, relevance, grammar, and argument strength (Taghipour & Ng, 2016). Automated grading not only reduces the workload for educators but also provides instant feedback to students, allowing for immediate reflection and improvement.

Adaptive Testing: Adaptive testing adjusts the difficulty level of questions in real time based on the student's performance. AI algorithms analyze each response, determining the student's knowledge level and adapting subsequent questions to maintain an optimal challenge. This approach ensures a more accurate assessment of a student's capabilities and learning progress.

Learning Analytics: AI-driven learning analytics track students' interactions with educational materials, identifying patterns that reveal learning preferences, strengths, and areas needing improvement (Dawson et al., 2017). By analyzing data from various sources such as quizzes, assignments, and classroom participation, AI provides insights that help educators make informed decisions about instructional strategies.

Exploring about the user experience of AI-driven evaluation tools for students and educators in promoting equitable educational practices:

Student Experience: AI tools offer personalized, instant feedback and adaptive learning, which may increase engagement. However, for an inclusive experience, accessibility features such as screen readers, closed captions, and alternate inputs are necessary to support diverse learners, including those with disabilities.

Educator Experience: The AI tools made grading easier and saved time, which could be directed toward differentiated support. The transparency of AI in assessment-making is essential to the trust and eventual adoption of such tools by an educator. Educator professional development also helps educators understand AI better and interpret insights that lead to issues with accessibility or bias from AI tools.

Accessibility and Equity: Universal design principles applied in flexible formats for assessments and multisensory feedback create accessibility. Bias can be detected and corrected through regular auditing of AI tools to make them more fair for any demographics or learning styles.

1.4.3 Case Studies of Institutions Successfully Implementing AI-Driven Evaluation Techniques

- **University of Southern California—AI-Powered Feedback Systems:**
  The University of Southern California makes use of AI-based writing tools such as Grammarly and Turnitin to make immediate responses in their writing programs in response to student writing assignments. Students submit their papers to a site where grammar, style, and originality will be reviewed so that actionable responses can be made quickly and immediately. Such results of the use of these texts are improvements in the quality of student writing and engagement with the process.
- **Purdue University—Course Signals**
  Purdue University designed the Course Signals system, which uses predictive analytics to identify at-risk students using engagement and performance data. The system analyzes grades, attendance, and course interactions and sends alerts to the students and academic advisors so that they can intervene early. This initiative has increased retention rates and academic performance. In some cases, retention is reported to have risen by as much as 10%.
- **The University of Toronto—AI in Course Design**
  The University of Toronto has implemented AI-based tools in the course development and assessment process. The machine learning algorithms help the university assess the continuous feedback received from students and their performance data for improvement in both the course materials and assessment methods. Thus, this constant improvement loop yielded a better course delivery and performance among students and thus demonstrates the potential of AI in teaching.

1.4.4 Challenges and Solutions of "AI-Based Assessment Tools"

AI-based assessment tools, including automated grading systems, adaptive testing, and learning analytics, present several challenges when implemented in educational settings. These challenges range from technical limitations to ethical concerns, which need to be addressed to maximize the benefits of AI in student assessment. Here is an analysis of key challenges and potential solutions, with supporting references:

- **Challenge: Limited Contextual Understanding**
  AI-based assessment tools, particularly those relying on NLP, often struggle with understanding the nuanced context of students' written responses. For example, automated grading systems may misinterpret the quality of arguments or creativity in essays, leading to inaccurate scores. This limitation arises because AI models primarily rely on pre-trained algorithms that may not fully capture the diversity and complexity of human thought (Taghipour & Ng, 2016).

  Solution: Enhancing AI models with more sophisticated, context-aware NLP algorithms can improve their ability to understand student responses more accurately. Integrating human–AI hybrid systems, where AI conducts an initial assessment followed by a review by human educators, can also address limitations in contextual understanding. Continuous training of AI models on diverse datasets that include various writing styles, cultural contexts, and subject areas can further enhance their accuracy and reliability.

- **Challenge: Risk of Over-Reliance on Automation**
  AI-based assessment tools, particularly automated grading systems, can lead to an over-reliance on technology, potentially undermining the educator's role in the evaluation process. Over-reliance on AI may result in a lack of critical human judgment, creativity, and empathy that are essential in holistic student assessment. Moreover, AI tools may miss certain qualitative aspects of student work, such as creativity, ethical considerations, and the application of knowledge in real-world contexts (Luckin & Holmes, 2016).

  Solution: Implementing AI-based assessment as a supportive tool rather than a standalone solution is crucial. Educators should be involved in the final evaluation, using AI-generated insights to inform and supplement their judgment. This hybrid approach ensures that qualitative aspects of student performance are not overlooked. Additionally, educators should receive training to understand AI's capabilities and limitations, allowing them to use AI tools effectively and critically.

1.5 Critical Analysis of Existing AI Applications in Education: Examining Both Successes and Failures

Best Practice: Adaptive Learning Systems: DreamBox and Knewton have been able to adapt their content to individual students, adjusting the degree of difficulty based on real-time performance. Such systems have been proven to increase the engagement and even achievements of students in learning mathematics and language skills where mastering specific steps is essential.

Automated Grading Systems: AI-based grading tools such as Gradescope have streamlined grading processes, taking less time from instructors' hands in assessment and making scoring much more consistent. They are especially helpful for large classes, where teachers can concentrate more on instruction and interaction with students.

AI-Powered Coaching: Virtual coaches similar to those offered in Duolingo provide immediate feedback in addition to steering students through their practice by corrective recommendations and motivational feedback, for instance. Such systems are already becoming popular for engagement building and retention in the likes of language learning applications as well as test preparation.

Predictive Analytics for Student Success: This is how institutions are employing AI-driven analytics tools that identify at-risk students regarding dropping out or failing a course. Systems like Purdue University's Course Signals provide timely interventions, leading to improved retention rates and better academic success.

1.5.1 Notable Failures and Challenges

- **Bias in Automated Grading:** Some AI grading systems, such as standardized testing or admissions, have come under criticism for biasing against certain demographics or against non-standard writing styles. For example, automated scoring of essays may go awry with unconventional syntax or cultural references, resulting in unfair judgments.

- **Privacy and Data Security:** AI systems significantly depend on large amounts of student data to deliver personal learning experiences. Issues related to privacy and data security have cropped up, as students' personal and academic information could be at the risk of being misused or breached.

- **Lack of Contextual Understanding:** While AI tutoring systems are handy in many areas, it is not really very good at nuanced understandings of complex subjects such as literature or ethics. Thus, feedback may often be too simplistic, or it may even lead to rote learning experiences without developing critical thinking or creativity.

- **Over-Dependence on AI:** In a few cases, schools have overly relied on AI-driven tools, downplaying the human educator. For example, some low-budget institutions have used automated systems to cut costs, which has done away with meaningful teacher–student interaction, essential for all-rounded development and engagement.

1.5.2 Scope for Improvement and Directions for the Future

In the near future, AI in education may be expected to improve, with better management of context and bias.

Strengthen the Future Outlook by Proposing Specific Research Directions:

1 **Bias and Fairness:** Research could develop standardized methods for detecting and reducing AI biases in educational settings.

2 **Holistic Assessment:** Studies could explore AI's role in assessing qualitative skills like creativity and collaboration, providing a more complete view of student growth.
3 **Adaptive Learning for Diverse Contexts:** Research could focus on adapting AI tools for diverse cultural and linguistic backgrounds, supporting global inclusivity.
4 **Ethics and Data Privacy:** Developing ethical frameworks for handling student data responsibly would be essential, especially across different regulatory environments.
5 **Human–AI Collaboration:** Future studies could explore effective teacher–AI collaboration models that blend AI insights with educator expertise.
6 **Scalability and Affordability:** Research could aim to create affordable, scalable AI solutions, such as lightweight or open-source models for resource-limited schools.

Weakness:
It has risks of privacy while emotion and voice analytics, bias in the collaborative grading process, no transparency about grading when done with AI, and an over-reliance on AI for real-time interventions. Their weaknesses are in need of being addressed through focused research in using AI without compromising ethics and effectiveness.

1.6 Technical and Infrastructure Limitation

Implementing AI-based assessment tools requires advanced digital infrastructure, including reliable internet connectivity, data storage, and processing power.

In regions with limited access to such infrastructure, the adoption of AI-driven assessment tools may be challenging, leading to disparities in educational opportunities (Azevedo et al., 2021).

Solution: Developing lightweight, mobile-friendly AI assessment tools can enhance accessibility in low-resource environments. Offline functionalities and cloud-based solutions can further reduce the dependence on high-end infrastructure. Partnerships between educational institutions, governments, and technology-providers can facilitate investment in digital infrastructure, particularly in underprivileged areas. Additionally, open-source AI tools can provide cost-effective solutions for institutions with limited resources.

1.7 Benefits of AI-Driven Evaluation

AI-driven evaluation techniques offer several advantages over traditional assessment methods:

Personalized Feedback: AI can generate personalized feedback tailored to individual student performance, providing specific recommendations for improvement. This level of detail is often challenging to achieve through manual grading alone (Zawacki-Richter et al., 2019).

Reducing Bias: AI algorithms, when designed and implemented with care, have the potential to minimize human biases in evaluation. Unlike human assessors, AI can apply consistent criteria across all assessments, promoting fairness and objectivity in grading (West, Kraut, & Chew, 2019).

Scalability: AI-driven evaluation systems can efficiently handle large volumes of student data, making them suitable for institutions with high enrollment. This scalability is particularly beneficial for online education platforms and massive open online courses (MOOCs) (Raza et al., 2021).

In Figure 1.1, beginning with the student's submission of work, the flowchart illustrates the steps involved in AI-driven student assessment. The AI system then creates an initial score after analyzing the contribution using a variety of techniques (text analysis, code assessment, etc.). It offers thorough, tailored feedback that identifies both areas of strength and room for development.

1.7.1 Types of Real-Time Feedback Mechanisms

Automated Grading and Instant Scoring: Talk about tools that can provide instant feedback on quizzes and assignments to help students recognize their areas of strength and improvement.

Adaptive Feedback: Discuss how platforms can modify the content difficulty level according to the student's responses in order to allow individualized pacing and promote mastery of concepts.

Skill-Based Feedback: Describe the skill-based feedback concerning the language and STEM subjects in order to help the learner understand the areas where improvement is needed.

Delivery Channels:

Dashboard Views: Suggest how the dashboard views may be utilized for tracking and monitoring the students' performance trend in real time.

Mobile and Email Alerts: The alerts are suggested to use when there is poor performance or missing assignments as an alert for the student well in advance.

In-Platform Hints and Explanations: Explain how in some platforms, there will be hints or explanations in case of wrong answers given that promote immediate reflection and self-correction.

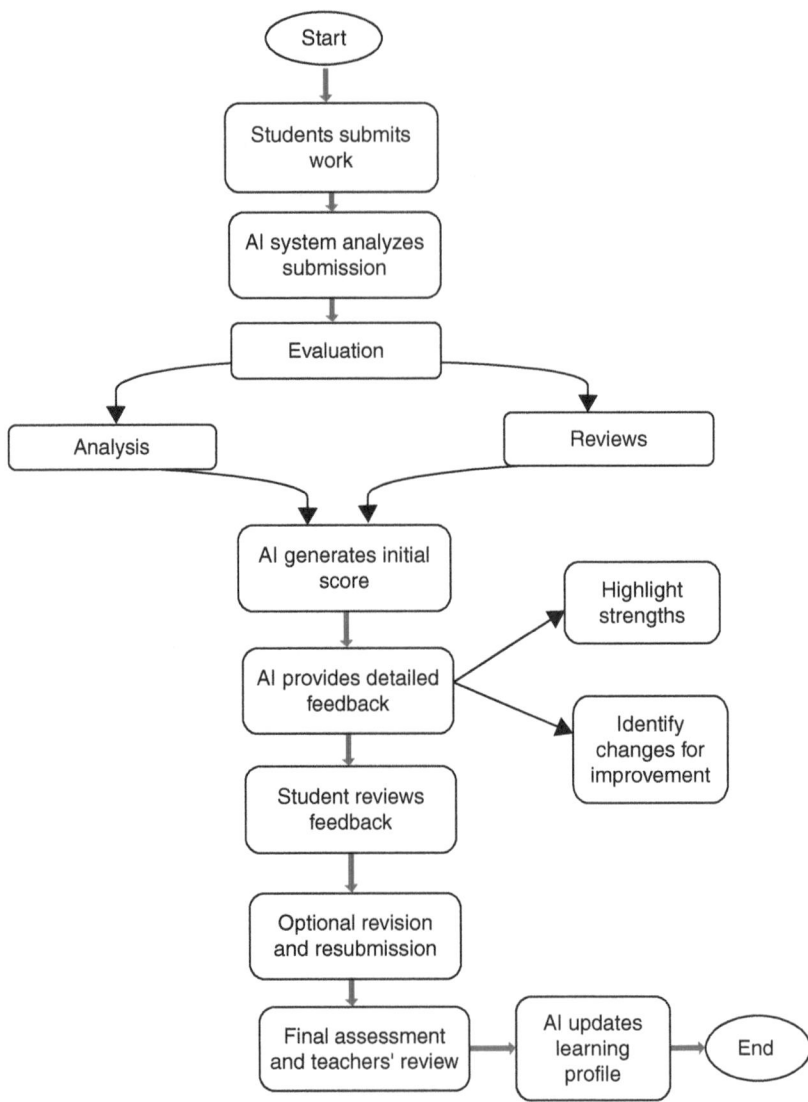

Figure 1.1 AI-based Student Assessment Practices.

Student Learning Impact:

Increased Participation: Instant feedback holds students captive as they learn because instant results and places where to improve are reflected back at them.

Boosting Motivation: Immediate feedback encourages motivation since the learner understands their progress, leading them to continue learning more.

Better Retention: Since corrections are immediate, they become cemented for learners before they continue so they can retain the concept longer and understand it.

Effectiveness and Best Practices:

Timeliness and Frequency: Feedback must be frequent and timely in order to keep students engaged and to improve performance.

Personalization: Feedback is personalized so that individual learning gaps are addressed, keeping the student focused on the challenge at hand.

Balanced Feedback: Positive reinforcement should always be balanced with constructive criticism in order not to discourage the student's confidence and motivation.

1.7.2 Challenges and Solutions

AI-driven evaluation offers several benefits, including personalized learning, efficient grading, and insightful analytics. However, realizing these benefits comes with challenges related to implementation, bias, data privacy, and technical limitations. Here is a detailed analysis of these challenges and potential solutions, along with references.

- **Challenge: Bias in Personalized Learning**
  One of the key benefits of AI-driven evaluation is its ability to provide personalized learning experiences. However, the algorithms that drive personalization can inadvertently reinforce biases. AI systems often rely on historical data to tailor learning content, and if this data contains biases, it may result in discriminatory outcomes. For example, an AI system might recommend advanced materials to students based on their past performance, which could disadvantage those from underrepresented groups if the system misinterprets differences in learning styles (Holstein et al., 2019).

  Solution: To mitigate bias, it is essential to train AI models on diverse and representative datasets that encompass a variety of learning styles, demographics, and educational backgrounds. Regular audits of AI-driven evaluation tools can identify and address bias in their recommendations and outputs. Implementing fairness constraints within AI algorithms can help ensure that students from different backgrounds receive equitable recommendations and opportunities. Additionally, including educators in the personalization process can provide a human perspective to counteract any potential algorithmic bias.

- **Challenge: Data Privacy Concerns**

  AI-driven evaluation tools often collect and analyze large amounts of student data to offer personalized learning paths and insights into academic progress. However, this reliance on data raises concerns about privacy and security. Protecting sensitive information, such as students' performance records, personal information, and learning behaviors, is crucial to prevent misuse or unauthorized access. Privacy concerns can also create resistance among educators and students towards the adoption of AI tools (Williamson & Eynon, 2020).

  Solution: Robust data protection measures, such as data encryption, anonymization, and secure data storage, should be implemented to safeguard student information. Educational institutions should be transparent about data collection practices, providing students and guardians with clear information on how data will be used. Obtaining informed consent is essential to ensure ethical use of data. Furthermore, adopting privacy-by-design principles—embedding privacy considerations into the architecture of AI systems—can enhance compliance with data protection regulations like the GDPR.

- **Challenge: Overemphasis on Measurable Outcomes**

  AI-driven evaluation systems often excel in assessing quantifiable aspects of learning, such as grades, test scores, and engagement metrics. However, this focus on measurable outcomes can overlook critical qualitative aspects of education, such as creativity, problem-solving abilities, social skills, and emotional intelligence. Consequently, students may not receive a holistic evaluation that captures their full range of competencies (Luckin & Holmes, 2016).

  Solution: AI-driven evaluation tools should be designed to support a more holistic assessment approach, incorporating multiple modalities of evaluation, such as peer assessments, project-based learning, and qualitative feedback from educators. For instance, AI algorithms can be trained to analyze student interactions in collaborative projects, giving insights into teamwork and communication skills. Combining AI-driven assessments with human-led evaluations ensures that both quantitative and qualitative aspects of student learning are considered.

1.7.3 Ethical Challenges and Considerations

The integration of AI in educational settings, particularly in evaluation and assessment, raises several ethical considerations and challenges. These range from concerns about student data privacy, biases in AI algorithms, to the ethical implications of automating aspects of student evaluation. Addressing these issues is critical for ensuring that AI systems support equitable and responsible education. Here is an exploration of key ethical challenges and potential solutions, supported by references.

- **Challenge: Student Data Privacy and Consent**
  AI-driven educational tools collect and analyze a vast amount of student data, including academic performance, behavioral patterns, and personal information. This data is essential for tailoring educational experiences, but it also raises significant privacy concerns. Inadequate handling of student data can lead to unauthorized access, misuse, or even identity theft, potentially putting students at risk. Additionally, students and parents may not always fully understand how their data is being used, raising issues around informed consent (Williamson & Eynon, 2020).

  Solution: Educational institutions must prioritize data privacy by implementing strict data protection measures, such as data encryption, secure storage, and anonymization. Policies regarding data usage should be transparent, and informed consent must be obtained from students or guardians, ensuring that they understand how their data will be used. Moreover, AI systems should be designed following privacy-by-design principles, embedding privacy considerations into the system's architecture to protect sensitive student information. Compliance with relevant regulations, such as the GDPR in Europe, is also essential to safeguard student privacy rights.

Challenge: Algorithmic Bias and Fairness

AI algorithms used in educational evaluation may inherit biases from their training data. This bias can result in unfair assessments, particularly for students from underrepresented or minority groups. For example, an AI grading system trained on responses from a specific demographic may disproportionately penalize students who use different linguistic or cultural expressions. This can perpetuate inequality in educational outcomes and undermine the principles of fairness and inclusivity (Holstein et al., 2019).

Solution: To address algorithmic bias, AI models should be trained on diverse and representative datasets that include inputs from various demographics, linguistic backgrounds, and cultural contexts. Regular audits of AI systems can help identify and correct biases in their assessments. Incorporating fairness constraints into the AI algorithms can ensure more equitable evaluation outcomes. Furthermore, a human–AI collaborative approach, where educators review AI-generated assessments, can help mitigate biases and promote fairness by incorporating human judgment into the evaluation process.

- **Challenge: Transparency and Explainability**
  AI-driven assessment tools often operate as "black boxes," making decisions and evaluations through complex algorithms that may not be easily understood by educators, students, or parents. This lack of transparency can lead to mistrust in AI systems and make it difficult to identify and address errors or biases in the evaluation process. Students and

educators may find it challenging to contest or seek explanations for the AI's assessments, raising ethical concerns about accountability and fairness (Selbst & Barocas, 2018).

Solution: AI systems used in education should be designed with explainability in mind, providing clear insights into how assessments and decisions are made. Explainable AI (XAI) techniques can help create models that offer understandable feedback, enabling educators and students to comprehend and question the AI's evaluation process. Incorporating user-friendly interfaces that provide detailed explanations of assessment criteria and outcomes can enhance transparency. Additionally, involving educators in the development and implementation of AI systems can improve the system's alignment with educational goals and ethical standards.

1.8 The Future of AI-Driven Student Evaluation

As AI technology continues to evolve, its role in student evaluation is likely to expand. Future developments may include more sophisticated adaptive learning systems that not only assess but also actively support personalized learning pathways. AI could enable ongoing, formative assessments embedded in daily learning activities, providing a continuous feedback loop that enhances student practices and outcomes (Luckin & Holmes, 2016). Moreover, AI has the potential to support holistic evaluation approaches, incorporating cognitive, emotional, and social factors into the assessment process. By analyzing student behavior, participation, and collaboration, AI-driven systems can provide a more comprehensive view of student performance beyond academic achievement.

1.8.1 Challenges and Solutions

As AI-driven student evaluation tools continue to evolve, they promise a more personalized and efficient educational landscape. However, realizing this future involves overcoming several challenges related to technological development, ethical considerations, scalability, and human–AI interaction. Here is a discussion of the key challenges in advancing AI-driven student evaluation and potential solutions, backed by references.

- **Challenge: Ensuring Adaptability and Flexibility of AI Systems**
  The future of education demands AI systems that can adapt to diverse learning environments, subjects, and individual student needs. Current AI-driven evaluation tools often focus on specific subjects or learning modalities, limiting their applicability across different educational contexts. This lack of flexibility could hinder the integration of AI into a broad range of curriculums and student demographics, potentially excluding certain types of learners (Zawacki-Richter et al., 2019).

Solution: Developing adaptable AI models that can handle various content areas and student learning styles is crucial. This requires creating AI systems based on modular and scalable frameworks that can be customized according to different educational needs. Incorporating adaptive learning algorithms capable of continuously evolving with new data and educational trends will enhance their flexibility. In addition, co-creating AI tools with educators, students, and content experts can ensure that these systems are responsive to the specific demands of different educational settings.

- **Challenge: Ethical Use of AI in Predictive Analytics**
  AI's growing ability to use predictive analytics in student evaluation, such as identifying at-risk students or forecasting academic success, raises ethical concerns. Predictive analytics could lead to labeling or tracking students in ways that affect their self-perception and opportunities. The risk is that such predictions may become self-fulfilling, potentially reinforcing inequalities rather than promoting equitable educational practices (Holstein et al., 2019).

Solution: Implementing ethical guidelines for the use of predictive analytics in AI-driven evaluation is vital. These guidelines should include principles of fairness, accountability, and transparency. AI systems must be designed to avoid deterministic labels or tracking while focusing on providing constructive support and interventions. Furthermore, educators should be involved in interpreting AI-generated predictions, ensuring that decisions based on analytics are made within a broader educational context. Periodic audits of predictive analytics systems can identify and address potential biases, promoting ethical use.

To enhance the discussion on AI-driven evaluation techniques by integrating insights from education, psychology, and computer science, consider the following solutions:

1 **Interdisciplinary Frameworks:** Create a framework illustrating how each discipline contributes to understanding AI in education.
2 **Collaborative Research:** Promote joint studies among researchers from these fields to analyze AI's impact on learning outcomes.
3 **Curriculum Development:** Design interdisciplinary curricula that cover AI applications, incorporating psychological and educational theories.
4 **Workshops and Seminars:** Organize events for educators, psychologists, and computer scientists to foster dialog and share insights.
5 **Case Studies:** Present examples of successful AI implementation in education, highlighting theoretical underpinnings and outcomes.
6 **AI Literacy Programs:** Enhance AI literacy for educators and students to understand its technical, psychological, and educational dimensions.
7 **Ethical Considerations:** Discuss ethical implications of AI in education, focusing on data privacy, equity, and biases.

8 **Feedback Mechanisms:** Establish systems for continuous feedback from users of AI tools to assess their effectiveness and impact.

1.9 Conclusion

The future of AI-driven student evaluation holds great promise, but it also presents challenges that need to be addressed to ensure ethical, adaptable, and equitable education. Solutions lie in developing flexible AI systems, fostering human–AI collaboration, ensuring ethical use of predictive analytics, and promoting global scalability with a focus on inclusivity. Continuous ethical governance and proactive involvement of educators in AI development will be critical in shaping a future where AI-driven evaluation enhances the educational experience for all students.

AI-driven evaluation techniques are revolutionizing student practices by offering personalized, efficient, and equitable assessment methods. While challenges remain, particularly in terms of data privacy and potential biases, the benefits of AI in education are clear. By leveraging AI's capabilities, educators can create more dynamic and responsive learning environments that cater to individual student needs, ultimately enhancing educational outcomes. As research and technology continue to advance, the future of AI in student evaluation holds great promise for transforming educational practices.

1.10 Future Work and Challenges

AI-driven student evaluation should focus on addressing the existing challenges while expanding the scope and potential of these technologies. Research should prioritize developing AI systems that are transparent, explainable, and adaptable to diverse educational contexts. This includes refining algorithms to minimize biases, ensuring fairness in evaluation, and improving data privacy safeguards. Collaboration between AI developers, educators, policymakers, and students will be essential to ensure that AI tools align with the needs of real-world classrooms and that educators have the training and resources to integrate AI effectively. Additionally, exploring AI's potential to assess more complex skills such as creativity, critical thinking, and emotional intelligence could broaden the application of AI in education. Long-term studies on the impact of AI-driven assessments on learning outcomes and student well-being are also needed to continuously refine these tools. By fostering interdisciplinary research and innovation, the future of AI in education can evolve to create more inclusive, ethical, and effective learning environments.

Table 1.1 outlines emerging AI techniques for educational evaluation, detailing their potential applications, expected advancements, and challenges. Examples include emotion recognition to adjust learning support, voice analysis for language assessment, and explainable AI to make grading

Table 1.1 Future Directions in AI-Driven Evaluation Techniques for Education

Emerging AI technique	Potential application	Advancements expected	Challenges to address
Emotion recognition in learning	Identifies student emotions during learning to adjust difficulty or support	Enhances engagement, supports emotional well-being	Ethical concerns, risk of misinterpretation
Voice and speech analysis	Assesses language proficiency or public-speaking skills via AI-based analysis	Improves assessment of spoken skills, instant feedback	Privacy of voice data, need for nuanced language models
AI for collaborative skills assessment	Evaluates group dynamics and teamwork in collaborative projects	Captures social skills, teamwork, and leadership	Complex data integration, potential privacy issues
Explainable AI (XAI) for grading	Transparent grading models that educators and students can interpret	Builds trust, promotes understanding of grading	Balancing transparency with model complexity
Real-time intervention suggestions	AI offers live prompts to educators on effective interventions for students	Supports timely intervention, fosters responsive teaching	Avoiding over-reliance, preserving educator's role

transparent. Each technique addresses specific educational needs while also presenting ethical, privacy, and transparency challenges.

References

Ahmad, K., Iqbal, W., El-Hassan, A., Qadir, J., Benhaddou, D., Ayyash, M., & Al-Fuqaha, A. (2023). Data-driven artificial intelligence in education: A comprehensive review. *IEEE Transactions on Learning Technologies*. DOI: https://doi.org/10.35542/osf.io/zvu2n

Azevedo, J. P., Hasan, A., Goldemberg, D., Geven, K., & Iqbal, S. A. (2021). Simulating the potential impacts of COVID-19 school closures on schooling and learning outcomes: A set of global estimates. *The World Bank Research Observer, 36*(1), 1–40. DOI: https://doi.org/10.1596/40037

Baral, S., Botelho, A. F., Erickson, J. A., Benachamardi, P., & Heffernan, N. T. (2021). Improving automated scoring of student open responses in mathematics. *International Educational Data Mining Society*. DOI: https://doi.org/10.1111/jcal.12793

Dawson, S., Jovanovic, J., Gašević, D., & Pardo, A. (2017, March). From prediction to impact: Evaluation of a learning analytics retention program. In *Proceedings of the seventh international learning analytics & knowledge conference* (pp. 474–478). DOI: https://doi.org/10.1145/3027385.3027405

Fahmy, Y. (2024). *Student Perception on AI-Driven Assessment: Motivation, Engagement and Feedback Capabilities* (Bachelor's thesis, University of Twente). DOI: https://doi.org/10.52783/eel.v14i2.1635

Holstein, K., McLaren, B. M., & Aleven, V. (2019). Co-designing a real-time classroom orchestration tool to support teacher-AI complementarity. *Grantee Submission.* DOI: https://doi.org/10.18608/jla.2019.62.3

Hooda, M., Rana, C., Dahiya, O., Rizwan, A., & Hossain, M. S. (2022). Artificial intelligence for assessment and feedback to enhance student success in higher education. *Mathematical Problems in Engineering*, 2022(1), 5215722. DOI: https://doi.org/10.1155/2022/5215722

Luckin, R., & Holmes, W. (2016). Intelligence unleashed: An argument for AI in education. DOI: https://doi.org/10.4236/ijaa.2011.14023.

Raza, S. A., Qazi, W., Khan, K. A., & Salam, J. (2021). Social isolation and acceptance of the learning management system (LMS) in the time of COVID-19 pandemic: An expansion of the UTAUT model. *Journal of Educational Computing Research*, 59(2), 183–208. DOI: https://doi.org/10.1177/0735633120960421

Selbst, A. D., & Barocas, S. (2018). The intuitive appeal of explainable machines. *Fordham Law Review*, 87, 1085. DOI: https://doi.org/10.2139/ssrn.3126971

Sutton, A., Clowes, M., Preston, L., & Booth, A. (2019). Meeting the review family: exploring review types and associated information retrieval requirements. *Health Information and Libraries Journal*, 36(3), 202–222. https://doi.org/10.1111/hir.12276

Taghipour, K., & Ng, H. T. (2016, November). A neural approach to automated essay scoring. In *Proceedings of the 2016 conference on empirical methods in natural language processing* (pp. 1882–1891). DOI: https://doi.org/10.18653/v1/d16-1193

West, M., Kraut, R., & Ei Chew, H. (2019). I'd blush if I could: closing gender divides in digital skills through education. UNESCO: Equals skills coalition.

Williamson, B., & Eynon, R. (2020). Historical threads, missing links, and future directions in AI in education. *Learning, Media and Technology*, 45(3), 223–235. DOI: https://doi.org/10.1080/17439884.2020.1798995

Zawacki-Richter, O., Marín, V. I., Bond, M., & Gouverneur, F. (2019). Systematic review of research on artificial intelligence applications in higher education–Where are the educators?. *International Journal of Educational Technology in Higher Education*, 16(1), 1–27. DOI: https://doi.org/10.1186/s41239-019-0171-0

2 Inclusive Learning and Assessment in the Era of AI

*Minal Patil, R. H. Goudar, Anand Nayyar,
G. M. Dhananjaya, and
Vijayalaxmi N. Rathod*

2.1 Introduction

The field of higher education is changing swiftly, propelled by the revolutionary capabilities of artificial intelligence (AI) technologies. These tools show a glimpse into a future of personalized learning, where educational experiences are tailored to individual student strengths and weaknesses (Jain, 2023). In addition to automating tasks like feedback generation and progress monitoring, AI can enable real-time adjustments in the learning journey, fostering deeper student engagement and promoting a stronger grasp of learning objectives (Memarian & Doleck, 2024). This personalized approach ultimately aims to improve academic performance (De Witte Chénier, 2023). Nonetheless, utilizing AI in education requires a dedication to ensuring inclusivity and accessibility for every learner (Baker & Hawn, 2022). However, traditional assessment methods, often reliant on standardized tests, have frequently perpetuated inequalities by being inflexible and harboring cultural biases, potentially disadvantageous to students from diverse backgrounds or with different learning styles (Alam et al., 2022). For instance, standardized exams often prioritize specific cultural knowledge or language styles, which can unfairly disadvantage students from marginalized communities. This chapter delves into the exciting potential of AI for fostering inclusive learning and assessment in higher education, with a specific focus on mitigating cultural bias within AI algorithms. We will examine the obstacles that must be tackled to guarantee fair access to educational opportunities and attain favorable results for every student.

This study seeks to investigate how AI can promote inclusive assessment and overcome the shortcomings of conventional approaches.

Specific research objectives include

- To explore how AI can personalize learning for diverse students
- To explore how AI can reduce bias in assessment
- To explore how AI can personalize student support and feedback
- To analyze the ethical implications of AI in education and identify strategies for responsible and equitable implementation

DOI: 10.1201/9781003470304-2

This study expands available research on AI in education by integrating the sensory learning framework to create a more comprehensive approach to inclusive assessment. Our novel approach leverages multimodal interaction and a human-centered perspective to provide personalized and accessible learning experiences, addressing the limitations of previous research that concentrated solely on cognitive aspects of learning. However, while AI offers significant potential for inclusive assessment, it also presents unique challenges.

Key Terms

Personalized Learning: A pedagogical approach that tailors instruction to meet the individual needs and preferences of each learner.

Adaptive Learning: A type of personalized learning that uses technology to automatically adjust the difficulty and pace of instruction based on a student's performance.

Algorithmic Bias: The systematic and unfair treatment of certain groups by algorithms, often due to biases in the data used to train them.

2.2 Challenges of AI in Inclusive Assessment

AI has great potential in assessment and is an exciting area of work on the horizon, but we also need to recognize the challenges it presents when considering inclusion for all learners. Some of these challenges are the result of shortcomings in common assessment practices but they also grow out of various complications AI faces.

2.2.1 Limitations of Traditional Assessment Methods

2.2.1.1 Lack of Flexibility

When it comes to assessments, standardized tests—one of the most widely used forms—have a tendency not only to favor rote memorization over understanding and application in general. Some are rigid, not catering for different learning styles or the needs of disability students needing more time or special types of examination (Bray et al., 2024).

2.2.1.2 Cultural Bias

Additionally, traditional assessments often embed cultural biases that can disadvantage students from underrepresented backgrounds. For example, language choices, question framing, and cultural references might favor students belonging to particular cultural backgrounds (Walker et al., 2023). This can lead to inaccurate assessments of student knowledge and potential.

2.2.1.3 *Potential Biases in AI Algorithms*

Unfortunately, the potential for bias is not limited to traditional assessment methods. AI algorithms, while powerful tools, can also inherit biases from the data they are trained on. This can lead to stereotyping and algorithmic bias, negatively impacting student assessment and perpetuating educational inequalities. Figure 2.1 illustrates the contrast between traditional and AI-based assessment methods, highlighting the potential for bias in both approaches. To address these challenges and promote fairness in AI-powered assessment, various data curation methods can be employed.

2.3 Mitigating Bias in AI Assessment

As discussed, potential biases within AI algorithms pose a significant challenge to ensuring fairness in student assessment. Comparison of traditional and AI-based assessment methods is shown in Figure 2.1. Fortunately, various data curation methods can be employed to reduce these prejudices and promote more equitable AI-powered assessment.

2.3.1 *Data Curation for Fairer AI Assessment*

Data curation is a critical step in building fair and unbiased AI models. By carefully cleaning, organizing, and enriching data, we can address potential issues in the training data and mitigate bias in AI assessment.

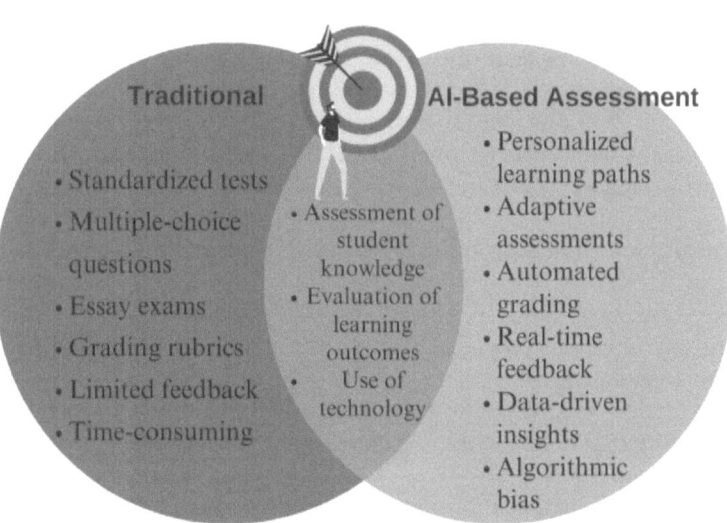

Figure 2.1 Traditional and AI-Based Assessment Methods—Comparative Analysis.

2.3.1.1 Data Cleaning

Data cleaning involves identifying and addressing issues such as missing values, outliers, and inconsistencies. By removing or imputing missing values, handling outliers appropriately, and standardizing data formats, we can ensure that the training data is accurate and reliable (Hanna et al., 2020).

2.3.1.2 Data Balancing

To mitigate the impact of imbalanced datasets, techniques like oversampling, undersampling, and synthetic data generation can be employed. These methods help ensure that the AI model is exposed to a diverse range of examples, reducing the risk of bias (Ferrara, 2023).

2.3.1.3 Data Augmentation

Data augmentation involves creating new, synthetic data points to expand the training dataset. This technique can be particularly useful for tasks like image and text classification, where generating additional training examples can improve model performance and robustness. By effectively applying these data curation techniques, we can significantly improve the fairness, accuracy, and robustness of AI assessment models (Mumuni & Mumuni, 2022).

By ensuring that AI algorithms are trained on diverse and unbiased data, we can create a foundation for fair and equitable assessment practices. This, in turn, leads to fairer assessment practices that accurately measure student knowledge and potential, regardless of background or learning style. By meticulously curating training data to mitigate bias, we lay a crucial foundation for equitable AI-powered assessment. Fair and unbiased assessment is an indispensable component of creating inclusive learning environments. To fully realize the potential of AI in fostering personalized and accessible education, we must shift our focus to designing learning experiences that provide diverse learners with their unique needs. The sensory learning framework offers a promising approach to achieving this goal.

Key strategies for mitigating cultural bias in AI-powered assessment include

1 **Diverse Training Data:** Ensuring that the datasets used to train AI algorithms represent a diverse student population to avoid perpetuating existing biases.
2 **Bias Detection and Mitigation:** Implementing techniques to identify and address potential biases within AI algorithms, such as bias detection tools and fairness metrics.
3 **Transparent Algorithms:** Promoting transparency in AI algorithms to enable understanding and scrutiny of decision-making processes.
4 **Human Oversight:** Ensuring that human educators have oversight over AI-powered assessments to recognize and correct any biases that may arise.

By adopting these strategies, we can work toward creating AI-powered assessments that are fair, inclusive, and free from cultural bias. To further enhance the inclusivity of learning experiences, we can leverage the sensory learning framework.

2.4 Designing Inclusive Learning Experiences

2.4.1 *The Sensory Learning Framework: Engaging Learners through Multiple Channels*

This name emphasizes the diverse ways students can interact with learning materials through their senses. The sensory learning framework stresses the significance of offering learners various methods to engage with course materials and demonstrate their understanding. This structure recognizes that students possess distinct learning preferences, and by involving different senses, teachers can establish a more comprehensive and efficient learning setting. To further enhance the potential of the sensory learning framework, AI can be leveraged to create more engaging and personalized learning experiences.

2.4.2 *Multimodal Interaction*

AI can revolutionize the sensory learning framework by offering a wider range of multimodal interaction options.

- **Speech Recognition and Synthesis:** AI can transcribe spoken words into text, allowing students to dictate responses or engage with educational resources via voice commands. Additionally, text-to-speech capabilities can provide auditory availability of information for students who have visual impairments or learning preferences.
- **Gesture Recognition and Visual Feedback:** The combination of gesture recognition and visual stimulation is a powerful means of improving the learning process, and therefore an AI can be employed. The AI can analyze the gestures performed by students on touchscreens or tablets in order to deliver alternative means of interaction with the learning materials. As an example, students may move virtual models, use images to depict ideas, or draw important details. This type of technique encourages more active participation and comprehension. At the same time, it is fair to note that students' movements can trigger constructive visual responses from AI. These can be various animated explanations, interactive models, or learning simulations. In this way, both gestures and images act together with voice communication to improve the educational process by active participation in placing voice and showing images.
- **Adaptive Interfaces:** By analyzing student data, including performance, learning styles, and preferences, AI can tailor the learning environment

to individual needs. This includes adjusting the difficulty level of content, providing alternative explanations or examples, and offering different presentation formats (text, audio, visual). For instance, students with visual impairments can learn well from text-to-speech choices, while learners who have difficulties in auditory processing may feel more comfortable when using tools that use visual cues. Personalized interfaces ensure that all students can also reach the information and help required to assist their needs. By leveraging these multimodal interaction techniques, AI can create more inclusive and engaging learning experiences for students with diverse needs.

2.4.3 Designing Inclusive Learning Experiences with AI: The Sensory Learning Framework in Action

The sensory learning framework, as shown in Figure 2.2, emphasizes providing learners with diverse ways to interact with learning materials and express their knowledge. Here's how AI can enhance each aspect of this framework through multimodal interaction:

- **Multimodal Interaction:** This involves capturing information from students through various channels and delivering learning experiences tailored to each student.
- **Input:** AI can analyze student input through speech recognition, gesture recognition, and adaptive interfaces.
- **Speech Recognition:** AI can convert spoken words into text, allowing students to dictate responses to questions, essays, or creative writing assignments. Participate actively in discussions without needing to write everything down. Access learning materials through audio recordings, lectures, or audiobooks.
- **Gesture Recognition:** AI can analyze student gestures on touchscreens or tablets to provide alternative ways to solve problems by manipulating virtual objects or diagrams. Express understanding by drawing, highlighting, or circling key concepts. Engage in interactive simulations or virtual labs.
- **Adaptive Interfaces:** AI can personalize the learning interface based on student needs. For example, students with visual impairments can utilize text-to-speech options or haptic feedback for non-visual cues about graphs, charts, or images. Students with motor skill limitations can use voice commands or eye-tracking technology to interact with learning materials. The interface can adjust difficulty levels or present information in alternative formats based on student responses and performance data.

Output: Based on the processed information, the system delivers learning experiences tailored to each student. This can include personalized learning

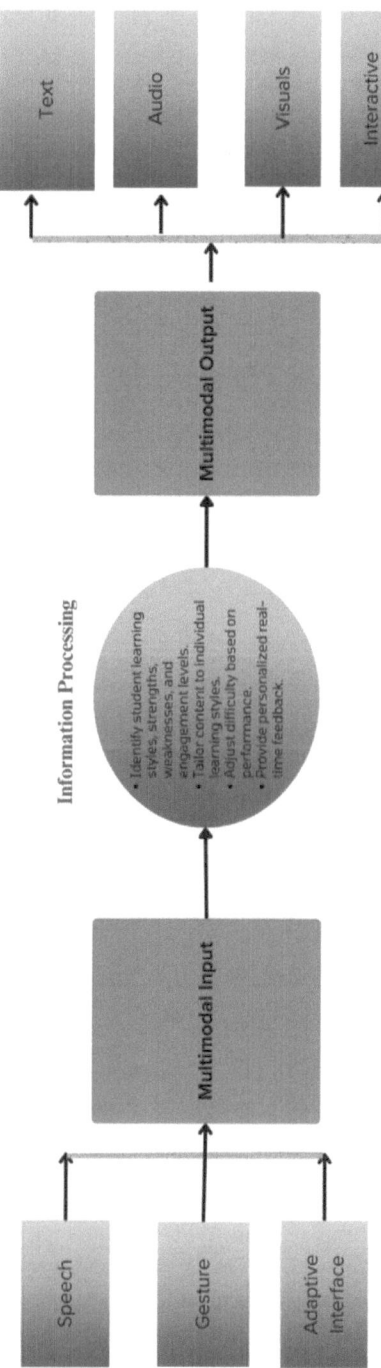

Figure 2.2 AI-enhanced Sensory Learning Framework.

materials with different formats (text, audio, visuals), interactive simulations and virtual reality experiences, and real-time feedback in various forms (audio, visual, personalized messages).

Due to AI's assisted multimodal interaction, the sensory learning framework enables learners to have a more interactive and inclusive environment. By integrating different input systems such as our speech or gesture-recognition systems as well as our adaptive interfaces, each pupil is able to engage with study materials in a way that fits their personal needs and preferences as well as their sensory strengths. Under normal conditions, students dictate on speech recognition systems and interact with visual objects to show that they understand the task or complete it through gesture recognition. Adaptive interfaces refine the experience even more, for instance, by presenting a more appropriate level of difficulty or providing a different mode for students with visual or motor skill impairments.

This approach translates to a richer learning experience through multimodal output as well. AI tailors the learning materials using various formats like text, audio, visuals, and even interactive simulations. Real-time feedback in the form of audio prompts, visual cues, or personalized messages further enhances understanding and engagement. The result is a dynamic and inclusive environment of learning that includes all students who actively participate, receive immediate feedback, and access information in formats that suit their individual needs.

Evaluation Metrics
To access the effectiveness of our AI-powered inclusive assessment approach, we can collect data on the following parameters:

- **Student Engagement Metrics:** Time on task, completion rates, and click-stream analysis
- **Learning Outcomes:** Knowledge retention, problem-solving skills, and critical thinking
- **Accessibility Metrics:** Student satisfaction and inclusive features
- **Cost–Benefit Analysis:** Resource utilization and return on investment

Additional Benefits and the Role of Educators
This AI-powered approach offers several advantages. Disabled students achieve increased accessibility due to alternative input and output methods. Multimodal learning materials capture student attention more effectively, leading to improved retention. Interactive simulations and personalized feedback foster enhanced comprehension of complex concepts. However, it's important to remember that AI serves as a powerful tool, not a replacement for educators. Educators remain essential in creating engaging learning activities, selecting appropriate AI-powered resources, and providing personalized guidance to students. Building on this concept of personalized learning,

AI-powered adaptive learning offers a promising approach to tailoring education to individual needs.

2.5 AI-Powered Adaptive Learning for Inclusion

Traditional, one-size-fits-all learning approaches often fail to accommodate the various requirements and preferences of students. Here's where AI-powered adaptive learning emerges as a transformative force, fostering inclusivity and custom learning experiences. Adaptive learning is an education approach that uses technology to tailor the learning experience to the individual needs and preferences of each student. It uses information about students' skills, their ability to learn, what they are good at, and what needs improvement to customize the educational process. To effectively implement adaptive learning, AI plays a crucial role in analyzing student data and making real-time adjustments to the learning experience.

2.5.1 Benefits of Adaptive Learning

2.5.1.1 Personalized Learning Paths

Adaptive learning platforms examine student data and deliver content that is tailored to be the most relevant and engaging for each individual. This can include adjusting the difficulty level, providing alternative learning resources, or offering personalized feedback (Fadieieva, 2023).

2.5.1.2 Improved Engagement and Motivation

Adaptive learning platforms improve students' engagement and motivation by meeting different requirements and preferences. Students are in control of their pace and decide which aspects need more help (Mumuni & Mumuni, 2022).

2.5.1.3 Knowledge-Gap Identification and Remediation

Adaptive learning systems can help pinpoint which knowledge gaps students need to address—and provide targeted pathways for intervention. This will likely be helpful, especially for those students that need a slower pace in some topics or were dusted halfway through (Gligorea et al., 2023).

2.5.2 AI Tailoring Learning for Diverse Learners

AI plays a crucial role in powering adaptive learning by analyzing vast amounts of student data and making real-time adjustments to the learning experience. To provide personalized and effective learning experiences, AI can be used to identify individual learning styles, generate tailored feedback, and predict potential challenges.

2.5.2.1 *Identifying Learning Styles*

AI can analyze student interactions within the learning platform to identify their preferred learning styles (visual, auditory, kinesthetic). This allows the system to tailor content delivery and activities to best suit each student's learning preferences (Salas-Pilco et al., 2022).

2.5.2.2 *Personalized Feedback Loops*

Using AI, feedback can be automatically created and uploaded into the system, with the system's eyes, with the specific purpose of supporting the student's strong sides and working on the required concepts. That improves performance and educational results (Luzano, 2024).

2.5.2.3 *Predictive Analytics for Learning Difficulties*

Early identification of potential challenges before students face learning issues through academic advisors using AI on student data. This allows educators to spot students who may be falling behind, enabling them to intervene sooner and provide additional support (Ravichandran et al., 2023).

An AI-driven individualized approach to schooling balances out opportunities for a variety of students by tailoring the teaching strategy to learner needs. Students' differences in learning styles, experience, or knowledge levels can be catered for through the Personalized Learning and Smart Education (PSLE) approach that targets their specific needs. It also fosters a positive learning environment where every student has the chance to succeed. To effectively implement and leverage AI-powered personalized learning, it is essential to empower educators with the necessary tools and training.

2.6 Empowering Educators with AI Tools: A Human-Centered Approach

Although AI has great potential for evaluation, it's important to recognize that educators still play a central role in the learning process. Prioritizing a user-focused strategy for incorporating AI into evaluation is essential for successful deployment and ethical practice. This is how AI can support teachers in helping students and enhancing educational outcomes. By leveraging AI-powered tools, educators can gain valuable insights into student learning and tailor their instruction accordingly.

2.6.1 *Individualized Support through AI-Powered Insights*

AI-powered products can process students' data derived from a number of tests, online courses' progress, practical classes, etc. This information has valuable significance to teachers with regards to each student's abilities, gaps, and learning preferences (Salas-Pilco et al., 2022). Armed with these insights, educators can

2.6.1.1 Tailor Instruction

Design personalized learning plans that address each student's specific needs. This might involve providing additional support for struggling students, offering enrichment activities for advanced learners, or adapting teaching methodologies to cater to diverse learning styles.

2.6.1.2 Targeted Interventions

Identifying who would need help and getting it to them proactively before they slipped through the cracks. Able to provide timely support and personalized guidance so all students will always remain on track for success.

2.6.1.3 Formative Assessment and Feedback

Deploy AI-based feedback systems that can analyze student work and furnish immediate, personalized feedback. Educators can use this information to provide additional instruction and support around the content (Luzano, 2024).

2.6.2 Benefits of AI-Powered Feedback Systems

By automating routine tasks such as grading multiple-choice questions, AI-powered feedback systems significantly reduce educators' workload. This frees up valuable time for more personalized interactions with students, including providing in-depth feedback, addressing individual learning needs, and fostering a supportive learning environment. Additionally, AI-powered feedback systems offer real-time insights into student understanding. By analyzing student responses, these systems can provide immediate, targeted feedback, allowing students to adjust their learning approach and improve their understanding as they progress. This proactive approach encourages students to take charge of their learning and cultivate metacognitive skills.

Second, AI-powered feedback systems provide actionable data for students and educators. By understanding our strengths and weaknesses in these four quadrants (knowledge, comprehension, application, analysis), we can follow systems that will help us be conscious of where to put more or less effort. Insights that educators can use to offer personalized instruction and support. Although AI-powered feedback systems bring a slew of advantages to your work, always bear in mind that not even the best spark will ever replace great human touch. Educators are important in the upbuilding of respect, encouragement, and good analytical thinking. AI should be viewed as a tool to enhance, rather than replace, the educator's role in the learning process. While AI-powered feedback systems offer a wealth of advantages, it's crucial to remember that effective implementation requires further exploration. Understanding the long-term impact on student development and identifying potential biases within the algorithms are important areas for ongoing research.

2.7 Discussion

Our analysis supports the inclusion of AI-mediated assessment in education, suggesting that it can be applied inclusively. It is important to recognize that relying too much on technology can sometimes create barriers. However, it is important to recognize the potential challenges and limitations of relying too heavily on technology. For instance, students lacking the necessary devices or reliable internet access may struggle to engage in the learning experiences we propose. Additionally, the effectiveness of our findings could be influenced by various external factors, such as the institutional environment, teacher training practices, and the unique traits of the students themselves. There remain questions that need answers on the best practices for implementing our model in other education systems and on the barriers to accessibility.

Case Study: AI-Powered Personalized Learning in LAUSD (psico-smart.com., October 26, 2023)

Building on the promise of AI-powered personalized learning, the Los Angeles Unified School District (LAUSD) serves as a valuable case study. Their successful integration of AI tools like DreamBox and Knewton demonstrates the potential for increased student engagement and improved academic outcomes. As highlighted earlier, LAUSD educators achieved a 40% increase in student engagement and a 15% rise in math proficiency through personalized learning pathways.

Role of educators in integrating AI tools while maintaining meaningful interactions with students

AI can automate the overworked static job roles of grading and even attendance, enabling educators to focus their energy on personalizing interactions and feedback. Through personalized learning pathways, instantaneous feedback, and collaborative group work, AI drives engagement to enable educators with more time for deeper intellectual inclination. Students engage with interactive AI-driven material and are reassured that the use of academic work is fair.

Educators also play a crucial role in equipping students with digital literacy skills. This empowers students to effectively utilize AI tools and navigate the learning environment.

In the same vein, teachers looking to maximize this discreet form of AI now face an imperative: ensure student experience remains a priority in teaching and learning by using feedback from students on their interaction with it as they mold its use into something that supplements—not substitutes for—the interactions found between teacher and learner.

While our research demonstrates the potential benefits of AI-powered inclusive assessment, it's important to acknowledge that overreliance on technology can create accessibility issues. Students who lack access to necessary devices or reliable internet connectivity may face challenges in fully engaging with the learning experiences we propose. Additionally, the generalizability of our findings may be influenced by contextual factors such as institutional policies, teacher training, and student demographics. Further research is needed to explore how our approach can be adapted to diverse educational settings and to address potential barriers to accessibility. To ensure that AI is used ethically and responsibly in education, it is crucial to consider the following ethical implications, as discussed in the next section.

2.8 Ethical Considerations and Future Directions for AI in Inclusive Learning

The integration of AI into assessment necessitates a commitment to ethical considerations. Responsible development and deployment of these tools are paramount to ensuring fairness, transparency, and positive outcomes for all students. To ensure the ethical use of AI in education, it is crucial to address the following key areas:

2.8.1 Responsible and Ethical Use of AI

2.8.1.1 Fairness, Bias Mitigation, and Educator Empowerment

As mentioned earlier, AI algorithms can carry biases from the data used in their training. To address these biases and promote fair assessment practices, it's essential to adopt data curation techniques and create ethical guidelines for developing algorithms. Furthermore, educators should play an active role in choosing and applying AI tools to make sure they fit their teaching philosophies and meet their students' needs.

2.8.1.2 Transparency, Explainability, and Educational Agency

AI assessment tools should be sufficiently transparent for educators and students to comprehend the process of assessments and decision-making. This helps build confidence and approval of AI in the educational setting. By understanding how these tools make decisions, educators will be able to better understand how to incorporate AI algorithms into their instructional practices.

2.8.1.3 Data Privacy and Security

Student data used to train and power AI assessment tools must be treated with utmost care. Robust data security protocols and clear privacy policies are essential to ensuring student data is protected and used ethically. Educators play a crucial role in safeguarding student information by understanding data privacy regulations and collaborating with institutions to implement appropriate measures. By actively involving educators in the development, implementation, and monitoring of AI tools, institutions can promote ethical AI practices and ensure that these technologies are used to enhance, rather than hinder, the learning experience. While addressing these immediate ethical considerations is crucial, it is equally important to consider the long-term implications of AI in education.

2.8.2 Long-Term Implications of AI in Education

While AI offers immense potential for transforming education, it is crucial to consider its long-term implications. One key area of concern is the potential for AI to exacerbate existing educational inequalities. If not implemented carefully, AI-powered tools could further widen the gap between privileged and disadvantaged students. Therefore, it is essential to ensure equitable access to AI-powered education and to develop strategies to mitigate potential biases in AI algorithms.

Another important consideration is the impact of AI on the role of teachers. While AI can automate routine tasks and provide personalized support to students, it is important to emphasize that human educators remain essential for fostering critical thinking, creativity, and social–emotional skills. AI should be seen as a tool to enhance, rather than replace, the role of teachers.

Finally, AI has the potential to empower students by providing them with personalized learning experiences and opportunities for creative expression. However, it is crucial to ensure that students develop the necessary digital literacy skills to critically evaluate information and use AI tools responsibly.

By carefully considering these long-term implications, we can harness the power of AI to create a more equitable, inclusive, and effective education system.

2.8.3 Future Directions for AI in Inclusive Learning

While AI has immense potential, it's still an evolving field. Future advancements can explore areas like

- **Natural Language Processing (NLP) for Personalized Feedback:** AI could provide more nuanced and personalized feedback on open-ended assessments, catering to diverse writing styles and learning objectives.

- **AI-Powered Assistive Technologies:** AI tools can be further developed to support students with disabilities, providing accommodations that enhance accessibility and participation in assessments.
- **Culturally Responsive AI Design:** Creating AI algorithms that recognize cultural differences, and various learning styles can greatly improve inclusivity and ensure fair educational opportunities for every student. By focusing on a human-centered approach and prioritizing ethical considerations, AI can empower both teachers and learners. This could ultimately result in a more inclusive and effective educational experience in higher education.

2.9 AI Applications in Inclusive Education

AI has the potential to transform inclusive education by providing creative solutions to meet the diverse learning needs of students. While personalized learning and the sensory learning framework have been explored before, the AI applications highlighted here demonstrate the progress being made toward fostering a more inclusive educational setting. To realize the full potential of AI in inclusive education, several specific applications can be leveraged:

2.9.1 Personalized Learning Platforms

These platforms utilize AI to assess each student's performance, preferences, and learning speed, which aligns with the idea of personalized learning. By customizing instructional materials and approaches to address individual needs, these platforms foster a more inclusive educational experience.

2.9.2 Speech Recognition and Text-to-Speech (TTS) Technologies

These tools enhance accessibility by providing various input and output options, in line with the principles of the sensory learning framework. They can be particularly helpful for students facing different learning challenges, such as dyslexia or speech impairments.

2.9.3 Adaptive Assessment and Feedback Systems

By offering immediate feedback and adjusting to each student's performance, these systems support the ideas of personalized learning and help create a more inclusive assessment process.

2.9.4 Augmented Reality (AR) for Accessibility

AR applications offer additional sensory input, enhancing the sensory learning framework by providing virtual support and information. This technology benefits students with diverse learning needs by providing alternative ways to access and understand information.

2.9.5 Emotion Recognition for Social Interaction

While not directly tied to the previous sections, this application highlights the potential of AI to create more inclusive and supportive learning environments. By understanding students' emotional states, educators can provide targeted support, promoting social and emotional well-being.

2.9.6 Early Intervention and Support

The ability of AI to analyze patterns in student performance and pinpoint potential challenges supports the goals of personalized learning and inclusive education. By using early intervention strategies, teachers can offer specific help to overcome academic difficulties. This approach guarantees that every student has the chance to thrive and succeed. Ultimately, these AI-powered tools have the potential to create a more inclusive and equitable educational environment. These AI tools together demonstrate the potential to create a more inclusive and fair educational environment, catering to various learning needs while providing customized support. By building upon the foundations established in previous sections, these applications contribute to a holistic approach to inclusive education.

2.10 Conclusion

This study has demonstrated the potential of AI-powered inclusive assessment in revolutionizing higher education. By integrating the sensory learning framework and leveraging multimodal interaction, we have developed a personalized and accessible approach that caters to diverse student needs. Our findings highlight the importance of providing students with multiple ways to interact with learning materials and receive feedback. The implications of our research extend beyond the immediate benefits for students.

By addressing the limitations of traditional assessment methods and leveraging the power of AI, we can create a more equitable and inclusive learning environment for all students.

Our findings suggest that AI-powered inclusive assessment can

- **Promote Equity:** By addressing the limitations of traditional assessment methods, our approach can help to reduce educational disparities and ensure that all students have equal opportunities to succeed.
- **Enhance Student Engagement:** The personalized and interactive nature of our approach can foster greater student motivation and engagement, leading to improved learning outcomes.

• **Inform Future Research:** Our study provides a foundation for further research on AI-powered inclusive assessment. Future studies could explore the long-term impacts of our approach, investigate scalability, and investigate the effectiveness of our methods in different educational contexts.

Future research should concentrate on exploring the long-term impacts of AI-enhanced inclusive assessments on student learning outcomes, engagement, and overall well-being. Additionally, it is essential to ensure that these methods can be seamlessly integrated into large educational environments. By delving into these research paths, we can push forward the field of AI-driven inclusive assessment and ensure that all students have access to fair and effective learning opportunities. This study represents a significant opportunity to reshape higher education into a more inclusive and equitable environment. In conclusion, this research offers a promising chance to make higher education more welcoming and just. Leveraging AI alongside the sensory learning framework enables us to create personalized learning experiences that empower every student to reach their full potential.

References

Alam, S., Mahmud, I., Hoque, S. M. S., Akter, R., & Rana, S. M. S. (2022). Predicting students' intention to continue business courses on online platforms during COVID-19: An extended expectation confirmation theory. *International Journal of Management Education, 20*(3), 100706. https://doi.org/10.1016/j.ijme.2022.100706

Baker, R. S., & Hawn, A. (2022). Algorithmic bias in education. *International Journal of Artificial Intelligence in Education, 32*(4), 1052–1092. https://doi.org/10.1007/s40593-021-00285-9

Bray, A., Devitt, A., Banks, J., Sanchez Fuentes, S., Sandoval, M., Riviou, K., Byrne, D., Flood, M., Reale, J., & Terrenzio, S. (2024). What next for universal design for learning? A systematic literature review of technology in UDL implementations at the second level. *British Journal of Educational Technology, 55*(1), 113–138. https://doi.org/10.1111/bjet.13328

De Witte, K., & Chénier, M. A. (2023). Learning analytics in education for the twenty-first century. In E. Bertoni, M. Fontana, L. Gabrielli, S. Signorelli, & M. Vespe (Eds.), *Handbook of computational social science for policy* (pp. 305–326). Springer: Cham. https://doi.org/10.1007/978-3-031-16624-2_16

Fadieieva, L. O. (2023). Adaptive learning: A cluster-based literature review. *Educational Technology Quarterly, 2023*(3), 319–366. https://doi.org/10.55056/etq.613

Ferrara, E. (2024). Fairness and bias in artificial intelligence: A brief survey of sources, impacts, and mitigation strategies. *Science, 6*(1), 3. https://doi.org/10.3390/sci6010003

Gligorea, I., Cioca, M., Oancea, R., Gorski, A.-T., Gorski, H., & Tudorache, P. (2023). Adaptive learning using artificial intelligence in e-learning: A literature review. *Education Sciences, 13*(12), 1216. https://doi.org/10.3390/educsci13121216

Hanna, A., Denton, E., Smart, A., & Smith-Loud, J. (2020). Towards a critical race methodology in algorithmic fairness. In *Proceedings of the 2020 Conference on Fairness, Accountability, and Transparency (FAT'20)* (pp. 501–512). Association for Computing Machinery. https://doi.org/10.1145/3351095.3372826

Jian, M. (2023). Personalized learning through AI. *Advances in Engineering Innovation, 5*, 16–19. https://doi.org/10.54254/2977-3903/5/2023039

Luzano, J. (2024). An integrative review of AI-powered STEM education. *International Journal of Academic Pedagogical Research, 8*(4), 113–118.

Memarian, B., & Doleck, T. (2024). A review of assessment for learning with artificial intelligence. *Computers in Human Behavior: Artificial Humans, 2*(1), 100040. https://doi.org/10.1016/j.chbah.2023.100040

Mumuni, A., & Mumuni, F. (2022). Data augmentation: A comprehensive survey of modern approaches. *Array, 16*, 100258. https://doi.org/10.1016/j.array.2022.100258

Ravichandran, K., Virgin, B. A., Tiwari, A., Javheri, S. B., Fatma, G., & Lourens, M. (2023). Predictive analysis in education: Using artificial intelligence models to identify learning difficulties early. In *Proceedings of the 2023 10th IEEE Uttar Pradesh Section International Conference on Electrical, Electronics and Computer Engineering (UPCON)* (pp. 1754–1758). IEEE. https://doi.org/10.1109/UPCON59197.2023.10434783

Salas-Pilco, S. Z., Xiao, K., & Hu, X. (2022). Artificial intelligence and learning analytics in teacher education: A systematic review. *Education Sciences, 12*(8), 569. https://doi.org/10.3390/educsci12080569

Walker, M. E., Olivera-Aguilar, M., Lehman, B., Laitusis, C., Guzman-Orth, D., & Gholson, M. (2023). Culturally responsive assessment: Provisional principles. *ETS Research Report Series, 2023*(1), 1–24. https://doi.org/10.1002/ets2.12374

3 Automated Grading Systems
Enhancing Efficiency and Consistency in Student Assessments

S. C. Vetrivel, V. P. Arun, Ramya Ambikapathi, and T. P. Saravanan

3.1 Introduction

3.1.1 Overview of Automated Grading Systems

Automated grading systems utilize advanced technologies such as artificial intelligence (AI), machine learning (ML), and natural language processing (NLP) to evaluate and score student assessments. These systems are designed to replicate the grading process traditionally performed by human educators, analyzing various forms of student work including multiple-choice tests, essays, and even complex problem-solving tasks (Alqadi & Maletic, 2017). Automated grading systems can process large volumes of data quickly and accurately, identifying patterns and assessing student performance based on predefined criteria. By leveraging algorithms and data analytics, these systems provide objective and consistent grading, reducing the potential for human error and bias. The development of automated grading systems has revolutionized the educational landscape, offering scalable solutions for institutions to manage assessments efficiently, particularly in environments with large student populations.

3.1.2 Importance of Consistency and Efficiency in Assessments

Consistency and efficiency are critical components of effective educational assessments. Consistency ensures that all students are graded according to the same standards, thereby promoting fairness and equity in the educational process. In traditional grading, human factors such as fatigue, bias, and subjective judgment can lead to inconsistencies. Automated grading systems mitigate these issues by applying uniform grading criteria across all assessments, ensuring that every student is evaluated equally. Efficiency is equally important, as timely feedback is essential for the learning process. Automated systems can deliver immediate results, allowing students to quickly understand their performance and areas for improvement (Aziz et al., 2015). This prompt feedback loop aids in reinforcing learning concepts and helps educators identify and address student needs more swiftly. By enhancing

DOI: 10.1201/9781003470304-3

both consistency and efficiency, automated grading systems support a more transparent and effective educational environment.

3.2 History and Evolution of Grading Systems

3.2.1 Traditional Grading Methods

Traditional grading methods have been the cornerstone of educational assessment for centuries. These methods typically involve manual evaluation by educators who assess student performance based on a set of criteria outlined in rubrics or scoring guidelines. Grading can encompass a variety of assessment types, including multiple-choice tests, essays, projects, and oral presentations (Becker, 2016). The process relies heavily on the teacher's expertise and judgment, which can be influenced by subjective factors such as personal bias, fatigue, and varying levels of strictness. Traditional grading methods are time-consuming, particularly with large class sizes, and can lead to delays in providing feedback to students. Despite these challenges, traditional grading remains a widely used approach due to its ability to offer personalized feedback and nuanced evaluation that can take into account the individual student's learning context.

3.2.2 Emergence of Automated Grading

The emergence of automated grading systems represents a significant shift in the landscape of educational assessment. This shift began in earnest in the late 20th century with the advent of computer-based testing and scoring. Early automated grading systems were primarily used for multiple-choice tests, employing optical mark recognition (OMR) technology to quickly and accurately score answer sheets. As technology advanced, so did the capabilities of automated grading systems (Börstler, 2018). The integration of AI and ML enabled these systems to handle more complex assessment types, such as essays and short answer questions. NLP technologies allowed for the analysis of written responses, evaluating grammar, coherence, and content relevance (Chou & Chen, 2021). The development of sophisticated algorithms and neural networks further enhanced the ability of automated grading systems to replicate human grading standards with high accuracy. Today, automated grading systems are increasingly adopted across educational institutions, driven by the need for efficiency, scalability, and consistency in assessments. These systems not only streamline the grading process but also provide valuable analytics and insights into student performance, aiding in the overall improvement of educational outcomes.

3.2.3 Milestones in Automated Grading Technology

The evolution of automated grading technology has been marked by several key milestones, each contributing to the advancement and refinement of these systems.

1960s – Introduction of OMR: The initial development of automated grading technology began with OMR, a method used to score multiple-choice tests. OMR technology allowed for the rapid processing of answer sheets by detecting marks made on paper and converting them into electronic data (De Souza et al., 2017). This was one of the first instances of automation in grading, significantly speeding up the assessment process and reducing manual errors.

1980s – Development of Computerized Test Scoring: With the rise of personal computers, educational institutions began adopting computerized test scoring systems. These systems expanded beyond OMR to include basic data analysis capabilities, enabling more sophisticated grading and reporting. This period saw the integration of databases and software that could handle a variety of test formats and produce detailed performance reports.

1990s – Emergence of AI and Early Essay Scoring: The 1990s marked the introduction of early AI techniques in grading. Initial systems used simple algorithms to assess essay responses, focusing on structural elements like grammar and syntax. These systems laid the groundwork for more advanced NLP capabilities.

2000s – Advancements in NLP: The early 2000s saw significant progress in NLP, which enabled automated grading systems to analyze and evaluate more complex aspects of written text, such as coherence, content relevance, and argument structure (De Souza et al., 2005). Systems like the educational testing service's (ETS) e-rater were developed to assess essays and other open-ended responses with increasing accuracy.

2010s – Integration of ML and Deep Learning: The 2010s witnessed the integration of ML and deep learning algorithms into automated grading systems. These technologies enhanced the ability of systems to understand context, infer meaning, and evaluate nuanced aspects of student responses (Dixson & Worrell, 2016). The use of neural networks and advanced statistical models allowed for more sophisticated grading capabilities, including the ability to handle a broader range of assessment types.

2020s – Widespread Adoption and Refinement: The current decade has seen widespread adoption of automated grading systems across educational institutions. Enhanced by continuous improvements in AI and ML, these systems now offer real-time feedback, personalized learning insights, and integration with digital learning platforms (Dong et al., 2020). Innovations such as adaptive learning technologies and predictive analytics are being incorporated to further refine assessment accuracy and provide actionable insights into student performance.

2024 – Holistic Assessment Approaches: Automated grading technologies have evolved to support holistic assessment methods, incorporating formative and summative assessments while providing real-time feedback to support learning processes. Advanced models now also consider emotional and engagement metrics to provide a comprehensive understanding of student learning.

3.3 Technologies behind Automated Grading

3.3.1 Machine Learning and Artificial Intelligence

ML and AI are at the core of modern automated grading systems. ML algorithms are designed to learn from data and improve their performance over time without being explicitly programmed for each task. In the context of automated grading, ML models are trained on large datasets of student responses and corresponding grades to recognize patterns and make predictions about the quality of new submissions (Eleyan et al., 2020). AI enhances these systems by enabling more complex decision-making processes, such as evaluating the relevance and accuracy of student answers. These technologies allow automated grading systems to handle a wide range of assessment types, from multiple-choice questions to open-ended essays, with increasing accuracy and efficiency.

3.3.2 Natural Language Processing for Text Analysis

NLP is a critical technology in automated grading, particularly for evaluating written text. NLP involves the application of algorithms to understand, interpret, and generate human language. In automated grading systems, NLP techniques are used to analyze the content, structure, and coherence of student essays and written responses (Gerdes et al., 2010). NLP tools can assess grammar, spelling, and punctuation while also evaluating the semantic meaning of the text. Advanced NLP models can understand context and nuance, allowing for a more nuanced assessment of complex responses. This technology enables automated systems to provide feedback on both the technical and conceptual aspects of written work.

3.3.3 Image Recognition for Handwritten and Graphical Assessments

Image recognition technology plays a vital role in grading assessments that include handwritten responses and graphical elements. This technology involves the use of algorithms to interpret visual data from images, such as scanned test papers or handwritten assignments (Gulwani et al., 2018). Image recognition systems can identify and classify characters, symbols, and shapes, enabling the automated grading of handwritten answers and mathematical equations. For graphical assessments, such as diagrams or art projects, image recognition can assess the accuracy and completeness of visual representations. This technology allows for the automation of grading tasks that were previously time-consuming and labor-intensive, providing a more efficient and scalable solution.

3.3.4 Algorithm Design and Functionality

The design and functionality of algorithms underpin the effectiveness of automated grading systems. Algorithms are the set of rules and calculations used by grading systems to evaluate and score student submissions (Gusukuma et al., 2018). The design of these algorithms involves defining the criteria and weights for different aspects of the assessment, such as accuracy, relevance, and presentation. Functionality encompasses how these algorithms process input data, apply grading rules, and generate scores. Sophisticated algorithms may use techniques such as regression analysis, classification, and clustering to interpret data. The effectiveness of an automated grading system depends on the quality of its algorithmic design, which must balance accuracy, fairness, and scalability to meet educational needs.

3.4 Implementation of Automated Grading Systems

3.4.1 Integration with Existing Educational Systems

Integrating automated grading systems with existing educational frameworks requires a careful and strategic approach to ensure seamless functionality and compatibility (Haendler et al., 2020). The process begins with assessing the current technological infrastructure of the educational institution, including learning management systems (LMS), student information systems, and assessment platforms. Automated grading systems must be compatible with these existing systems to facilitate smooth data transfer and interoperability.

Technical Integration: This involves aligning the automated grading system's technical specifications with those of the institution's current systems. Application programming interfaces (APIs) and middleware solutions are often employed to enable data exchange between systems (Haldeman et al., 2018). For example, grades and feedback generated by the automated system need to be accurately recorded in the LMS, where students and educators can access them.

Data Management: Ensuring that data flows correctly between systems is crucial. Automated grading systems must handle various data formats and structures, such as student submissions, grading rubrics, and feedback. Data synchronization processes must be established to maintain consistency and accuracy across platforms.

User Training and Support: Successful integration also requires training for educators and administrators. This includes familiarizing them with the new system's features, functionalities, and potential issues (Hameer & Pientka, 2019). Ongoing technical support is essential to address any integration challenges that may arise and to ensure that the system operates effectively.

Testing and Evaluation: Before full-scale deployment, comprehensive testing is necessary to identify and resolve any issues. Pilot programs or phased rollouts can help evaluate the system's performance in real-world conditions, ensuring that it meets the institution's needs and integrates smoothly with existing processes.

3.4.2 *Customization for Different Subjects and Assessment Types*

Customization is a key aspect of implementing automated grading systems, as different subjects and assessment types require tailored approaches to accurately evaluate student performance.

Subject-Specific Adaptations: Different subjects have unique grading criteria and evaluation standards. For instance, grading an essay in literature involves evaluating arguments and style, while grading a math problem focuses on accuracy and problem-solving steps (Hao, 2022). Automated grading systems must be customized to address these subject-specific requirements. This may involve developing specialized algorithms or modifying existing ones to accommodate the nuances of various disciplines.

Assessment Type Variations: The system must be adaptable to various types of assessments, including multiple-choice questions, short answers, essays, projects, and practical exercises. Each assessment type has its own grading challenges (Hao et al., 2019). For example, automated grading of essays requires sophisticated NLP capabilities, while grading multiple-choice questions is relatively straightforward.

Scoring Rubrics and Criteria: Customization also involves defining scoring rubrics and criteria specific to each type of assessment. Automated systems must be configured to interpret these rubrics accurately and apply them consistently (Hao & Tsikerdekis, 2019). This may require collaboration with subject matter experts to ensure that the grading criteria reflect the educational objectives and standards.

Feedback Mechanisms: Providing meaningful and actionable feedback is another aspect of customization. Automated grading systems should be designed to generate feedback that is relevant and helpful to students. This involves programming the system to identify common errors and provide constructive comments that guide students in improving their performance.

Flexibility and Scalability: As educational needs evolve, automated grading systems must be flexible and scalable. The system should support updates and adjustments to grading criteria, accommodate new assessment types, and scale to handle varying numbers of students and assessments.

3.4.3 *Training and Calibration of Grading Algorithms*

Training and calibration of grading algorithms are crucial steps in ensuring the accuracy and reliability of automated grading systems. These processes involve fine-tuning the algorithms to accurately reflect educational standards and provide fair evaluations of student work.

Training of Algorithms: The training process involves exposing the grading algorithms to large datasets of student assessments and their corresponding grades. This dataset serves as a reference for the algorithm to learn the patterns and criteria used in grading (Haque et al., 2022). During training, the system adjusts its parameters based on the feedback it receives, gradually improving its ability to assess new submissions. ML techniques, such as supervised learning, are often employed, where the algorithm learns from labeled examples to make predictions about unseen data. This process is iterative and requires continuous refinement to ensure that the algorithm captures the nuances of various assessment types and subjects.

Calibration: Calibration ensures that the automated grading system aligns with the established grading standards and rubrics. This step involves validating the algorithm's performance against a set of benchmark assessments and comparing its results with those of human graders. Calibration helps identify any discrepancies between the automated system's output and human judgments, allowing for adjustments to improve accuracy (Hart et al., 2023). This may include tweaking the algorithm's parameters, modifying the grading criteria, or incorporating additional training data. Effective calibration ensures that the system provides consistent and reliable grades, enhancing its credibility and acceptance among educators.

Ongoing Maintenance: Once the initial training and calibration are complete, ongoing maintenance is necessary to keep the grading algorithms up to date. This involves periodically retraining the system with new data, incorporating feedback from users, and adapting to changes in educational standards or assessment formats (Hegarty-Kelly & Mooney, 2021). Continuous monitoring and evaluation help maintain the system's accuracy and relevance over time.

3.4.4 User Interface and Accessibility

The user interface (UI) and accessibility of automated grading systems play a significant role in their effectiveness and adoption. A well-designed UI ensures that both educators and students can interact with the system intuitively and efficiently, while accessibility features guarantee that all users, including those with disabilities, can utilize the system effectively.

User Interface Design: The UI of an automated grading system should be user-friendly and intuitive, allowing users to navigate through different features and functionalities with ease. For educators, this includes interfaces for configuring grading criteria, reviewing student submissions, and analyzing grading reports (Ihantola et al., 2010). For students, it involves accessing their grades, feedback, and performance analytics. Key elements of a good UI design include clear layout, easy navigation, and responsive design that adapts to different devices and screen sizes. Customizable dashboards and streamlined workflows also enhance usability, enabling users to perform tasks efficiently.

Accessibility Features: Accessibility is a critical consideration in designing automated grading systems. The system should comply with accessibility standards, such as the Web Content Accessibility Guidelines (WCAG), to ensure that it is usable by individuals with disabilities (Insa & Silva, 2015). This includes providing alternative text for images, keyboard navigation options, and compatibility with screen readers. Accessibility features ensure that all users, regardless of their physical abilities, can interact with the system effectively and benefit from its functionalities.

Training and Support: Effective training and support resources are essential for helping users adapt to the automated grading system. This includes providing comprehensive documentation, tutorials, and help resources to guide users through the system's features. Support channels, such as help desks or online forums, should be available to assist users with any issues or questions they may encounter.

Feedback Mechanisms: Incorporating feedback mechanisms within the UI allows users to report issues, suggest improvements, and share their experiences. This feedback is valuable for ongoing system enhancement and ensuring that the system meets the needs of its users.

3.5 Benefits of Automated Grading

3.5.1 Enhancing Efficiency in Grading

Automated grading systems significantly enhance the efficiency of the grading process by streamlining and accelerating the evaluation of student assessments. Traditional grading methods, particularly for large classes, often require substantial time and effort from educators, as they manually review and score each student's work (Insa & Silva, 2018). Automated grading systems, by contrast, can process a vast number of assessments swiftly, thanks to their ability to handle and analyze data at high speeds.

Speed and Scalability: One of the primary advantages of automated grading is its capacity to provide rapid feedback. Automated systems can grade assessments almost instantaneously, which is particularly beneficial for large-scale standardized testing and online courses. This quick turnaround time allows students to receive timely feedback on their performance, facilitating a more dynamic and responsive learning environment.

Reduction in Administrative Burden: By automating the grading process, educators can significantly reduce their administrative workload (Insa et al., 2021). This reduction allows teachers to focus more on instructional activities, student engagement, and personalized support, rather than spending hours on grading. Automated systems handle repetitive tasks efficiently, freeing up valuable time for educators to concentrate on other aspects of teaching.

Consistency in Scoring: Automated grading systems provide consistent and reliable evaluation of assessments. Once programmed with specific grading criteria and algorithms, these systems apply the same standards uniformly across all submissions. This consistency ensures that all students are evaluated according to the same parameters, which is particularly useful in large classes or standardized testing scenarios.

3.5.2 Ensuring Consistency and Objectivity

Ensuring consistency and objectivity in grading is a fundamental benefit of automated grading systems. Traditional grading methods can be susceptible to various forms of bias and variability, which may impact the fairness of the assessment process. Automated grading systems address these concerns by providing a standardized approach to evaluation.

Uniform Application of Criteria: Automated grading systems apply pre-defined grading criteria consistently to all student submissions. Unlike human graders, who may vary in their interpretation of grading rubrics or be influenced by subjective factors, automated systems adhere strictly to the established parameters (Krusche et al., 2020). This uniform application ensures that every student's work is evaluated based on the same standards, promoting fairness and equity in the grading process.

Reduction of Bias: Automated grading systems help mitigate personal biases that can affect human graders. Factors such as grading fatigue, personal preferences, or unconscious bias can influence traditional grading. By removing these subjective elements, automated systems contribute to a more impartial evaluation of student performance (Leinonen et al., 2022). This objectivity is particularly important in maintaining the integrity of assessments and ensuring that all students are judged solely on the merit of their work.

Transparency and Accountability: Automated grading systems enhance transparency by providing clear and consistent criteria for assessment. Educators and students can review the grading algorithms and understand how scores are determined. This transparency fosters accountability and helps ensure that the grading process is fair and aligned with educational objectives.

Scalability and Standardization: Automated grading systems are scalable and can handle large volumes of assessments without compromising the quality of evaluation. This scalability is crucial for standardized testing and large educational institutions, where maintaining consistency across a high number of assessments is challenging (McBurney, 2015). Automated systems facilitate standardization, ensuring that grading practices are uniform across different sections, campuses, or even institutions.

3.5.3 Reducing Teacher Workload

Automated grading systems play a crucial role in alleviating the workload of teachers by automating repetitive and time-consuming grading tasks (Messer, 2022). Traditional grading, particularly in subjects requiring extensive written responses or complex problem-solving, can be labor-intensive and demanding. Automated systems significantly reduce this burden, enabling educators to focus on more impactful aspects of teaching.

Time Savings: One of the most direct benefits of automated grading is the substantial reduction in the time required for grading. Automated systems can process and evaluate large volumes of student work rapidly, completing tasks that would otherwise take educators several hours or even days. This efficiency allows teachers to manage their time more effectively, balancing their responsibilities between instruction, lesson planning, and student support.

Reduced Administrative Burden: By handling the grading process, automated systems decrease the administrative load on teachers. This reduction in administrative tasks frees up time for educators to engage more deeply with their students, develop creative lesson plans, and participate in professional development activities. As a result, teachers can enhance their teaching effectiveness and job satisfaction.

Consistency in Grading: Automated grading systems ensure that grading is consistent and impartial, eliminating the variability that can arise from different human graders. This consistency not only helps maintain fairness but also reduces the need for teachers to spend additional time reconciling discrepancies in grading across different sections or assignments.

Support for Diverse Assessment Types: Automated grading systems can manage various assessment types, including multiple-choice questions, short answers, and even essays. This versatility means that teachers are not required to manually grade each type of assessment individually, further reducing their workload and allowing them to focus on other instructional activities.

3.5.4 Providing Immediate Feedback

Providing immediate feedback is a significant advantage of automated grading systems, greatly enhancing the learning experience for students (Messer et al., 2023). Timely feedback is essential for effective learning, as it helps students understand their performance, identify areas for improvement, and make necessary adjustments to their study strategies.

Real-Time Feedback: Automated grading systems can deliver grades and feedback to students almost instantly after submission. This immediacy allows students to quickly review their performance, address mistakes, and reinforce their understanding of the study material (Narciss, 2008). Real-time feedback supports a more dynamic and responsive learning environment, where students can immediately apply corrective measures and enhance their learning.

Enhanced Learning Opportunities: Immediate feedback enables students to engage in iterative learning. By receiving prompt responses on their work, students can identify gaps in their knowledge and make adjustments before moving on to new topics. This iterative process helps deepen their understanding and improves overall learning outcomes.

Increased Motivation and Engagement: Timely feedback can also boost student motivation and engagement. When students receive prompt and constructive feedback, they are more likely to stay motivated and invested in their learning (Nayak et al., 2022). Immediate feedback provides students with a clear understanding of their progress and encourages them to take an active role in their educational journey.

Support for Personalized Learning: Automated grading systems can provide personalized feedback based on individual student performance. By analyzing patterns in student responses, these systems can offer targeted suggestions and resources tailored to each student's needs. This personalized approach helps address specific learning challenges and supports differentiated instruction.

3.6 Challenges and Limitations

3.6.1 Technical Challenges and Limitations

Automated grading systems, while promising, face several technical challenges and limitations that can affect their performance and reliability. One major challenge is ensuring the accuracy of grading algorithms. These algorithms must be meticulously designed and trained to handle various types of assessments and subjects. Inaccuracies can arise from insufficient training data, flawed algorithmic design, or discrepancies in grading criteria. For instance, while grading multiple-choice questions might be straightforward, assessing complex essays or nuanced responses requires sophisticated NLP techniques (Ouzzani et al., 2016). Ensuring that algorithms can effectively evaluate diverse responses is technically demanding and requires ongoing refinement. Another significant technical challenge is the integration of automated grading systems with existing educational technologies. Compatibility issues can arise, necessitating custom solutions or modifications to ensure seamless functionality (Page et al., 2021). This integration involves aligning the new system with current learning management systems (LMS), student information systems, and other educational platforms. Additionally, scalability is a concern, as the system must efficiently handle large volumes of assessments without compromising performance or accuracy. Addressing these technical challenges requires careful planning, robust solutions, and continuous technical support to ensure smooth operation and integration.

3.6.2 Addressing Bias in Automated Grading

Addressing bias in automated grading systems is a critical issue that impacts fairness and effectiveness. Automated systems can inadvertently perpetuate or introduce biases present in their training data. For example, if the dataset used to train the algorithms contains biases related to specific writing styles or content types, these biases can be reflected in the system's evaluations (Paiva et al., 2022). This is particularly problematic in ensuring equitable treatment of all student submissions. To address algorithmic bias, it is essential to carefully curate training data and conduct regular audits of the grading algorithms. Transparency in the grading process is also crucial; educators and students need to understand the criteria and methods used by the system. This transparency helps in identifying and correcting biases. Incorporating human oversight into the grading process can further mitigate bias by allowing educators to review and validate the system's results (Parihar et al., 2017). Continuous monitoring and feedback from users are necessary to detect and address any emerging biases, ensuring that the system remains fair and equitable.

3.6.3 Security and Privacy Concerns

Security and privacy are paramount when implementing automated grading systems, as they handle sensitive student data. Protecting this data from unauthorized access and cyber threats is a major concern. Automated grading systems must implement robust security measures, such as encryption and secure authentication protocols, to safeguard personal and academic information. Compliance with privacy regulations, such as the Family Educational Rights and Privacy Act (FERPA) and the General Data Protection Regulation (GDPR), is also essential (Qian & Lehman, 2017). Automated grading systems must ensure that data is collected, stored, and used in accordance with these regulations to protect student privacy. This involves establishing clear data-handling practices, including data anonymization and secure storage, to minimize privacy risks.

3.6.4 Acceptance and Adoption by Educators and Students

The acceptance and adoption of automated grading systems by educators and students can present significant challenges. Educators may be resistant to change due to concerns about the accuracy of the system, potential loss of personal judgment, or the need for additional training. To overcome this resistance, it is important to address these concerns through comprehensive training programs, demonstrate the benefits of the system, and provide ongoing support (Rahman et al., 2020). Building trust and confidence in the automated grading system is crucial for its successful adoption. Educators and students must be assured that the system provides fair and accurate evaluations. Transparency in how the system operates, regular updates, and feedback mechanisms can help build this trust.

3.7 Case Studies and Real-World Applications

3.7.1 Successful Implementations in Various Educational Institutions

The adoption of automated grading systems has proven beneficial in a range of educational institutions globally. These case studies, including those from Indian contexts, highlight how automated grading can enhance grading efficiency, improve feedback quality, and support educators in managing large volumes of student assessments.

3.7.1.1 University of California, Berkeley

At the University of California, Berkeley, automated grading systems have been successfully implemented in several large-scale courses, including introductory computer science and mathematics classes. The institution uses automated tools to grade multiple-choice questions, programming assignments, and even some types of essays. By integrating these systems with their existing LMS, UC Berkeley has streamlined the grading process and significantly reduced turnaround times for student feedback (Rai et al., 2022). The system's ability to handle large volumes of assessments efficiently has been particularly beneficial for high-enrollment courses, allowing instructors to focus more on personalized teaching and student engagement.

3.7.1.2 Georgia Institute of Technology

Georgia Tech has implemented an automated grading system in its online master's in computer science program. The system is used to grade coding assignments and projects, which are a significant component of the program. Georgia Tech's automated grading platform, known as "Autograder," provides immediate feedback on student submissions, helping learners identify and correct errors in real time. This approach has enhanced the learning experience by allowing students to receive timely, actionable feedback, thus accelerating their progress through the program. The successful deployment of Autograder has also reduced the grading workload for instructors, enabling them to devote more time to curriculum development and student interaction.

3.7.1.3 Stanford University

At Stanford University, automated grading systems have been integrated into various engineering and business courses. The university employs a combination of ML and NLP to evaluate complex assignments, such as essays and case studies. Stanford's system is designed to assess both the content and structure of written responses, providing detailed feedback on areas such as argumentation, coherence, and style. This implementation has not only improved grading efficiency but also enhanced the quality of feedback provided to students. The university has noted that the automated system's consistency and objectivity have helped in maintaining high grading standards across different sections of the same course.

3.7.1.4 Carnegie Mellon University

Carnegie Mellon University has utilized automated grading in its online courses through the use of advanced algorithms for assessing student performance in quizzes and written assignments. The university's system incorporates adaptive learning technologies that adjust the difficulty of assessments based on individual student performance (Savelka et al., 2023). This personalized approach has allowed Carnegie Mellon to provide targeted feedback and support to students, improving their learning outcomes. The successful integration of automated grading has also facilitated better data analysis and reporting, enabling instructors to track student progress more effectively and identify areas for improvement in the course design.

3.7.1.5 Singapore University of Technology and Design

The Singapore University of Technology and Design has implemented an automated grading system for its design and engineering courses, where students submit project work and prototypes. The system uses image recognition and ML algorithms to evaluate and provide feedback on the design quality and functionality of student projects. This innovative application of automated grading has helped streamline the evaluation process for complex, practical assignments, allowing instructors to manage large numbers of submissions more efficiently (Sendjaja et al., 2021). The university's experience highlights the potential of automated grading to support creative and technical assessments beyond traditional multiple-choice or written exams.

3.7.1.6 Indian Institute of Technology (IIT) Bombay

The Indian Institute of Technology (IIT) Bombay has integrated automated grading systems in several of its undergraduate and postgraduate courses. For example, in computer science and engineering programs, IIT Bombay uses automated tools to grade programming assignments and projects. The system, developed in-house, leverages both automated scripts and ML algorithms to assess code functionality, efficiency, and adherence to project specifications. This approach has streamlined the grading process, allowing for faster feedback and enabling instructors to manage large classes more effectively (Sharmin, 2021). The system's success at IIT Bombay underscores the potential for automated grading to enhance educational efficiency in India's top technical institutions.

3.1.1.7 *National Institute of Technology (NIT), Warangal*

At NIT Warangal, automated grading systems have been deployed for online quizzes and assignments across various engineering disciplines. The system utilizes a combination of automated algorithms and manual oversight to ensure accurate grading and timely feedback. The integration of automated grading has been particularly beneficial in handling the high volume of assessments typical in large engineering courses. By reducing the grading burden on faculty and accelerating feedback, NIT Warangal has improved the overall learning experience for students and facilitated more efficient course management.

3.7.1.8 *Amity University*

Amity University has implemented automated grading systems in its online and blended learning courses. The university uses these systems to grade assignments and quizzes, particularly in large, multi-section courses. The automated system provides immediate feedback to students, helping them understand their performance and areas for improvement quickly. Additionally, it assists faculty in managing grading efficiently, allowing them to focus on interactive teaching methods and student support. The implementation at Amity University highlights the adaptability of automated grading systems to diverse educational contexts within India.

3.7.2 *Impact on Student Performance and Teacher Workload*

The implementation of automated grading systems has had a noticeable impact on both student performance and teacher workload across various educational institutions. These effects are evident in the improvements in grading efficiency, the timeliness of feedback, and the overall quality of education.

Impact on Student Performance: Automated grading systems contribute significantly to enhanced student performance by providing timely and actionable feedback. For instance, students who receive immediate feedback on their assignments can quickly identify areas for improvement and adjust their study strategies accordingly. This rapid response helps students learn more effectively and reinforces their understanding of the material. Case studies from institutions such as Georgia Tech and IIT Bombay reveal that students benefit from the quicker turnaround of grades and constructive comments, which leads to better academic performance and higher engagement levels. The ability to continuously track and respond to feedback allows students to address issues promptly, fostering a more iterative and responsive learning process.

Impact on Teacher Workload: The reduction in teacher workload is one of the most pronounced benefits of automated grading systems. By automating repetitive tasks such as grading multiple-choice questions and programming assignments, educators are freed from the time-consuming aspects of assessment. This alleviation of grading burdens enables teachers to allocate more time to instructional activities, such as developing course content, engaging in one-on-one student interactions, and participating in professional development (Vetrivel et al., 2024). Institutions like Stanford and Carnegie Mellon have reported that automated grading systems have allowed faculty to concentrate on enhancing the quality of their teaching and providing more personalized support to students. The efficiency gained through automation helps instructors manage large classes more effectively, contributing to a more balanced and fulfilling teaching experience.

3.7.3 Lessons Learned and Best Practices

The successful deployment of automated grading systems reveals several crucial lessons and best practices essential for optimizing their effectiveness. Ensuring the accuracy and reliability of grading algorithms is paramount, requiring extensive testing and continuous refinement to maintain high standards. Comprehensive training for educators and students facilitates smoother adoption and effective use of the system. Addressing and mitigating biases is vital to ensure fairness and equity in assessments, necessitating regular evaluations and transparency. Seamless integration with existing educational technologies is crucial for operational efficiency, and maintaining robust data security measures is essential to protect student information. By adhering to these best practices, institutions can leverage automated grading systems to enhance grading efficiency, provide timely feedback, and support personalized learning experiences.

3.8 Future Directions and Innovations

3.8.1 Advances in AI and ML

The future of automated grading systems is closely intertwined with advances in AI and ML. As these technologies evolve, they promise to enhance the capabilities of automated grading systems, making them more sophisticated and effective. Recent advancements in AI and ML enable more accurate and nuanced assessments by improving algorithms that can understand and evaluate complex student responses. For example, the development of deep learning models and NLP techniques allows systems to better grasp context, sentiment, and subtle nuances in written assignments (Vetrivel et al., 2024). These advancements not only increase the reliability of automated grading but also enable the system to adapt to various types of assessments, providing more personalized and precise feedback. Continued progress in AI and ML will likely lead to more intelligent grading systems that can handle a broader range of evaluation tasks and deliver richer insights into student performance.

3.8.2 Potential for Personalized Learning

Automated grading systems have significant potential to support personalized learning by tailoring educational experiences to individual student needs. With the ability to analyze large volumes of data, these systems can identify patterns in student performance and adapt instructional content accordingly. For instance, based on performance metrics, automated systems can recommend additional resources, suggest specific areas for improvement, and adjust the difficulty level of assignments to better match each student's proficiency. This personalized approach can enhance learning outcomes by addressing gaps in knowledge and providing targeted support. The integration of automated grading with adaptive learning platforms is likely to offer more customized educational experiences, fostering a learning environment where students can progress at their own pace and receive tailored feedback that supports their unique learning journey.

3.9 Conclusion

Automated grading systems represent a transformative advancement in educational assessment, offering significant improvements in efficiency and consistency. By leveraging technologies such as AI and ML, these systems streamline the grading process, providing timely and objective evaluations of student work. The ability to handle large volumes of assessments with precision and speed reduces the administrative burden on educators, allowing them to focus more on instructional quality and student engagement. Additionally, automated grading systems offer the potential for personalized learning experiences, adapting to individual student needs and enhancing educational outcomes. However, the successful implementation of these systems requires careful consideration of challenges such as algorithmic bias, data security, and integration with existing educational technologies. As educational institutions continue to explore and adopt automated grading solutions, ongoing advancements in technology and best practices will play a crucial role in addressing these challenges and maximizing the benefits. Ultimately, automated grading systems hold the promise of a more efficient, equitable, and responsive education system, driving improvements in both teaching and learning.

References

Alqadi, B. S., & Maletic, J. I. (2017). An empirical study of debugging patterns among novice programmers. In *Proceedings of the 2017 ACM SIGCSE Technical Symposium on Computer Science Education (SIGCSE '17)* (pp. 15–20). Association for Computing Machinery. https://doi.org/10.1145/3017680.3017761

Aziz, M., Chi, H., Tibrewal, A., Grossman, M., & Sarkar, V. (2015). Auto-grading for parallel programs. In *Proceedings of the Workshop on Education for High-Performance Computing (EduHPC'15)* (Article 3). Association for Computing Machinery. https://doi.org/10.1145/2831425.2831427

Becker, B. A. (2016). An effective approach to enhancing compiler error messages. In *Proceedings of the 47th ACM Technical Symposium on Computing Science Education (SIGCSE'16)* (pp. 126–131). Association for Computing Machinery. https://doi.org/10.1145/2839509.2844584

Börstler, J., Störrle, H., Toll, D., van Assema, J., Duran, R., Hooshangi, S., et al. (2018). "I know it when I see it": Perceptions of code quality: ITiCSE'17 working group report. In *Proceedings of the 2017 ITiCSE Conference on Working Group Reports (ITiCSE-WGR')* (pp. 70–85). Association for Computing Machinery. https://doi.org/10.1145/3174781.3174785

Chou, C. Y., & Chen, Y. J. (2021). Virtual teaching assistant for grading programming assignments: Non-dichotomous pattern-based program output matching and partial grading approach. In *2021 IEEE 4th International Conference on Knowledge Innovation and Invention (ICKII)* (pp. 170–175). https://doi.org/10.1109/ICKII51822.2021.9574713

De Souza, D. M., Kölling, M., & Barbosa, E. F. (2017). Most common fixes students use to improve the correctness of their programs. In *2017 IEEE Frontiers in Education Conference (FIE)* (pp. 1–9). https://doi.org/10.1109/FIE.2017.8190524

De Souza, S. C. B., Anquetil, N., & de Oliveira, K. M. (2005). A study of the documentation essential to software maintenance. In *Proceedings of the 23rd Annual International Conference on Design of Communication: Documenting & Designing for Pervasive Information (SIGDOC'05)* (pp. 68–75). Association for Computing Machinery. https://doi.org/10.1145/1085313.1085331

Dixson, D. D., & Worrell, F. C. (2016). Formative and summative assessment in the classroom. *Theory into Practice, 55*(2), 153–159. https://doi.org/10.1080/00405841.2016.1148989

Dong, Y., Hou, J., & Lu, X. (2020). An intelligent online judge system for programming training. In Y. Nah, B. Cui, S.-W. Lee, J. Xu Yu, Y.-S. Moon, & S. E. Whang (Eds.), *Database Systems for Advanced Applications* (pp. 785–789). Springer International Publishing. https://doi.org/10.1007/978-3-030-59419-0_57

Eleyan, D., Othman, A., & Eleyan, A. (2020). Enhancing software comments readability using Flesch reading ease score. *Information, 11*(9), 1–25. https://doi.org/10.3390/info11090430

Gerdes, A., Jeuring, J. T., & Heeren, B. J. (2010). Using strategies for assessment of programming exercises. In *Proceedings of the 41st ACM Technical Symposium on Computer Science Education (SIGCSE'10)* (pp. 441–445). Association for Computing Machinery. https://doi.org/10.1145/1734263.1734412

Gulwani, S., Radiček, I., & Zuleger, F. (2018). Automated clustering and program repair for introductory programming assignments. *SIGPLAN Notices, 53*(4), 465–480. https://doi.org/10.1145/3296979.3192387

Gusukuma, L., Bart, A. C., Kafura, D., & Ernst, J. (2018). Misconception-driven feedback: Results from an experimental study. In *Proceedings of the 2018 ACM Conference on International Computing Education Research (ICER'18)* (pp. 160–168). Association for Computing Machinery. https://doi.org/10.1145/3230977.3231002

Haendler, T., Neumann, G., & Smirnov, F. (2020). Refactutor: An interactive tutoring system for software refactoring. In H. C. Lane, S. Zvacek, & J. Uhomoibhi (Eds.), *Computer Supported Education* (pp. 236–261). Springer International Publishing, Cham. https://doi.org/10.1007/978-3-030-58459-7_12

Haldeman, G., Tjang, A., Babeş-Vroman, M., Bartos, S., Shah, J., Yucht, D., & Nguyen, T. D. (2018). Providing meaningful feedback for autograding of programming assignments. In *Proceedings of the 49th ACM Technical Symposium on Computer Science Education (SIGCSE'18)* (pp. 278–283). Association for Computing Machinery, Baltimore, MD. https://doi.org/10.1145/3159450.3159502

Hameer, A., & Pientka, B. (2019). Teaching the art of functional programming using automated grading (experience report). In *Proceedings of the ACM on Programming Languages, 3(ICFP)*, Article 115. https://doi.org/10.1145/3341695

Hao, Q. (2022). Towards understanding the effective design of automated formative feedback for programming assignments. *Computer Science Education, 32*(1), 105–127. https://doi.org/10.1080/08993408.2020.1860408

Hao, Q., & Tsikerdekis, M. (2019). How automated feedback is delivered matters: Formative feedback and knowledge transfer. In *2019 IEEE Frontiers in Education Conference (FIE)* (pp. 1–6). https://doi.org/10.1109/FIE43999.2019.9028686

Hao, Q., Wilson, J. P., Ottaway, C., Iriumi, N., Arakawa, K., & Smith, D. H. (2019). Investigating the essential of meaningful automated formative feedback for programming assignments. In *2019 IEEE Symposium on Visual Languages and Human-Centric Computing (VL/HCC)* (pp. 151–155). https://doi.org/10.1109/VLHCC.2019.8818922

Haque, S., Eberhart, Z., Bansal, A., & McMillan, C. (2022). Semantic similarity metrics for evaluating source code summarization. In *Proceedings of the 30th IEEE/ACM International Conference on Program Comprehension (ICPC'22)* (pp. 36–47). Association for Computing Machinery. https://doi.org/10.1145/3524610.3527909

Hart, R., Hays, B., McMillin, C., Rezig, E. K., Rodriguez-Rivera, G., & Turkstra, J. A. (2023). Eastwood-tidy: C linting for automated code style assessment in programming courses. In *Proceedings of the 54th ACM Technical Symposium on Computer Science Education V. 1 (SIGCSE 2023)* (pp. 799–805). Association for Computing Machinery. https://doi.org/10.1145/3545945.3569817

Hegarty-Kelly, E., & Mooney, A. (2021). Analysis of an automatic grading system within first year computer science programming modules. In *Proceedings of the 5th Conference on Computing Education Practice (CEP'21)* (pp. 17–20). Association for Computing Machinery, Durham, United Kingdom. https://doi.org/10.1145/3437914.3437973

Ihantola, P., Ahoniemi, T., Karavirta, V., & Seppälä, O. (2010). Review of recent systems for automatic assessment of programming assignments. In *Proceedings of the 10th Koli Calling International Conference on Computing Education Research (Koli Calling'10)* (pp. 86–93). Association for Computing Machinery. https://doi.org/10.1145/1930464.1930480

Insa, D., Pérez, S., Silva, J., & Tamarit, S. (2021). Semiautomatic generation and assessment of Java exercises in engineering education. *Computer Applications in Engineering Education, 29*(5), 1034–1050. https://doi.org/10.1002/cae.22443

Insa, D., & Silva, J. (2015). Semi-automatic assessment of unrestrained Java code: A library, a DSL, and a workbench to assess exams and exercises. In *Proceedings of* the 2015 ACM Conference on Innovation and Technology in Computer Science Education (ITiCSE'15) (pp. 39–44). Association for Computing Machinery. https://doi.org/10.1145/2729094.2742615

Insa, D., & Silva, J. (2018). Automatic assessment of Java code. *Computer Languages, Systems & Structures, 53*, 59–72. https://doi.org/10.1016/j.cl.2017.09.001

Krusche, S., von Frankenberg, N., Reimer, L. M., & Bruegge, B. (2020). An interactive learning method to engage students in modeling. In *Proceedings of the ACM/IEEE 42nd International Conference on Software Engineering: Software Engineering Education and Training (ICSE-SEET'20)* (pp. 12–22). Association for Computing Machinery, Seoul, South Korea. https://doi.org/10.1145/3377814.3381701

Leinonen, J., Denny, P., & Whalley, J. (2022). A comparison of immediate and scheduled feedback in introductory programming projects. In *Proceedings of the 53rd ACM Technical Symposium on Computer Science Education – Volume 1 (SIGCSE 2022)* (pp. 885–891). Association for Computing Machinery, Providence, RI. https://doi.org/10.1145/3478431.3499372

McBurney, P. W. (2015). Automatic documentation generation via source code summarization. In *2015 IEEE/ACM 37th IEEE International Conference on Software Engineering* (Vol. 2, pp. 903–906). https://doi.org/10.1109/ICSE.2015.288

Messer, M. (2022). *Automated Grading and Feedback Tools: A Systematic Review.* https://doi.org/10.17605/OSF.IO/VXTF9

Messer, M., Brown, N. C. C., Kölling, M., & Shi, M. (2023). Machine learning-based automated grading and feedback tools for programming: A meta-analysis. In *Proceedings of the 2023 Conference on Innovation and Technology in Computer Science Education V. 1 (ITiCSE 2023)* (pp. 491–497). Association for Computing Machinery, Turku, Finland. https://doi.org/10.1145/3587102.3588822

Narciss, S. (2008). Feedback strategies for interactive learning tasks. In Spector, J. M., Merrill, M. D., van Merrienboer, J., & Driscoll, M. P. (Eds.), *Handbook of Research on Educational Communications and Technology* (pp. 125–143). Taylor and Francis, New York. https://doi.org/10.4324/9780203880869

Nayak, S., Agarwal, R., & Khatri, S. K. (2022). Automated assessment tools for grading of programming assignments: A review. In *2022 International Conference on Computer Communication and Informatics (ICCCI)* (pp. 1–4). https://doi.org/10.1109/ICCCI54379.2022.9740769

Ouzzani, M., Hammady, H., Fedorowicz, Z., & Elmagarmid, A. (2016). Rayyan–A web and mobile app for systematic reviews. *Systematic Reviews, 5*(1), 1–10. https://doi.org/10.1186/s13643-016-0384-4

Page, M. J., McKenzie, J. E., Bossuyt, P. M., Boutron, I., Hoffmann, T. C., Mulrow, C. D., et al. (2021). The PRISMA 2020 statement: An updated guideline for reporting systematic reviews. *Systematic Reviews, 10*(1), 89. https://doi.org/10.1186/s13643-021-01626-4

Paiva, J. C., Leal, J. P., & Figueira, Á. (2022). Automated assessment in computer science education: A state-of-the-art review. *ACM Transactions on Computing Education, 22*(3), 34. https://doi.org/10.1145/3513140

Parihar, S., Dadachanji, Z., Singh, P. K., Das, R., Karkare, A., & Bhattacharya, A. (2017). Automatic grading and feedback using program repair for introductory programming courses. In *Proceedings of the 2017 ACM Conference on Innovation and Technology in Computer Science Education (ITiCSE'17)* (pp. 92–97). Association for Computing Machinery, Bologna, Italy. https://doi.org/10.1145/3059009.3059026

Qian, Y., & Lehman, J. (2017). Students' misconceptions and other difficulties in introductory programming: A literature review. *ACM Transactions on Computing Education, 18*(1), 1. https://doi.org/10.1145/3077618

Rahman, M. M., Watanobe, Y., & Nakamura, K. (2020). Source code assessment and classification based on estimated error probability using attentive LSTM language model and its application in programming education. *Applied Sciences, 10*(8), 1–21. https://doi.org/10.3390/app10082926

Rai, S., Belwal, R. C., & Gupta, A. (2022). A review on source code documentation. *ACM Transactions on Intelligent Systems and Technology, 13*(5), 84. https://doi.org/10.1145/3519312

Savelka, J., Agarwal, A., Bogart, C., Song, Y., & Sakr, M. (2023). Can generative pre-trained transformers (GPT) pass assessments in higher education programming courses? In *Proceedings of the 2023 Conference on Innovation and Technology in Computer Science Education V. 1 (ITiCSE 2023)* (pp. 117–123). Association for Computing Machinery, Turku, Finland. https://doi.org/10.1145/3587102.3588792

Sendjaja, K., Rukmono, S. A., & Perdana, R. S. (2021). Evaluating control-flow graph similarity for grading programming exercises. In *2021 International Conference on Data and Software Engineering (ICoDSE)* (pp. 1–6). https://doi.org/10.1109/ICoDSE53690.2021.9648464

Sharmin, S. (2021). Creativity in CS1: A literature review. *ACM Transactions on Computing Education, 22*(2), 16. https://doi.org/10.1145/3459995

Vetrivel, S. C., Sowmiya, K. C., Gomathi, T., & Arun, V. P. (2024). Engaging online classes through gamification: Leveraging innovative tools and technologies. In R. Bansal, A. Chakir, A. Hafaz Ngah, F. Rabby, & A. Jain (Eds.), *AI Algorithms and ChatGPT for Student Engagement in Online Learning* (pp. 171–191). IGI Global, Hershey, PA. https://doi.org/10.4018/979-8-3693-4268-8.ch012

4 The Potential and Drawbacks of Machine Learning for Student Assessment

K. Kartheeban, V. Aanandaram,
D. Lakshminarasimman, and D. Kabalishwaran

4.1 Introduction

The way that student assessments are carried out is changing dramatically as a result of the introduction of machine learning (ML) into higher education. Conventional evaluation techniques, which are frequently defined by standardized testing and set review intervals, have long faced criticism for their incapacity to accommodate the unique demands and learning preferences of individual students. ML algorithms, on the other hand, present an innovative method by utilizing massive amounts of data to deliver continuous, personalized, and adaptable assessments that may dynamically adjust to each student's individual learning path. The educational experience can be greatly improved by using ML algorithms to offer personalized student assessments. To generate customized evaluations, these algorithms examine comprehensive data on learning practices, preferences, and student success. With the help of this customized method, teachers can pinpoint students' individual strengths and shortcomings and provide focused interventions that advance their learning. An ML-driven assessment system, for example, can maintain the ideal degree of challenge and engagement by dynamically adjusting the questions' complexity based on the students' answers. This flexibility helps to sustain students' enthusiasm and interest while also increasing the accuracy of examinations. AI has a variety of educational applications, such as personalized learning platforms to promote students' learning, automated assessment systems to aid teachers, and facial recognition systems to generate insights about learners' behaviors (Akgun & Greenhow, 2022).

Furthermore, the ability of ML to deliver insights based on data is revolutionizing decision-making in education. Deeper understanding of the ways in which various elements influence learning outcomes can be gained by ML algorithms through the analysis of patterns and trends in student performance data. With the use of these insights, educators are better equipped to decide on curriculum development, instructional techniques, and resource allocation. Teachers might update lesson plans or offer more assistance to students who have persistent difficulties with a particular idea, for instance,

DOI: 10.1201/9781003470304-4

if data indicates that this is the case. A data-driven strategy like this guarantees the efficacy, timeliness, and targeting of educational initiatives. Another important benefit of ML in education is continuous assessment. Conventional evaluations, such as midterms and finals, are frequently given at set times and might not fairly represent a student's continuous learning. On the other hand, ML algorithms provide ongoing evaluation by continuously tracking student performance. With a more thorough and nuanced knowledge of student learning made possible by this continuous evaluation, prompt feedback and assistance are made possible. By identifying learning gaps early on, continuous assessment enables teachers to take remedial action before these gaps become major obstacles to students' academic progress. The use of artificial intelligence (AI) and ML into education has created new opportunities for personalized and adaptable learning experiences. These technologies offer the potential to respond to individual learners' requirements, provide focused support, and empower instructors to make data-driven decisions (Goel et al., 2024).

The use of ML in customized student assessments is not without difficulties, despite its many advantages. To guarantee that the application of ML technologies is just and responsible, ethical considerations including privacy, bias, and openness must be properly taken into account. The massive amount of data collecting necessary for ML algorithms to work well gives rise to privacy problems. Sensitive information regarding students' conduct, academic standing, and personal traits is frequently included in this data. It is critical to safeguard sensitive data from unwanted access and to maintain its confidentiality. To protect student privacy, educational institutions need to put strong data security measures in place and create explicit policies on data usage and storage. Another crucial concern is algorithmic bias. Because ML algorithms are trained on historical data, they could be biased by nature. If these prejudices are not dealt with, they may result in unjust evaluations that harm particular student groups. For instance, an algorithm may reinforce biases in gender or race in its evaluations if it was trained on data reflecting such biases. It is crucial to employ representative and diverse training data, put bias mitigation techniques into practice, and routinely check algorithms for bias in order to guarantee fairness. By taking these actions, assessment systems that are more egalitarian and give fair and accurate evaluations to all students can be developed.

The use of ML algorithms in individualized student assessments has significant potential for changing higher education. ML has the potential to transform how we test and support student learning by providing tailored, adaptive, and data-driven assessments. However, it is critical to address the ethical issues of privacy, bias, and transparency in order to ensure that these technologies are utilized ethically and fairly. Educators and politicians may use ML to provide a more personalized, effective, and equitable educational experience by applying innovative solutions while adhering to ethical standards.

4.2 Related Works

Yağcı (2022) presented a novel approach that uses ML algorithms to predict undergraduate students' final test marks based on midterm exam outcomes. The author evaluated random forests, nearest neighbor, support vector machines, logistic regression, naïve Bayes, and k-nearest neighbor (KNN) algorithms on data from 1854 Turkish Language-I students at a state university in Turkey during the 2019–2020 fall semester. With a categorization accuracy of 70–75%, the model used midterm grades, departmental and teacher data as predictive parameters. Such data-driven techniques are critical for establishing educational analytics frameworks and helping institutional decision-making processes. This study makes a substantial contribution by identifying effective ML algorithms for early detection of pupils at danger of failing.

Kamalov et al. (2023) studied to evaluate the possible impact of AI on education by reviewing and analyzing existing literature along three primary axes: applications, benefits, and obstacles. Authors review focused on the application of AI to collaborative teacher–student learning, intelligent tutoring systems, automated assessment, and personalized learning. They also discussed the potential drawbacks, ethical concerns, and future directions for AI use in education. Authors concluded that the best path ahead is to welcome new technology while putting safeguards in place to prevent it from being abused.

Alier et al. (2024) investigated the use of GenAI in education, with a focus on ethical concerns, best practices, and opportunities. GenAI can improve traditional teaching methods by creating interactive and personalized learning experiences, such as custom quizzes and essay grading, which reduces teachers' workload. However, it raises concerns about academic integrity, as students might misuse GenAI for assignments. Maintaining academic standards and originality is crucial.

Vashishth et al. (2024) investigated AI-driven learning analytics in higher education, focusing on its function in providing individualized feedback and assessments. Students receive individualized feedback based on AI algorithms and data analytics that address their strengths and areas for improvement. AI provides adaptive and formative assessments, which ensure accurate evaluations of student knowledge and skills. Ethical problems, implementation challenges, and faculty training are all important considerations for successful integration. In the face of changing technology environments, adopting AI-driven learning analytics has the potential to improve student engagement, promote individualized learning experiences, and optimize educational results.

Ayeni et al. (2024) reviewed and explored the AI-powered personalized learning, concentrating on adaptive content delivery, real-time feedback, and intelligent tutoring systems. It investigates their impact on student performance, stressing their ability to resolve learning gaps and accommodate a variety of learning styles. AI's incorporation into curriculum development, evaluation methodologies, and administrative chores is examined, as well as ethical concerns such as privacy and algorithmic biases. The review calls for collaborative efforts to establish ethical principles and provide fair access to AI-enhanced educational resources, with the goal of informing future developments in AI integration in education.

Fenu et al. (2024) investigated the student interactions with ChatGPT in C programming education, finding various engagement patterns and problem-solving methodologies using manual clustering analysis. It shows the importance of tailored educational interventions based on individual learning styles and preferences. Despite advances in AI-supported learning, there are still gaps in understanding how students respond to AI-driven cues and activities. The study fills this gap by providing insights into effective pedagogical practices and instructional design for AI integration. It helps to improve student engagement, learning results, and educational experiences using technology.

Gligorea et al. (2023) examined the current usage of AI/ML in e-learning for adaptive learning by examining 63 articles published since 2010. It emphasizes AI/ML's role in personalizing learning routes, increasing engagement, and improving academic success, including higher exam scores. Despite problems such as data privacy, these technologies provide substantial contributions to tailored and successful education, demonstrating their ability to alter learning by meeting the requirements of individual learners.

Owan et al. (2023) also investigated the AI technologies applications in educational measurement and assessment, with a focus on their integration at several phases such as test formulation, item production, administration, scoring, and result interpretation. The authors also investigated the roles of teachers in AI-based assessments and addresses issues such as data privacy and algorithmic bias. Strategies for increasing AI's efficacy in educational assessments are presented. Despite its potential to alter education and improve learning outcomes, rigorous coordination among educators, policymakers, and stakeholders is required to maximize AI's benefits while mitigating associated risks.

Badal and Sungkur (2023) studied to predict students' performance and engagement by applying an ML model to data from an online learning platform. The study took a quantitative approach, focusing on the random forest classifier's superior performance over other techniques. The model, which included student profile traits and platform interaction data, achieved 85% accuracy for grade prediction and 83% for engagement prediction, indicating its efficacy in educational analytics.

Kooli (2023) studied the fundamental insights into AI systems and chatbots, examining their benefits, drawbacks, and ethical concerns in education and research. It stresses their significance in increasing human competence while also addressing ethical concerns like misuse and exploitation. The study predicts a dramatic shift in educational assessments with the introduction of AI, calling for creative adaptation and legal measures to ensure ethical standards and long-term integration. It emphasizes the importance of raising awareness, establishing ethical rules, and adapting continuously in order to use AI systems and chatbots as developmental chances in education.

Rızvı (2023) explored and reviewed works on AI-powered tutoring systems, focusing on design, implementation methodologies, and effectiveness with ML, natural language processing, and data mining and also explored how they affect academic achievement and learner engagement, as well as ethical considerations and communication challenges. The project intends to identify gaps, offer changes, and raise awareness about how AI technology may improve individualized educational experiences.

Rane et al. (2023) addressed the adaptive learning and Education 5.0, emphasizing the role of AI systems in dynamically altering educational tactics in response to real-time input and learner development. It tries to improve educational outcomes by tailoring content, pace, and tests to students' skills and learning styles. The study also examines ethical issues surrounding AI adoption, such as data privacy, algorithmic prejudice, and the effects on teacher–student interactions. The findings, which emphasize responsible integration, highlight the necessity of balancing technological innovation with ethical considerations for effective personalized and adaptable learning environments.

Alqahtani et al. (2023) also investigated the AI's potential to shape future educational and research practices by assessing its benefits, limitations, and applications. It covers important research applications like text generation, data analysis, and peer review, as well as educational applications including feedback, evaluation, personalized curriculum, and mental health support. Addressing ethical concerns and algorithmic biases is critical for optimizing AI's impact on education and research outcomes, and we hope to contribute to discussions about its transformative role for students, educators, and researchers.

Dieterle et al. (2024) started their examination by looking at the ethical implications of algorithms and solutions for reducing bias in AI-driven instructional decisions and learning result forecasts. Then they investigated upstream issues such as access and representation, which contribute to the algorithmic divide by determining who may use AI technologies and how data biases influence outcomes. Later, the authors examined how interpretation and citizenship influence educational decisions and societal results. These gaps reinforce structural prejudices in education unless they are addressed via constant reflection and action. At last they recommended strengthening human oversight to initiate a virtuous cycle that promotes diversity, equity, and inclusion, followed by initiatives for boosting educational chances through progressive bias mitigation.

The AI4K12 Initiative is creating nationwide guidelines for AI teaching in K–12, based on the "Five Big Ideas in AI." These principles are based on best practices from Learning Sciences and CS Education research and are consistent with the CSTA's K–12 Computer Science Standards, Common Core, and NGSS. The standards provide grade band progression charts to ensure that knowledge and skills are developmentally suitable. A thorough examination of Big Idea 3 (Learning) reveals the expected knowledge of topics at each grade band, both horizontally and vertically within the band. Examples demonstrate these progressions, and the guidelines provide techniques for constructing interconnected learning experiences with free online tools (Touretzky et al., 2023).

Wang et al. (2023) investigated into the impact of AI on international student education, with an emphasis on applications such as personalized learning, adaptive testing, predictive analytics, and chatbots. They also investigated how AI may improve learning efficiency and provide personalized help while simultaneously addressing issues such as privacy, cultural diversity, language proficiency, and ethical considerations. By examining these factors, the article sheds light on the integration of AI in educational administration and learning processes, resulting in a deeper understanding of AI's potential impact on international students' educational experiences.

Shi et al. (2023) examined college students' learning practices and developed a predictive model for learning outcomes using information literacy behavior traits. Using data from 320 Chinese university students, the study applies the Pearson algorithm to establish a substantial relationship between information thinking qualities and learning outcomes. Supervised classification techniques, such as decision tree, KNN, naïve Bayes, neural net, and random forest, are used to forecast learning effects. The random forest model performs the best, with an accuracy of 92.50%, precision of 84.56%, recall of 94.81%, F1-score of 89.39%, and Kappa value of 0.859. The authors also provided diversified intervention recommendations as well as management decision-making resources to help improve information literacy instruction.

Sridharan and Sequeira (2024) also studied that AI methods were employed to develop student learning outcomes (SLOs) that are consistent with current medical education principles. These methods are especially useful for medical academics, who frequently lack formal educational credentials, particularly early in their careers. According to data, only roughly one-third of medical school academics have received formal medical education instruction. Their study assesses AI's credibility in producing appropriate course learning outcomes and discovers that AI platforms generate high-quality test items suited for a variety of evaluations. The generative AIs utilized generated fresh content from their training datasets, with only minimal changes across the results.

Tang and Su (2024) investigated the ethical concerns of utilizing AI models in the classroom, emphasizing the importance of a comprehensive understanding and guidelines for mitigating these issues. A systematic literature assessment of 1,445 papers from 2013 to 2023 yielded 32 articles, highlighting 5 major ethical implications: algorithmic bias and prejudice, data privacy leakage, a lack of transparency, reduced autonomy, and academic misconduct. The most important ethical values identified were justice, privacy, transparency, accountability, autonomy, and beneficence. Algorithmic bias and fairness were the most researched topics, while autonomy and beneficence were comparatively understudied. This study indicated that future research should focus on a more in-depth examination of ethical implications, the explanation and implementation of ethical standards, and an accurate assessment of AI's ethical impacts in education.

Awad and Oueida (2024) also investigated the opportunities and problems of using AI into education. This highlights the possible benefits such as assisting teachers in creating tailored courses and offering individualized teaching to students. Their report also addressed the issues like privacy and algorithmic bias. A review of current literature and case studies using AI in education is given. Authors studied both the benefits and drawbacks of AI interventions and suggest areas for future investigation.

Alfertshofer et al. (2024) investigated a worldwide perspective on ChatGPT's test-taking ability, indicating its weakest performance on questions with multiple correct answers, as shown in the French medical licensure exam. Mean test question length was not a good predictor of ChatGPT's performance. The report recommends conducting additional research in other countries to produce comprehensive, country-specific rules to minimize AI-assisted cheating in medical licensing tests.

Li et al. (2024) also presented a detailed introduction to the ethical implications of employing AI in higher education, building on findings from 20 recent studies. This covers the proper approach and attitude toward AI, emphasizing its potential benefits for students while also addressing dangers such as electronic plagiarism, black box theory, and decreased creativity. The research also investigates whether AI should be disallowed in higher education in order to offset these harmful consequences. This report contributed to the continuing discourse about AI's role in education, laying the groundwork for future research.

Naseer et al. (2024) investigated the use of generative AI in higher education assessment, focusing on how AI might overcome the constraints of existing techniques while also meeting the demands of diverse learners. It explains how AI technologies such as natural language processing and computer vision may give tailored, scalable, and informative evaluations. The authors also critically evaluates AI's expanded capabilities and the ethical challenges they pose in education. It emphasizes a balanced approach, combining AI's analytical strengths with human expertise to achieve fair and successful judgments. This work seeks to educate educators, administrators, and legislators through the complexity of AI adoption in academic evaluation, with a focus on preserving academic integrity and inclusivity while maximizing AI's transformative potential.

Fagbohun et al. (2024) investigated the use of large language models (LLMs) in grading processes, emphasizing its potential to transform the assessment landscape through individualized feedback, consistency, and scalability. They examined the limitations of standard grading methods, highlighting the need for more complex alternatives. Authors introduced LLMs and describe their extensive capabilities in natural language processing and ML for analyzing various student answers. Case studies of real-world applications, such as automated grading systems and adaptive testing platforms, show how successful LLMs are. Despite their potential, the study critically explores issues such as data privacy and biases in AI algorithms. The authors also proposed strategies to address these concerns, emphasizing the importance of ethical standards, human oversight, and constant model refining. The paper also sees a future in which grading processes use continuous LLM breakthroughs to build more efficient, fair, and tailored assessment techniques, in line with the larger aims of individualized learning and educational justice.

Onesi-Ozigagun et al. (2024) thoroughly investigated AI's disruptive impact on education, with a focus on individualized learning, improved teaching approaches, and better educational administration. AI facilitates personalized learning by designing adaptive systems that tailor information to particular student needs, increasing engagement and academic success. It also provides instructors with tools to automate chores such as grading and providing real-time feedback, allowing them to focus more on teaching critical thinking skills. AI-driven assessment systems provide dynamic evaluation, which goes beyond standard tests to effectively assess comprehension. Despite the benefits, issues such as data privacy and algorithmic bias remain, necessitating attention for fair educational access. Overall, the evolution of AI in education promises to improve learning results and administrative efficiency, equipping students for success in the digital age.

AlAli et al. (2024) also investigated the application of generative AI in education, with a focus on its ability to automate processes such as lesson design, feedback creation, and individualized learning. The literature study highlights advantages such as efficiency and individualized education, as well as drawbacks such as ethical concerns and privacy concerns. The authors proposed ways for incorporating generative AI into classrooms while remaining consistent with educational goals. Case studies of successful AI deployments offer useful insights for educators and policymakers looking to improve teaching and learning experiences with AI technology.

Williams (2024) discussed the ethical concerns about platforms like ChatGPT in education, concentrating on privacy problems, algorithmic prejudice, and the implications for student autonomy and academic integrity. It promotes clear policies, effective plagiarism detection, and new assessment methods to ensure ethical AI use in education.

Tang (2024) summarized the broad implications of AI in education, building on over 55 studies. The authors focused on AI's ability to improve learning through intelligent content generation, interactive tools, and adaptive tutoring systems. AI improves virtual learning environments by personalizing content and automating administrative duties such as grading. However, problems like infrastructure requirements, equality considerations, teacher preparedness, data protection, and ethical concerns must be solved in order to optimize AI's positive educational impact.

Finally, the literature survey highlights AI's transformative potential in education, focusing on intelligent content production, interactive tools, and adaptive tutoring systems to improve learning experiences. This also highlights the AI's role in customizing education via virtual learning environments and automating administrative work. However, constraints such as infrastructure requirements, equity considerations, and ethical concerns about data privacy and inclusion must be properly managed in order to effectively reap the benefits of AI in education.

4.3 Advantages of Machine Learning in Personalized Student Assessments

4.3.1 Enhanced Individualization

One of the most notable benefits of ML algorithms in education is the capacity to deliver highly personalized assessments (Figure 4.1). This capability stems from ML's ability to analyze large amounts of data, which includes not only test answers but also patterns of engagement, problem-solving approaches, time spent on each question, and even interactions with educational content outside of assessments.

4.3.2 Analyzing Performance Data

ML algorithms begin by gathering substantial performance data from a variety of sources, including online learning platforms, classroom interactions, and prior assessments. This data is then processed to reveal patterns and trends that human instructors might not notice at first glance. For example, an ML system may notice that a student repeatedly fails with algebraic ideas while excelling in geometry, even if these courses are taught as part of a

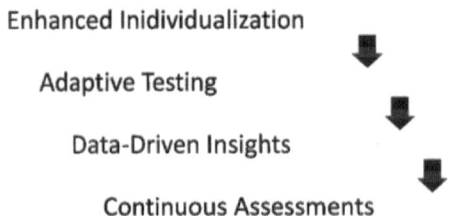

Figure 4.1 Advantages of ML in Personalized Student Assessment.

larger mathematics curriculum. This extensive research provides a more sophisticated insight of each student's learning profile.

4.3.3 *Identifying Strengths and Weaknesses*

By focusing on specific areas of performance, ML algorithms may accurately identify a student's strengths and limitations. Unlike traditional exams, which may yield a generic score or grade, ML-driven tests can determine which specific abilities or ideas a student has mastered and which they have not. For example, an ML algorithm could suggest that a student knows basic mathematical processes but struggles to apply them in word problems. This detailed information is invaluable for developing tailored educational interventions.

4.3.4 *Creating Personalized Learning Pathways*

Educators can design tailored learning routes using ML algorithms if they have extensive knowledge of each student's performance. These courses are designed to meet each student's specific needs, ensuring that they receive the appropriate level of challenge and assistance. Personalized learning routes may include a mix of tailored assignments, focused practice sessions, and specialized instructional resources. For example, a student who excels at reading comprehension but suffers with writing may be given more writing activities tailored to their interests, as well as comments focusing on their unique areas of difficulty.

4.3.5 *Tailoring Assessments to Student Needs*

The customized approach of ML algorithms extends to exams themselves. Adaptive testing, a fundamental feature offered by ML, ensures that the complexity of questions varies in real time based on student replies. If a student answers a question properly, the next question may be slightly more difficult, whereas a wrong answer may result in a simpler question. This dynamic adjustment keeps students engaged by presenting a proper amount of challenge, avoiding frustration and boredom.

4.3.6 *Promoting Effective and Engaged Learning*

The ultimate goal of tailored evaluations is to provide a more effective and interesting learning environment. When assessments are personalized to a student's individual requirements, they are more likely to find the learning process engaging and inspiring. This relevance is critical for keeping students engaged and encouraging active engagement in their education. Furthermore, individualized assessments can assist a student gain confidence by ensuring that they face a mix of obstacles and triumphs.

Case Study: Implementing ML-Driven Individualization

Consider a case study from a high school that has implemented an ML-driven assessment system. Students take regular online quizzes and interactive assignments, and the data from these activities is fed into an ML system. Over time, the system creates thorough profiles for every pupil. One student, Jane, is described as having a solid understanding of historical facts but difficulties with critical analysis and essay writing. Her individualized learning path includes interactive exercises to improve analytical skills and writing workshops. Furthermore, her tests are modified to include more possibilities for short-answer questions that gradually rise in complexity, allowing her to gain confidence and proficiency in these areas.

Table 4.1 shows the techniques that use ML to improve personalized student assessments by providing tailored insights, predicting performance trends, offering interpretable decision-making rules, dealing with complex data relationships, analyzing text for personalized feedback, recommending relevant resources, capturing intricate patterns, and detecting anomalies for timely interventions. Each technique makes a distinct contribution to creating a more effective and engaging learning experience that is suited to each student's specific needs.

4.3.7 Feedback and Continuous Improvement

The continuous feedback loop is an important component of tailored assessments. ML algorithms can give students with quick feedback, indicating areas for improvement and recommending resources or tactics to fill these gaps. This instant feedback enables students to alter their learning tactics in real time, resulting in more effective learning. For educators, the data collected from these assessments provides insights into the effectiveness of educational techniques and materials, allowing for ongoing improvement in teaching practices.

4.4 Adaptive Testing

The ML approaches enable adaptive testing by modifying question difficulty in real time based on student performance, providing ideal challenge levels, motivating students, improving assessment accuracy, and increasing learning efficiency. Each method makes a distinct contribution to the optimization of adaptive testing processes in educational contexts.

Table 4.1 ML techniques for enhanced personalized student assessments

Machine learning technique	Description and advantages
Clustering algorithms	**Description:** Grouping students based on similar performance patterns **Advantages:** Identifies clusters of students with similar learning needs, enabling targeted interventions and personalized learning paths
Regression analysis	**Description:** Predicting student performance based on historical data **Advantages:** Provides insights into future performance trends, aiding in proactive academic support and resource allocation
Decision trees	**Description:** Mapping out decision-making processes based on student data **Advantages:** Offers interpretable decision rules for educators to understand student progress and intervention points clearly
Neural networks	**Description:** Modeling complex relationships in student data through interconnected layers **Advantages:** Handles non-linear relationships effectively, enabling accurate predictions and personalized recommendations
Natural language processing (NLP)	**Description:** Analyzing text data such as student essays or feedback **Advantages:** Extracts insights from unstructured data, facilitating personalized feedback and language proficiency assessments
Collaborative filtering	**Description:** Recommending learning resources based on peer and collective behavior **Advantages:** Enhances engagement by suggesting relevant content aligned with individual learning preferences and peer interactions
Deep learning	**Description:** Learning from large volumes of data to improve predictions **Advantages:** Captures intricate patterns in student behavior and performance, refining personalized learning paths dynamically
Anomaly detection	**Description:** Identifying unusual or outlier student behaviors **Advantages:** Flags potential issues such as academic difficulties or personal challenges, enabling timely interventions for at-risk students

Adaptive testing, made possible by ML algorithms, is a significant improvement in educational evaluation. This approach adjusts the complexity of test questions in real time based on a student's performance, ensuring that each student is continually challenged at the right level. This dynamic modification provides various benefits, including increased student engagement, improved assessment accuracy, and a more personalized evaluation experience. Here's a detailed look at how adaptive testing works and its benefits.

4.4.1 Real-Time Adjustment of Question Difficulty

The ability to modify the difficulty of questions in real time is important to adaptive testing. ML algorithms examine each student response and utilize that information to evaluate the difficulty of upcoming questions. For example, if a student correctly answers a question, the subsequent question may be more difficult. If the learner replies incorrectly, the subsequent question may be simpler. This continuous adjustment results in a customized testing experience that conforms to the student's current level of comprehension.

4.4.2 Maintaining Appropriate Challenge Levels

One of the fundamental purposes of adaptive testing is to ensure that each student faces an appropriate level of challenge. Traditional tests frequently fail to engage all students equally; some may find the questions too simple and grow bored, whereas others may find them too challenging and become frustrated. Adaptive testing solves this problem by constantly modifying the difficulty to match the student's performance. This guarantees that all students are properly challenged, which is critical for maintaining their motivation and engagement during the test.

4.4.3 Reduce Frustration and Boredom

Adaptive testing reduces annoyance and boredom by giving questions that are neither too easy nor too complex. Students who meet too difficult questions may feel frustrated and disengaged, and those who face too simple questions may lose interest. By striking a balance, adaptive testing keeps students engaged in productive struggle, where they are challenged but not overwhelmed. This balance is critical for maintaining student involvement and providing a favorable testing experience.

4.4.4 Improving the Accuracy of Assessments

Adaptive testing's dynamic nature improves assessment accuracy. Traditional examinations frequently provide a limited perspective of a student's abilities since they feature a predetermined set of questions that may not fully capture the student's knowledge and capabilities. Adaptive testing, on the other hand, can provide a more exact measurement by responding to the student's performance in real time. This approach focuses the examination on the student's genuine skill level, resulting in a more accurate and complete evaluation of their strengths and weaknesses.

4.4.5 Personalized Evaluation Experience

Adaptive testing delivers a unique evaluating experience for each student. Adaptive testing ensures a unique assessment experience for each student by customizing the complexity of questions to the individual. This individualized approach not only makes the evaluation more relevant to the student's current knowledge and skills but it also helps to boost their confidence by posing appropriately tough questions. As a result, pupils are more likely to remain interested and perform to their full potential.

Case Study: Implementing Adaptive Testing

Consider a middle school that uses an adaptive testing system for mathematics examinations. Students take an online test, and the ML system analyzes their responses in real time. One student, Alex, begins with a moderately challenging question. After appropriately answering, the algorithm provides a little more difficult question. This approach continues until Alex confronts a difficult question. The computer then adjusts the level downward, ensuring that Alex is always pushed without becoming overwhelmed. By the end of the test, Alex has answered a variety of questions that accurately reflect his comprehension of mathematical concepts, presenting a comprehensive picture of his talents.

4.4.6 Feedback and Continuous Improvement

Adaptive testing also promotes continual improvement by providing quick feedback. As students proceed through an adaptive test, they are given immediate feedback on their responses. This real-time feedback allows kids to comprehend their mistakes and learn from them on the spot. For instructors, adaptive test data provides vital insights into student performance, allowing them to change curriculum and provide targeted help as needed. This continual feedback loop improves the entire learning process by ensuring that tests are both evaluative and informative.

Adaptive testing's instant feedback is a potent instrument for improving the learning process. Teachers are able to successfully incorporate this feedback into their lesson plans by providing instantaneous insights into this student performance. The adaptive testing system, for example, can not only deliver the right answer when a student answers a question poorly but it can also explain why. This focused feedback fosters mastery of the subject matter by helping students see their errors and reinforce their learning in real time.

Additionally, maintaining student motivation and engagement requires real-time question difficulty modifications. Students are more likely to stay focused and confident when they are regularly presented with questions that correspond to their level of proficiency. In order to create a more encouraging learning environment, the system can automatically modify the level of following questions if a learner is having trouble. This flexible method guarantees that tests are both instructive and evaluative. Through performance-monitoring data gathered from these assessments, teachers can make necessary curriculum modifications and give focused interventions by gaining important insights into individual and class-wide learning trends. Adaptive testing improves assessment and teaching efficacy by establishing an ongoing feedback loop, which results in a more individualized and significant educational experience.

4.4.7 Scalability and Efficiency

Adaptive testing is highly scalable and efficient, making it appropriate for a variety of educational environments. Because the complexity of questions adapts based on real-time performance, adaptive tests can be shorter while still producing accurate results. This efficiency is especially useful in large-scale testing situations, where reducing test length while maintaining accuracy can save time and resources. Furthermore, adaptive testing's scalability allows it to be used across multiple disciplines and grade levels, making it a versatile tool for tailored evaluation.

ML algorithms are particularly capable of digesting massive amounts of educational data and revealing important insights into student performance. By recognizing patterns and trends in this data, ML algorithms can help instructors gain a better understanding of how different factors influence learning results. This data-driven approach allows educators to make better informed decisions by implementing targeted interventions that support student achievement and improve overall educational effectiveness.

4.5 Data-Driven Insights

ML algorithms are particularly capable of digesting massive amounts of educational data and revealing important insights into student performance. By recognizing patterns and trends in this data, ML algorithms can help instructors gain a better understanding of how different factors influence learning results. This data-driven approach allows educators to make better informed decisions by implementing targeted interventions that support student achievement and improve overall educational effectiveness.

4.5.1 Analyzing Large Datasets

ML algorithms excel at evaluating massive datasets, which would be difficult for human instructors to do manually. These datasets can contain a wide range of information, including test scores, assignment completion rates, classroom engagement, learning management system interactions, and even non-academic elements like attendance records and socioeconomic status. By integrating and analyzing this different data, ML algorithms can provide a complete picture of a student's educational experience.

4.5.2 Identifying Patterns and Trends

ML algorithms can detect patterns and trends that are not immediately obvious by employing advanced data analysis methods. For example, an algorithm may determine that students who actively participate in class discussions score better on examinations. Similarly, it may discover which instructional approaches are more effective for specific student groups. These findings can help instructors better understand the underlying dynamics of student performance and learning behaviors.

4.5.3 Understanding Influential Factors

ML algorithms can explain how different factors influence learning results, giving instructors valuable insights. For example, an investigation could reveal that students who consistently use interactive learning tools perform better in scientific classes. Alternatively, it could mean that kids who consistently submit homework earn higher overall academic success. Understanding these key characteristics allows educators to customize their teaching approach to optimize good results.

4.5.4 Informing Decision-Making Data

Data-driven insights help instructors make more educated decisions. Rather than depending entirely on intuition or anecdotal evidence, educators can use concrete statistics to inform their decisions. For example, if data shows that a certain group of children is suffering with arithmetic, educators might provide more resources, such as tutoring or supplemental instructional materials, to meet this need. Similarly, if evidence indicates that students benefit from collaborative learning, educators might include more group activities in their lesson plans.

4.5.5 Targeted Interventions

One of the most significant benefits of data-driven insights is the capacity to carry out targeted interventions. Educators can provide tailored support to kids who are struggling in specific areas. For example, if an ML algorithm determines that a kid struggles with algebra but excels in geometry, educators can direct their efforts toward offering greater algebra instruction.

This tailored strategy guarantees that interventions are personalized and effective, resulting in better student outcomes.

4.5.6 Real-Time Monitoring and Feedback

Real-time monitoring of student performance using ML algorithms allows for quick feedback and timely interventions. For example, an algorithm may recognize that a student routinely underperforms in weekly quizzes. This real-time information enables educators to intervene quickly, possibly by providing one-on-one tutoring or modifying teaching approaches to better suit the student's learning style. Immediate feedback helps to keep minor issues from becoming big hurdles to academic success.

4.5.7 Enhancing Curriculum and Instruction

Data-driven insights can help improve curriculum and lesson design. By examining which topics students struggle with the most, educators can tailor the curriculum to provide more in-depth covering of difficult concepts. Furthermore, insights regarding the efficacy of various teaching approaches might assist educators in selecting the most successful instructional tactics. For example, if data demonstrates that project-based learning improves student engagement and comprehension, educators may include more project-based activities in their curriculum.

Case Study: Implementing Data-Driven Insights

Consider a high school that has adopted an ML-based data analysis system. The system collects and analyzes data from a variety of sources, including test results, homework submissions, class participation records, and interactions with the online learning platform. Over time, the ML system discovers that students who engage with multimedia resources (videos, interactive simulations) perform better in science classes. It also detects that students who participate in peer tutoring programs perform significantly better in math. Armed with these findings, the school plans to enhance the availability of multimedia tools in science classes and peer tutoring program in math. Furthermore, educators receive monthly reports identifying children who may require additional assistance, allowing them to act early and efficiently. As a result, the school notices a significant improvement in student performance in these disciplines, highlighting the value of data-driven decision-making.

4.5.8 Addressing Challenges

While data-driven insights have many advantages, it is critical to address potential issues. Ensuring data quality and accuracy is crucial, as inaccurate data can lead to incorrect conclusions and unproductive treatments. Additionally, educators must be educated to properly analyze and act on data insights. Data privacy and security are also critical, as sensitive student information must be safeguarded against unwanted access and breaches.

4.6 Continuous Assessment

Continuous evaluation is a substantial departure from standard assessment methods, which are often administered at defined intervals and may not capture the entirety of a student's learning experience. Continuous assessment, which uses ML algorithms, enables real-time monitoring of student progress, resulting in a more thorough and nuanced understanding of student learning. This strategy enables timely feedback and help, ultimately improving educational outcomes.

4.6.1 Limitations of Traditional Assessments

Traditional exams, such as midterms and finals, provide snapshots of student achievement across time. While these assessments can provide significant insights, they have several limitations:

- **Fixed Intervals:** Traditional assessments do not account for the continuous nature of learning and may overlook major swings in a student's performance.
- **Limited Feedback:** Students frequently receive feedback long after the evaluation, limiting the chance for immediate improvement.
- **Stress and Anxiety:** High-stake tests can induce severe stress, which can impair performance and misrepresent a student's genuine capabilities.

4.6.2 How ML Algorithms Facilitate Continuous Assessment

Continuous assessment is enabled by ML algorithms, which constantly analyze data from numerous sources, such as classroom interactions include information on participation, engagement, and collaboration.

- **Homework and Assignments:** Submittal rates, accuracy, and punctuality
- **Online Learning Platforms:** Usage trends, quiz results, and engagement analytics

- **Sensor Data:** In some advanced systems, biometric data from wearables can be included

By processing this constant stream of data, ML algorithms can provide a real-time picture of a student's learning path.

4.6.3 Real-Time Monitoring of Student Progress

Continuous assessment uses real-time monitoring to track students' development as it occurs. ML algorithms use continuous student behaviors and performance to identify trends and patterns. For example, an algorithm may note that a pupil is gradually increasing in reading comprehension, while suffering with writing tasks. This real-time monitoring enables educators to track a student's progress and identify difficulties as they arise.

4.6.4 Presenting a Comprehensive View of Student Learning

Continuous assessment provides a comprehensive view of student learning by combining data from various sources over time. This broad view includes

- **Academic Performance:** Monitoring scores and grades across a sequence of assignments and assessments
- **Behavioral Insights:** Tracking engagement levels, participation, and effort
- **Skill Development:** Assessing progress in specific skills and competences
- **Emotional and Social Factors:** Recognizing patterns in student well-being and social relationships

By merging these various data sources, instructors can gain a comprehensive view of each student's learning experience.

4.6.5 Enabling Timely Feedback and Support

One of the primary benefits of continuous evaluation is the ability to provide immediate feedback and support. ML systems can detect regions where pupils are underperforming and notify teachers in real time. The immediate feedback loop enables

- **Prompt Interventions:** Educators can address difficulties as they arise, providing focused assistance and resources to help pupils overcome obstacles.
- **Ongoing Adjustments:** Real-time data allows for the constant refinement of teaching tactics and learning materials.
- **Student Self-Regulation:** Students are given regular feedback on their progress, allowing them to take proactive efforts to improve their learning.

Case Study: Implementing Continuous Assessment

Consider a university that has implemented a continuous assessment system using ML algorithms. Students in an introductory computer science course use an online learning platform to track their activities, such as time spent on coding assignments, quiz outcomes, and participation in discussion boards. The ML algorithm continuously examines this data to find trends and patterns in student performance.

The system flags one student, Emily, for repeatedly struggling with debugging tasks. The algorithm notifies Emily's instructor, who assesses her progress and offers additional resources like tailored lessons and one-on-one coaching sessions. Emily's performance increases over the next few weeks, as she builds confidence in her debugging abilities. Emily's learning experience is considerably enhanced by the continuous evaluation system, which ensures that she receives the support she requires exactly when she needs it.

4.6.6 *Benefits of Continuous Assessment*

Continuous assessment provides numerous significant benefits:

- **Reduced Stress:** Because continuous assessment distributes assessment efforts throughout time, it reduces the pressure associated with high-stake tests.
- **Personalized Learning:** Continuous monitoring enables personalized learning experiences adapted to each student's specific needs.
- **Enhanced Engagement:** Regular feedback and modifications help students stay engaged and motivated.
- **Better Learning Outcomes:** Timely interventions and tailored help result in increased academic performance and a better knowledge of the content.

4.6.7 *Addressing Challenges*

While continuous assessment offers numerous benefits, it also poses challenges:

- **Data Privacy:** The security and privacy of student data is critical.
- **Implementation Complexity:** Integrating continuous assessment systems necessitates extensive technological infrastructure and training.
- **Over-Reliance on Data:** Educators must strike a balance between data-driven insights and their own professional judgment and expertise.

4.7 Ethical Implications

The use of ML algorithms into individualized student assessments raises various ethical concerns that must be carefully explored to guarantee that the technology is used responsibly. These include privacy issues, algorithmic unfairness, and the desire for transparency and responsibility.

4.7.1 Privacy Concerns

The use of ML in tailored assessments necessitates the collecting and analysis of large volumes of student data. This data comprises not only academic success measurements but also potentially sensitive personal information like learning habits, socioeconomic status, and even biometric data.

The privacy concerns provides the significance of installing stringent security measures, following legislative frameworks, and implementing best practices to safeguard student data confidentiality and privacy in ML-driven tailored evaluations.

Challenges:

- **Data Sensitivity:** The data acquired for ML algorithms may be exceedingly sensitive and intimate. Unauthorized access and data breaches can have serious consequences for students, such as identity theft, discrimination, and psychological suffering.
- **Data Collection Scope:** Continuous assessment systems collect data over long periods of time, possibly accumulating extensive profiles of students that could be exploited if not effectively protected.

Solutions:
Data anonymization and pseudonymization are techniques that remove or hide personally identifiable information to help secure student identities.

- **Robust Security Measures:** Implementing strong cybersecurity practices, including as encryption, secure data storage, and frequent security audits, is critical to protecting student data.
- **Explicit Privacy Policies:** Educational institutions should develop explicit policies that outline what data is gathered, how it is used, who has access to it, and how it is safeguarded. These regulations should be conveyed openly to students and parents.

Case Study: Remote Exam Monitoring Using ProctorU

When students voiced concerns about privacy infractions, such as the usage of webcam and microphone surveillance during tests, ProctorU, a remote exam monitoring service, came under fire. The degree of surveillance made many students uneasy because they thought their personal data would be misused.

Method of mitigation: In order to address these concerns, ProctorU improved data usage openness by clearly informing students about how their data would be retained and protected. Additionally, they gave students the choice to opt out of specific monitoring capabilities and put regulations in place to remove recordings after a predetermined amount of time.

4.7.2 Algorithmic Bias

ML algorithms learn from historical data, which may have existing biases. If these biases are not addressed, the algorithms can perpetuate or even exacerbate injustices, resulting in inaccurate judgments that penalize specific student groups.

Challenges:

- **Biased Training Data:** If the training data used to construct ML algorithms contains societal biases (e.g., racial, gender, socioeconomic), the algorithms' assessments may reflect these biases.
- **Disparate Impact:** Biased algorithms can result in disproportionate impacts, such as particular groups of pupils receiving routinely lower scores or less opportunities to advance.

Solutions:

- **Bias Detection and Mitigation:** Conduct regular audits and tests on ML algorithms for bias. Fairness constraints and reweighting can be used to reduce observed biases.
- **Varied Training Data:** When training ML systems, use datasets that are varied and reflective of all student populations.
- **Inclusive Development Practices:** These involve diverse teams in the development and testing of ML algorithms to discover and resolve any biases from various angles.

Case Study: The Use of AI in College Admissions at MIT

When the Massachusetts Institute of Technology (MIT) used ML algorithms to forecast which applicants would succeed in their programs, it came under fire in 2019. Historical admissions data, including test results, GPAs, and demographic data, were used to train the algorithm. Nonetheless, systematic biases from previous admittance procedures, such as the underrepresentation of particular ethnic and socioeconomic groups, were reflected in the training data. Because they had access to greater educational resources and could prepare for tests, candidates from affluent backgrounds were disproportionately preferred by the algorithm. The algorithm's recommendations unjustly harmed students from marginalized backgrounds, who frequently faced additional obstacles to success.

Mitigation Strategies:

- Data review and recalibration: The admissions committee carried out a comprehensive analysis of the historical data that was used to train the algorithm. By taking into account extra contextual elements, like the applicants' socioeconomic backgrounds, they were able to identify and mitigate bias.
- Putting fairness measures into practice: To make sure the algorithm did not unfairly disfavor any particular student group, fairness measures were created and used to assess the algorithm's results.
- Inclusive decision-making: To supervise the algorithm's use and guarantee that the admissions procedure remained fair, MIT formed an oversight committee with representation from a variety of stakeholders, including academics, students, and specialists in ethics and AI.
- Accountability and transparency: In order to enable stakeholders to hold the institution accountable, they published the results of their evaluation along with the measures they were doing to reduce bias.

Using a variety of training datasets is essential to addressing bias in ML models. Organizations can lessen the possibility of biases becoming ingrained in the algorithms by making sure that these datasets include a wide representation of various demographic groups. Because of this diversity, the model may learn from a range of viewpoints and experiences, which is crucial for producing predictions that are fair. Further improving equity is the application of fairness restrictions during model training. To ensure that the model works consistently for all demographics, strategies like adversarial debiasing can be employed to reduce differences in results between groups.

Another crucial procedure for preserving equity in ML systems is doing regular bias audits. Organizations can detect and evaluate biases in model predictions by carrying out these audits, examining results across different demographic groups to guarantee fair treatment. Model outputs can also be subjected to post-processing modifications, which enable corrections to satisfy fairness standards without compromising overall performance. In conclusion, the implementation of user feedback channels facilitates continuous assessment and enhancement of the model by allowing stakeholders to report observed biases or unfair treatment. When combined, these methods offer a thorough strategy for reducing bias and promoting equity in ML applications.

4.7.3 Transparency and Accountability

The complexity of ML algorithms can conceal how assessment judgments are made, making it difficult for educators, students, and parents to comprehend the reasoning behind specific outcomes. This lack of transparency may weaken trust in the assessment process.

Challenges:

- **Opaque Decision-Making:** Complex ML models, also known as "black boxes," can yield difficult-to-interpret findings, leaving it unclear how judgments are made.
- **Accountability Gaps:** Without a clear understanding, it can be difficult to hold the authors and users of ML systems responsible for incorrect or biased conclusions.

Solutions:

- **Explainable AI:** Create and implement explainable AI strategies that provide simple, intelligible explanations for how assessment choices are made. This can include employing simplified models or developing visualizations to make difficult decisions more understandable.
- **Transparent Procedures:** Make sure that the procedures and criteria employed by ML algorithms are transparent. Documentation and user guides should be made available to help educators and students understand how the algorithms work.
- **Stakeholder Involvement:** Involve educators, students, and parents in the development and implementation of ML-based evaluation systems. To retain trust and accountability, gather input on a regular basis and respond to any concerns.

Case Study: Automated Grading System in Higher Education

An automated essay grading system was introduced by a U.S. institution in 2018. Although the algorithm was designed to make grading more efficient, it was criticized for being opaque, which made it hard for teachers and students to comprehend how grades were assigned.

Students became anxious and worried about arbitrary judgments as a result of the algorithm's opaqueness, which damaged their confidence in the grading system.

Mitigation Strategies:

- Algorithm transparency: To improve comprehension, the institution supplied thorough documentation on the grading standards.
- Explainable AI: Functionalities were included to provide detailed comments on essay parts and to elucidate the rationale for ratings.
- Human oversight: To integrate human judgment with computer efficiency, faculty members examined a sample of graded essays.
- Feedback mechanism: For continuous assessment and development, students might offer input on the grading procedure.

The intricacy of ML algorithms may make it difficult to understand the logic behind the assessments they make, which results in a lack of transparency that erodes the confidence of parents, students, and teachers. This problem is addressed by explainable AI (XAI), which gives consumers insight into the decision-making processes of algorithms and helps them comprehend the variables that affect results. XAI can be extremely helpful in educational assessments by clarifying the rationale behind student evaluations, assisting teachers in determining the specific components of a student's performance that led to their results, and facilitating more insightful feedback.

Local interpretable model-agnostic explanations (LIME) are a useful illustration of how educators can interpret ML outcomes. For example, LIME can point out particular words or passages that contributed to a student's essay receiving a low grade from an ML model, such as poor grammar or unclear reasoning. This degree of detail enables teachers to have focused conversations with students regarding their performance and provide helpful criticism that targets the areas of weakness that have been discovered. In addition to promoting confidence in the evaluation procedure, this openness gives students the ability to take charge of their education by identifying their areas of weakness.

4.8 Innovative Solutions for Ethical Challenges in ML-Driven Assessments

4.8.1 Data Anonymization

Privacy problems occur when sensitive student data is collected and analyzed for ML-driven assessments.

Solution: Data anonymization techniques can be used to safeguard students' identities while still allowing for successful analysis.

Anonymization Methods:
To remove or obscure personally identifying information (PII) from datasets, use techniques such as data masking, tokenization, and aggregation.

- **Privacy-Preserving Technology:** Implement secure computation approaches, such as differential privacy, to ensure that aggregate insights can be extracted from data without revealing individual identities.
- **Policy Frameworks:** Create explicit policies and procedures for data anonymization techniques to ensure compliance with privacy requirements such as GDPR and the CCPA.

4.8.2 Bias Mitigation Strategies

ML algorithms can unintentionally propagate biases in training data, leading to biased judgments.

Solution: Implement techniques to reduce algorithmic bias and enhance fairness in assessments.

- **Diverse Training Data:** Make sure the training datasets are diverse and reflective of the student population, encompassing different demographic groupings.
- **Fairness Restrictions:** Include fairness restrictions in ML models to keep biases from influencing assessment results.
- **Bias Auditing:** Use statistical tests and fairness measures to discover and resolve any inequalities in algorithmic bias.
- **Algorithmic Adjustments:** Make adjustments to algorithms to ensure demographic parity and equal treatment across student groups, resulting in equitable outcomes.

4.8.3 Transparent Algorithms

A lack of openness in ML algorithms might harm confidence and accountability in assessment procedures.

Solution: Create transparent and explainable algorithms that provide insight into decision-making.

- **Explainable AI (XAI):** Use XAI techniques to make ML models interpretable, allowing instructors and students to better comprehend how assessments are administered.
- **Model Documentation:** Provide detailed documentation that defines the logic, inputs, and outputs of ML models, hence increasing transparency and understanding.
- **Visual Explanations:** Use visualizations and interactive tools to demonstrate the reasons behind assessment judgments, hence increasing transparency and user trust.
- **Education Resources:** Provide stakeholders with training and instructional resources on ML algorithms and their ramifications, with the goal of increasing understanding and involvement.

4.9 ML-Driven Assessments Transformative Pedagogical Implications

Teachers' approaches to teaching, learning, and student involvement are being drastically altered by the incorporation of ML into evaluations. For these technologies to be successfully implemented in educational settings, it is essential to comprehend the pedagogical impact in addition to the technological benefits.

4.9.1 Differentiated Instruction and Personalized Learning

Differentiated instruction and individualized learning are made possible by ML-driven exams, which offer information on each student's performance, learning preferences, and problem areas. This promotes varied education by enabling teachers to modify their lessons to fit the various needs of their students. Based on real-time data, educators can create personalized learning routes, modifying lesson plans to fill in knowledge gaps and reinforce ideas as needed. Consequently, ML technologies improve learning results by enabling a more student-centered approach.

4.9.2 Transition from Summative to Formative Assessment

Summative assessments, which offer a momentary view of student performance at a certain moment, are frequently the emphasis of traditional assessments. ML-driven evaluations, on the other hand, place more emphasis on ongoing, formative evaluation. These systems can provide continuous feedback by tracking students' progress in real time, assisting them in understanding their errors and making quick corrections. This change promotes a growth mentality, in which education is seen as a dynamic process rather than a fixed indicator of success. By using the information gathered from these tests, educators can provide prompt interventions and assistance, creating a more flexible and encouraging learning environment.

4.9.3 Encouraging Self-Directed Learning

The encouragement of self-directed learning is one of the major educational changes made possible by ML. With the help of ML-driven exams, students may set goals, track their progress, and take charge of their education by receiving quick, tailored feedback. These resources enable students to build critical thinking and self-assessment abilities by assisting them in determining their areas of strength and growth. Since students can see their learning path and comprehend how to reach their educational goals, this autonomy promotes deeper engagement and motivation.

4.9.4 Redefining the Role of Teachers

Teachers now play a more facilitative and guiding role, utilizing ML insights to help learning, rather than merely being assessors of students' performance.

Teachers can concentrate on deciphering information from ML systems, comprehending the subtleties of student learning styles, and creating focused interventions. The entire teaching and learning process is improved by this redefinition, which enables educators to devote more time to mentoring, individualized support, and innovative teaching techniques. ML is a tool that enhances teachers' comprehension and responsiveness to students' needs and not a substitute for them.

4.9.5 Scalable Support for Diverse Learning demands

In educational settings with a range of learning demands, ML-driven evaluations enable the provision of scalable, tailored support. ML systems may instantly modify the level of difficulty of activities and questions, whether they are intended for kids with learning difficulties or high achievers who require more challenging assignments. Every student is kept engaged at the right level, thanks to this flexibility, which keeps high performers from becoming bored and those who require more assistance from becoming frustrated. By doing this, ML enables a more diverse and inclusive learning environment that takes a larger range of skills and learning styles into consideration.

4.9.6 Ethical Issues in Pedagogy

Ethical issues like bias, openness, and data privacy must be addressed in the pedagogical application of ML in evaluations. To guarantee fair assessments, educators must be conscious of the drawbacks and possible biases of ML algorithms. In order to ensure that both instructors and students can comprehend and be informed by the decisions made by these systems, educators should also be involved in conversations around algorithm openness. Building trust and guaranteeing the equitable and appropriate application of ML in educational contexts require addressing these ethical issues.

4.9.7 Student Reaction: Autonomy, Engagement, and Motivation

ML-generated personalized assessments have a major impact on student autonomy, motivation, and engagement. Students are more likely to remain interested in the content when they receive prompt, personalized feedback since it makes the learning process more pertinent and directly meets their requirements. With this customized feedback, students can see real progress and know exactly where they need to improve, which boosts their confidence. Furthermore, the independence offered by ML-driven tests motivates students to take charge of their education by establishing objectives and monitoring their development. Higher motivation and greater engagement can result from this sense of control over their education, encouraging a more active and independent learning style.

4.9.8 Teacher Reaction: Changes in Methods of Instruction

A change in conventional teaching methods is required with the advent of ML-driven assessments. Instead of evaluating student performance alone, educators now work with ML algorithms to evaluate data and use it to inform instruction. Because of this change, educators must acquire new data literacy skills, such as how to interpret and act upon the insights produced by ML algorithms. Lesson plans can be modified in real time in response to student performance and feedback, which further promotes a more flexible teaching style. Ultimately, this enables teachers to provide more effective and customized help to their pupils, even though it could necessitate further training and professional development.

Effect on Teacher–Student Interactions: Assessments powered by ML may change how teachers and students interact. Teachers can have more meaningful and informed discussions with students about their progress if they have comprehensive insights into their unique learning styles. Teachers are better able to comprehend the individual requirements and difficulties of every student as a result of this change, which helps foster deeper relationships. Teachers can devote more of their time to mentoring, advising, and fostering the development of their students rather than grading assignments and other administrative work. It is crucial for educators to find a balance between utilizing technology and preserving a human touch in their teaching methods because there is a worry that a dependence on ML systems may result in less human engagement.

Scalable Support for Diverse Learning Demands: In educational settings with a range of learning demands, ML-driven evaluations enable the provision of scalable, tailored support. ML systems may instantly modify the level of difficulty of activities and questions, whether they are intended for kids with learning difficulties or high achievers who require more challenging assignments. Every student is kept engaged at the right level, thanks to this flexibility, which keeps high performers from becoming bored and those who require more assistance from becoming frustrated. By doing this, ML enables a more diverse and inclusive learning environment that takes a larger range of skills and learning styles into consideration.

4.10 Global Perspectives on the Adoption of Machine Learning in Education

Although schools and universities in high-income countries are more likely to have the resources to invest in advanced technologies, allowing for widespread use of ML for personalized learning, socioeconomic disparities can pose significant challenges to the implementation of these technologies in underfunded schools or developing countries. These factors, which include infrastructure, funding, and digital literacy, influence the adoption of ML-driven assessments in education.

Socioeconomic Disparities and Technology Access: The digital gap is still a major problem since low-resource schools might not have the hardware, high-speed internet, or skilled staff needed to successfully implement ML. Students in impoverished schools might not receive the same degree of specialized educational support as those in more affluent institutions as a result of these inequities, which might result in unequal access to the advantages of individualized learning. Infrastructure spending, teacher preparation, and reasonably priced technology solutions are all necessary to close these disparities.

Difficulties in Developing Countries: In developing nations, low levels of digital literacy, a lack of financing, and inadequate digital infrastructure frequently impede the adoption of ML in the classroom. Despite these obstacles, there are efforts to close the gap, like partnerships between tech companies, NGOs, and governments to offer reasonably priced educational technologies. For example, initiatives that provide affordable gadgets and learning platforms that are available offline can aid in introducing ML-driven education to isolated and rural regions. Developing inclusive policies that guarantee fair access to the advantages of ML in education requires an understanding of these geographical variations.

Case Studies from Various Locations: Including studies from various locations will show how various nations handle ML integration in education. While projects in some parts of Africa concentrate on creating low-tech, reasonably priced solutions that can function in places with poor internet connectivity, nations like Singapore and South Korea, for instance, have effectively incorporated ML by prioritizing teacher training and digital infrastructure. These kinds of instances can offer insightful information about best practices and methods for getting past implementation obstacles.

4.10.1 Critical Views on Machine Learning's Application in Education

Although there are many benefits to implementing ML in the classroom, it is important to consider opposing views that express worries about the overuse of technology in classrooms. According to academics, relying too much on ML can compromise the human component of education and pose a number of long-term hazards.

Dehumanization of Learning: According to critics, an excessive dependence on ML and automated tests could dehumanize education by lowering the number of meaningful interactions between instructors and students. In a technologically driven setting, the subtleties of human learning—like empathy, encouragement, and motivation—can be disregarded. It is vital to make sure that technology enhances rather than replaces human connection because this change may have an influence on students' social and emotional development.

Algorithmic Bias Risks: The possibility of algorithmic bias present in ML systems is another issue. These methods may reinforce inequality by giving minority students unfair assessments and chances if training data reflects preexisting biases. Critics contend that rather than fostering diversity, ML can exacerbate structural injustices in the absence of rigorous governance and diverse datasets.

Excessive Focus on Data: Concerns have also been raised about how an overemphasis on data-driven decision-making could minimize educational experiences to statistics while ignoring the larger context of student learning. Critics caution that this could result in a "teaching to the test" culture, in which teachers place more emphasis on performance measures and data collecting than on comprehensive teaching strategies that develop students' capacity for creativity, critical thinking, and problem-solving.

Dependency on Technology: Students' capacity to learn and adjust in settings devoid of technological assistance is called into doubt by their growing reliance on technology. Critics warn that depending too much on ML for evaluation and feedback could prevent students from developing self-control and intrinsic motivation, two qualities necessary for lifelong learning.

Seminal works in the domains of learning analytics, adaptive learning, and AI in education will provide insightful information about the evolution of these fields and how they influence contemporary procedures.

In the paper "Artificial Intelligence in Education: Promises and Implications for Teaching and Learning" by Wayne Holmes, Maya Bialik, and Charles Fadel, the possible advantages and difficulties of implementing AI in educational contexts are examined. It gives a basic grasp of the implications of AI and identifies important areas where it might improve teaching and learning.

The study "Learning Analytics: From Research to Practice" by George Siemens and Dragan Gasevic examines the development of learning analytics and highlights how crucial it is for using data to improve learning outcomes. It highlights the revolutionary potential of data-driven approaches by discussing how analytics may enhance student engagement and inform instructional strategies.

The book *Personalized Learning: A Guide for Engaging Students with Technology* by John Hattie and Gregory C. R. Yates describes adaptive learning techniques that use data to customize learning for each student. It addresses how student engagement and achievement are affected by individualized learning and offers a critical viewpoint on the use of adaptive technologies.

In the article "The Adaptive Learning Revolution" by Kevin McFarland the development of adaptive learning technologies and their effects on teaching methods are covered. It draws attention to the manner in which these technologies might meet the various needs of students and offer tailored learning paths, advancing the expanding subject of adaptive learning.

4.11 Best Practices for Data Anonymization and Security Protocols in Educational Institutions

Protecting student data is crucial as more and more educational institutions use ML technologies. The best practices for data anonymization and security measures to safeguard private information are listed:

1 Methods of data anonymization:
   - **Data Masking:** This is the process of replacing private information with fictitious or jumbled information that keeps its structure but makes it impossible to identify. For instance, distinct identifiers can be used in place of names.
   - **Aggregation:** For analysis, use aggregated data rather than data at the individual level. This method provides insights without disclosing private data. Reporting average test scores by class instead of by student is one example.
   - **K-Anonymity:** Verify that every dataset can be mistaken for at least k different records. This implies that if a piece of data from an individual occurs in a collection of at least k items with identical attributes, it cannot be re-identified.

2 Robust security procedures:
   - **Encryption:** Use robust encryption techniques for data in transit and at rest. This guarantees that without the right decryption keys, data will remain unreadable even if it is intercepted.
   - Enforce stringent access restrictions to ensure that only authorized personnel can access data. Role-based access control (RBAC), in which permissions are given according to the user's role within the organization, is one example of this.
   - **Frequent Audits:** To find and fix any possible flaws in data protection procedures, conduct frequent security audits and vulnerability assessments.

3 Observance of legal frameworks:
   - **Knowledge of Regulations:** Keep up of pertinent data-protection laws, such as the General Data Protection Regulation (GDPR) in Europe or the Family Educational Rights and Privacy Act (FERPA) in the United States, and make sure that all of their criteria are met.
   - **Impact Assessments of Data Protection (DPIAs):** To find and reduce risks related to processing personal data, do data protection impact assessments (DPIAs) when introducing new data processing technology.

4 Awareness and training:
- **Staff Education:** Regularly instruct teachers and staff on data privacy procedures and the value of safeguarding student information. This entails being aware of phishing attempts and comprehending data handling procedures.
- **Raising Student Awareness:** Inform students about their rights to privacy protection of their data as well as the precautions the school takes to keep it safe.

5 Planning for incident response:
- **Incident Response Team:** Create a special incident response team to handle security events or data breaches. Clear procedures for reporting and handling breaches should be in place for this team.
- **Crisis Communication Strategy:** In order to provide transparency and uphold confidence in the event of a data breach, create a communication strategy to notify all parties involved, including parents and students.

Educational institutions can greatly improve the security of student data and reduce the dangers related to the usage of ML technology by implementing these best practices for data anonymization and security policies.

4.12 Conclusion

The incorporation of ML algorithms into tailored student evaluations is an exciting development with the potential to greatly improve educational outcomes. By providing personalized, adaptive, and data-driven assessments, ML technology has the potential to transform how we measure and support student development. To guarantee that these technologies are used responsibly and fairly, it is critical to tackle the ethical issues of privacy, bias, and transparency. ML-driven evaluations necessitate the collection and analysis of substantial student data, raising privacy issues about the confidentiality and security of sensitive information. To protect student privacy rights, strong data anonymization techniques must be used along with strict privacy regulations. ML algorithms are subject to biases in training data, which might result in unjust judgments that harm specific student populations. Mitigating prejudice requires diverse and representative training data, fairness limitations, and regular bias audits to ensure equitable outcomes for all students. The complexities of ML algorithms can hide how assessment judgments are made, weakening trust and accountability in the educational system. Developing transparent and explainable algorithms, as well as giving educators and students with clear insights into assessment processes, is critical for fostering confidence and ensuring stakeholders can understand and critique assessment outputs.

Educational institutions can utilize the benefits of ML-driven assessments while adhering to ethical norms by deploying creative solutions such as data anonymization to preserve privacy, bias mitigation measures to promote fairness, and transparent algorithms to boost trust. This technique improves assessment accuracy and efficacy while also providing a more individualized and equal educational experience for all pupils.

4.13 Future Directions

The future of incorporating ML into tailored student evaluations is expected to see considerable gains and obstacles. Enhanced privacy protections, such as advanced data anonymization techniques and strong encryption protocols, will be critical in protecting sensitive student data in increasingly networked educational ecosystems. Addressing algorithmic bias through automated detection algorithms and ongoing auditing processes would ensure fair and equal assessments for a diverse student population. Interdisciplinary collaboration among educators, data scientists, and ethicists will be critical for negotiating complicated ethical issues and producing comprehensive standards for responsible AI use in education. User-centric design concepts will promote usability and acceptance, increasing the adoption of ML-based evaluation systems in educational contexts. Furthermore, integrating ML with adaptive learning systems promises to provide individualized educational experiences in real time, better adapting to individual learning needs. Establishing global norms and policy frameworks will be critical for harmonizing practices and maintaining ethical standards in various educational situations around the world. Finally, encouraging openness in AI models and supporting ethics education in STEM curricula would enable stakeholders to traverse the changing world of educational technology with confidence and integrity.

There are several chances to improve personalized student assessments through the use of ML algorithms in higher education. But as the area develops, there are still a number of important gaps in the literature that need to be filled. Examining algorithmic prejudice and its effects on various student populations is an important topic for further study. In order to guarantee that individualized assessments are fair and representative of all students' skills, research should specifically focus on creating and validating frameworks that evaluate and reduce bias in ML algorithms. In this effort, it will be essential to examine how well different training datasets and fairness criteria work in actual educational settings.

A thorough investigation of the ethical ramifications of data security and privacy in ML-driven evaluations is necessary. Future research should concentrate on determining and suggesting best practices for security procedures and data anonymization that educational institutions can use to safeguard private student data. This involves figuring out how to balance protecting students' privacy rights with using data for individualized learning. Additionally, research should concentrate on how XAI may advance accountability and transparency in ML systems. In the end, research in this field can promote trust in assessment results by offering insightful information about how teachers and students understand algorithmic decisions. A thorough analysis of educational strategies that optimize the advantages of ML is required for the integration of adaptive testing and real-time feedback. Future studies should examine how teachers might improve student engagement and learning results by utilizing real-time insights from adaptive assessments to guide their instructional tactics. It will also be crucial to comprehend how individualized learning experiences affect students' motivation and academic performance over the long run. In addition to improving the field's academic quality, filling these research gaps lays the groundwork for future investigations that will guarantee the ethical and equitable realization of ML's transformative promise in education.

References

Akgun, S., & Greenhow, C. (2022). Artificial intelligence in education: Addressing ethical challenges in K-12 settings. *AI and Ethics*, 2(3), 431–440. doi: /10.1007/s43681-021-00096-7.

AlAli, R., Wardat, Y., Al-Saud, K., & Alhayek, K. A. (2024). Generative AI in education: Best practices for successful implementation. *International Journal of Religion*, 5(9), 1016–1025. doi: https://doi.org/10.61707/pkwb8402

Alfertshofer, M., Hoch, C. C., Funk, P. F., Hollmann, K., Wollenberg, B., Knoedler, S., & Knoedler, L. (2024). Sailing the seven seas: A multinational comparison of ChatGPT's performance on medical licensing examinations. *Annals of Biomedical Engineering*, 52(6), 1542–1545. https://doi.org/10.1007/s10439-023-03338-3.

Alier, M., García-Peñalvo, F., & Camba, J. D. (2024). Generative artificial intelligence in education: From deceptive to disruptive. doi: 10.9781/ijimai.2024.02.011.

Alqahtani, T., Badreldin, H. A., Alrashed, M., Alshaya, A. I., Alghamdi, S. S., bin Saleh, K., ... & Albekairy, A. M. (2023). The emergent role of artificial intelligence, natural learning processing, and large language models in higher education and research. *Research in Social and Administrative Pharmacy*, 19(8), 1236–1242. doi: 10.1016/j.sapharm.2023.05.016.

Awad, P., & Oueida, S. (2024, March). The potential impact of artificial intelligence on education: Opportunities and challenges. In *Future of Information and Communication Conference* (pp. 566–575). Cham: Springer Nature Switzerland. https://doi.org/10.1007/978-3-031-53963-3_39.

Ayeni, O. O., Al Hamad, N. M., Chisom, O. N., Osawaru, B., & Adewusi, O. E. (2024). AI in education: A review of personalized learning and educational technology. *GSC Advanced Research and Reviews*, 18(2), 261–271. doi.org/10.30574/gscarr.2024.18.2.0062.

Dieterle, E., Dede, C., & Walker, M. (2024). The cyclical ethical effects of using artificial intelligence in education. *AI & Society*, 39(2), 633–643. https://doi.org/10.1007/s00146-022-01497-w.

Fagbohun, O., Iduwe, N., Abdullahi, M., Ifaturoti, A., & Nwanna, O. (2024). Beyond traditional assessment: Exploring the impact of large language models on grading practices. *Journal of Artificial Intelligence and Machine Learning & Data Science*, 2(1), 1–8. Doi: 10.51219/JAIMLD/OLUWOLE-FAGBOHUN/ 19.

Fenu, G., Galici, R., Marras, M., & Reforgiato, D. (2024, June). Exploring student interactions with AI in programming training. In *Adjunct Proceedings of the 32nd ACM Conference on User Modeling, Adaptation and Personalization* (pp. 555–560).

Gligorea, I., Cioca, M., Oancea, R., Gorski, A-T., Gorski, H., & Tudorache, P. (2023). Adaptive learning using artificial intelligence in e-learning: a literature review. *Education Sciences*, *13*(12), 1216. doi: 10.1145/3631700.3665227.

Goel, P. K., Singhal, A., Bhadoria, S. S., Saraswat, B. K., & Patel, A. (2024). AI and machine learning in smart education: Enhancing learning experiences through intelligent technologies. In *Infrastructure Possibilities and Human-Centered Approaches with Industry 5.0* (pp. 36–55). IGI Global. doi: 10.4018/979-8-3693-0782-3.ch003

Kamalov, F., Santandreu Calonge, D., & Gurrib, I. (2023). New era of artificial intelligence in education: Towards a sustainable multifaceted revolution. *Sustainability*, *15*(16), 12451. doi: 10.3390/su151612451.

Kooli, C. (2023). Chatbots in education and research: A critical examination of ethical implications and solutions. *Sustainability*, *15*(7), 5614. doi: 10.3390/su15075614

Li, Z., Dhruv, A., & Jain, V. (2024, February). Ethical considerations in the use of AI for higher education: A comprehensive guide. In *2024 IEEE 18th International Conference on Semantic Computing (ICSC)* (pp. 218–223). IEEE. doi: 10.1109/ICSC59802.2024.00041.

Naseer, F., Khalid, M. U., Ayub, N., Rasool, A., Abbas, T., & Afzal, M. W. (2024). Automated assessment and feedback in higher education using generative AI. In *Transforming Education With Generative AI: Prompt Engineering and Synthetic Content Creation* (pp. 433–461). IGI Global. doi: 10.4018/979-8-3693-1351-0.ch021.

Onesi-Ozigagun, O., Ololade, Y. J., Eyo-Udo, N. L., & Ogundipe, D. O. (2024). Revolutionizing education through AI: A comprehensive review of enhancing learning experiences. *International Journal of Applied Research in Social Sciences*, *6*(4), 589–607. doi: https://doi.org/10.51594/ijarss.v6i4.1011

Owan, V. J., Abang, K. B., Idika, D. O., Etta, E. O., & Bassey, B. A. (2023). Exploring the potential of artificial intelligence tools in educational measurement and assessment. *Eurasia Journal of Mathematics, Science and Technology Education*, *19*(8), em2307. doi.org/10.29333/ejmste/13428.

Rane, N., Choudhary, S., & Rane, J. (2023). Education 4.0 and 5.0: Integrating artificial intelligence (AI) for personalized and adaptive learning. *Available at SSRN 4638365*. doi: 10.2139/ssrn.4638365

Rızvı, M. (2023). Investigating AI-powered tutoring systems that adapt to individual student needs, providing personalized guidance and assessments. *Eurasia Proceedings of Educational and Social Sciences*, *31*, 67–73. doi: 10.55549/epess.1381518

Shi, Y., Sun, F., Zuo, H., & Peng, F. (2023). Analysis of learning behavior characteristics and prediction of learning effect for improving college students' information literacy based on machine learning. *IEEE Access*, *11*, 50447–50461. doi: 10.1109/ACCESS.2023.3278370.

Sridharan, K., & Sequeira, R. P. (2024). Artificial intelligence and medical education: Application in classroom instruction and student assessment using a pharmacology & therapeutics case study. *BMC Medical Education*, *24*(1), 431. https://doi.org/10.1186/s12909-024-05365-7.

Tang, K. H. D. (2024). Implications of artificial intelligence for teaching and learning. *Acta Pedagogia Asiana*, *3*(2), 65–79. doi: https://doi.org/10.53623/apga.v3i2.404.

Tang, L., & Su, Y. S. (2024). Ethical implications and principles of using artificial intelligence models in the classroom: A systematic literature review. https://doi.org/10.9781/ijimai.2024.02.010

Touretzky, D., Gardner-McCune, C., & Seehorn, D. (2023). Machine learning and the five big ideas in AI. *International Journal of Artificial Intelligence in Education*, *33*(2), 233–266. https://doi.org/10.1007/s40593-022-00314-1.

Vashishth, T. K., Sharma, V., Sharma, K. K., Kumar, B., Panwar, R., & Chaudhary, S. (2024). AI-driven learning analytics for personalized feedback and assessment in higher education. In *Using Traditional Design Methods to Enhance AI-driven Decision Making* (pp. 206–230). IGI Global. doi: 10.4018/979-8-3693-0639-0.ch009.

Wang, T., Lund, B. D., Marengo, A., Pagano, A., Mannuru, N. R., Teel, Z. A., & Pange, J. (2023). Exploring the potential impact of artificial intelligence (AI) on international students in higher education: Generative AI, chatbots, analytics, and international student success. *Applied Sciences*, *13*(11), 6716. https://doi.org/10.3390/app13116716.

Williams, R. T. (2024, January). The ethical implications of using generative chatbots in higher education. In *Frontiers in Education* (Vol. 8, p. 1331607). Frontiers Media SA. doi: https://doi.org/10.3389/feduc.2023.1331607.

Yağcı, M. (2022). Educational data mining: Prediction of students' academic performance using machine learning algorithms. *Smart Learning Environments*, *9*(1), 11. doi: 10.1186/s40561-022-00192-z

Yudish Teshal, B., & Sungkur, R. K. (2023). Predictive modelling and analytics of students' grades using machine learning algorithms. *Education and Information Technologies*, *28*(3), 3027–3057. doi: 10.1007/s10639-022-11299-8

5 NLP-Driven Approaches to Automated Essay Grading and Feedback

V. Nikhil, R. Annamalai, and Senthil Jayapal

5.1 Introduction

In the rapidly evolving landscape of education, natural language processing (NLP) stands out as a transformative force, reshaping how we understand and assess written communication. Traditionally, essay grading has been a tedious, time-consuming task, often burdening educators with unmanageable workloads. Today, however, NLP emerges as a powerful ally in the classroom, empowering both teachers and students through automation of essay evaluation and personalized feedback generation (FG). This chapter aims to explore the applications of NLP in educational contexts, specifically focusing on automated essay assessment (AEA), personalized FG, and the ethical implications of artificial intelligence (AI) in learning environments.

NLP encompasses a wide array of methods designed to help machines comprehend, interpret, and generate human language. Thanks to advances in deep learning models, such as transformers, the accuracy of language processing tasks has vastly improved, surpassing older methods in analyzing syntax, coherence, structure, and content in student essays. This approach enables consistent and objective assessment of large text volumes, making it invaluable for standardized testing and large educational environments.

Imagine a classroom where every student receives immediate, personalized feedback on their writing, guiding them through complex concepts like grammar, coherence, and argumentation. This is the promise of NLP—a shift from generic critiques to specific, actionable advice that empowers students to understand and improve their writing skills. As we navigate the nuances of automated assessment, this chapter will also consider the ethical dimensions of AI in education, examining how the integration of these tools affects creativity, authorship, and the essence of learning.

By blending cutting-edge technology with pedagogical principles, we aim to highlight the potential for NLP to revolutionize how we evaluate writing, enhance learning outcomes, and support both students and educators in achieving their goals. Join us as we delve into this fascinating intersection of language, technology, and education, revealing the transformative potential of NLP in shaping the future of learning.

DOI: 10.1201/9781003470304-5

5.2 Literature Review

Recent years have seen a surge in interest regarding NLP in education, leading to an expanding body of research on its applications and challenges. This literature review aims to summarize existing studies on NLP's role in automated essay evaluation and FG. By examining key advancements and methodologies, it assesses the current state of knowledge, identifies areas for improvement, and suggests future research directions.

This study implemented and evaluated an automated feedback system for German-speaking students' essays in an introductory educational psychology course. The objective was to assess the effectiveness and perception of highly informative feedback generated through a two-step NLP pipeline, employing GBERT and T5 models for essay segmentation and code prediction. Results indicated that transformer-based models effectively automated FG, with a randomized control trial showing that highly informative feedback enhanced students' perceptions of helpfulness and reflection but negatively impacted motivation. Limitations include potential challenges in aligning automated feedback with motivational needs, as highly informative feedback may highlight performance gaps, potentially reducing intrinsic motivation (Gombert et al., 2024).

This study explores the impact of essay assessments on student competency in science education, addressing Indonesia's lower PISA and TIMSS scores in literacy across linguistic, scientific, and mathematical domains. Using a literature review method, 16 articles from a pool of 1,000 were analyzed, focusing on studies published between 2019 and 2023. Results indicate that essay assessments are predominantly utilized at the high school (62.5%) and university (60%) levels, with biology and physics subjects showing a 60% usage rate. The study concludes that essay assessments positively influence students' competency achievement in science learning. Limitations include the narrow scope of articles and potential variability in assessment criteria across studies (Amanda et al., 2023).

This study developed an automatic essay assessment and plagiarism detection feature within the "MoLearn" learning management system (LMS) to streamline evaluation and reduce cheating in online learning. Using the software development life cycle (SDLC) waterfall model and latent semantic analysis (LSA) for answer comparison, MoLearn provides objective scoring and detects answer similarities among students. Testing showed that MoLearn improved grading speed by 8.04 times compared with manual grading, with an accuracy of 84.11%. Teachers rated MoLearn positively, citing its effectiveness in accelerating assessments and identifying plagiarism. Limitations include lower initial accuracy and a need for ongoing refinements based on user feedback (Lemantara et al., 2023).

This systematic literature review analyzes the development and effectiveness of automatic essay scoring systems, particularly in the context of the educational disruptions caused by the COVID-19 pandemic. By collatingg various studies, the authors explore different methodologies and datasets used in AEA. The review aims to enhance understanding of these systems, highlighting their potential contributions to future research and educational practices. Limitations noted include the need for diverse datasets and the continuous evolution of assessment methods to improve accuracy and reliability. Overall, the study emphasizes the importance of automation in supporting remote learning environments (Susanti et al., 2023).

This literature review systematically examines the advancements in Automatic Chinese Essay Evaluation (ACEE) technologies, focusing on their application in writing instruction and assessment. The authors employed a systematic literature review method, analyzing 29 high-quality studies published between 2004 and 2022. The primary objective was to assess the current state of ACEE, including corpus construction, feature extraction, and scoring models. Key results indicate significant progress in utilizing NLP for feature extraction, but challenges remain in corpus availability and the extraction of grammatical and rhetorical features. Limitations include insufficient publicly accessible corpora, inconsistencies in evaluation metrics, and the complexity of accurately assessing diverse writing styles in Chinese. The review emphasizes the need for collaborative efforts to enhance ACEE's effectiveness and adaptability in educational contexts (Yang et al., 2023).

Botelho et al. examine advancements in using NLP and machine learning for automated assessment and feedback on open-ended math responses. Their approach combines student log data with sentence-level semantic analysis to improve performance predictions and feedback relevance. By employing collaborative filtering, they achieve more accurate score predictions and personalized feedback than previous methods. The study demonstrates the potential for automated systems to enhance the evaluation of open-ended responses and support teachers, though further refinement is needed (Botelho et al., 2023).

Lagakis and Demetriadis review the evolution of automated essay scoring (AES) systems, focusing on the shift from mere scoring to providing detailed, actionable feedback. While AES has been researched for over five decades, traditional systems often fail to help students identify specific areas for improvement. Recent advancements aim to address this by offering feedback on various essay aspects, like consistency and technical accuracy, enhancing student learning. The review also examines the impact of these systems on students and educators, highlighting their potential to improve writing skills through constructive feedback (Lagakis & Demetriadis, 2022).

Bauer et al. explore the potential of NLP to enhance peer feedback in education. They propose a cross-disciplinary framework that integrates NLP techniques into the peer-feedback process, outlining learner activities, textual outputs, and adaptive support measures. The study highlights NLP's role in assisting throughout the feedback stages, from scoring to evaluation. Key challenges identified include data scarcity, biases in NLP models, and the need for improved interpretability of outputs. The authors suggest a research agenda focused on evaluating NLP's effectiveness in diverse contexts, proposing that addressing these issues could advance peer-feedback processes and educational practices (Bauer et al., 2023).

Yan et al. conducted a systematic scoping review of 118 peer-reviewed papers to explore the practical and ethical challenges of using large language models (LLMs) in educational technology. They identified nine main application areas, including grading, feedback, content generation, and recommendation. Despite their potential, challenges such as low technological readiness, lack of transparency, and privacy concerns were noted. Yan et al. recommend updating systems with advanced models like GPT-3/4, open-sourcing models, and adopting a human-cantered approach to enhance the practicality and ethicality of LLM-based educational tools. They also stress the importance of thorough testing and real-world implementation to address these challenges effectively, ensuring that the technology is both reliable and ethically sound in educational settings (Yan et al., 2024).

Alqahtani et al. examine the impact of AI, NLP, and LLMs like GPT-4 and BARD on higher education and research. Their review highlights benefits such as improved text generation, data analysis, and personalized support while addressing challenges like ethical concerns and algorithmic biases. The paper discusses applications in education—feedback, assessment, and tailored curricula—and in research, where AI enhances text generation and peer review. The authors stress that successful integration requires managing these challenges and recommend incorporating AI into curricula, hosting webinars, and providing resources for balanced implementation (Alqahtani et al., 2023).

5.2.1 Comparative Analysis

Transformer-based models, such as GBERT and T5, excel in providing nuanced, context-sensitive feedback, making them highly effective for personalized assessments in essay grading. However, these models require significant computational resources and may unintentionally impact student motivation by focusing on performance gaps. In contrast, models like LSA, as used in the MoLearn system, prioritize speed and efficiency, allowing rapid scoring and plagiarism detection, though they lack the semantic depth necessary for complex, context-driven evaluations. Hybrid approaches, like the collaborative filtering combined with semantic analysis, offer tailored feedback based on student performance patterns, but they demand extensive data and adaptation across subjects, which can limit their scalability. Additionally, LLMs such as GPT-4 bring adaptability and advanced text generation capabilities but pose ethical challenges related to transparency, privacy, and bias. Each model thus brings a unique balance of efficiency, depth, and ethical considerations, emphasizing the need for context-specific selection to optimize educational outcomes.

5.2.2 Limitations in the Literature Survey

The reviewed studies reveal several limitations. Many faced challenges in aligning automated feedback with students' motivational needs, as overly critical feedback can diminish intrinsic motivation. Additionally, the narrow scope of some literature and variability in assessment criteria can impact the generalizability of findings. More diverse, publicly accessible datasets are needed to enhance NLP models' robustness and broaden their adaptability to various writing styles. Lastly, ethical concerns and biases in AI and NLP systems require continuous attention to ensure fair and effective educational applications.

This review brings insights on automated feedback, essay assessment, and the integration of AI and NLP in education. Collectively, these studies underscore the potential of these tools to enhance learning outcomes, streamline assessments, and improve feedback mechanisms. However, they also highlight the importance of aligning these technologies with educational goals and addressing challenges to optimize AI and NLP's role in education.

5.3 Methodology

This section details the methodologies, processes, and technologies used for AEA and FG, focusing on the integration of NLP and machine learning techniques in a structured, continuous workflow. The approach centers on achieving accurate grading, robust FG, and user-friendly interaction.

To build an effective AEA and FG system, this study applies a comprehensive NLP pipeline, machine learning models, and detailed evaluation metrics to assess both essay quality and user interaction.

5.3.1 NLP Techniques for Essay Analysis

The AEA process begins with NLP techniques for essay analysis, which play a crucial role in preparing raw text data for subsequent analysis. These techniques allow for an in-depth understanding of the structure, sentiment, and originality of each essay. Key techniques employed in this initial phase include

- **Tokenization:** The process of breaking down text into smaller units, such as words and sentences, allows for more granular analysis of the content. Tokenization enables the system to examine linguistic elements, which contribute to an understanding of readability and sentence complexity.
- **Text Normalization:** This involves converting all text to lowercase, removing punctuation, and filtering out common stop words that do not contribute to the overall meaning. Normalization is essential for creating a consistent dataset and improves model performance by reducing noise.

- **Part-of-Speech (POS) Tagging:** Assigning parts of speech to each word aids in understanding sentence structure and grammatical usage, providing insights into composition quality and syntactical balance.
- **Sentiment Analysis:** Evaluating the tone of the essay helps gauge the emotional context and overall sentiment expressed in the writing. This can provide indirect insights into a writer's approach, style, and engagement with the topic.
- **Text Similarity Metrics:** Techniques such as cosine similarity or the Jaccard index assess how closely related essays are to one another. This is particularly useful for identifying originality and coherence, which can be important scoring factors in AEA.

The NLP techniques serve specific purposes within AEA, such as text normalization for readability scoring, POS tagging for structure assessment, and sentiment analysis for evaluating writing tone.

5.3.2 Machine Learning Models for Essay Scoring

Following NLP analysis, machine learning models are implemented to enhance grading accuracy and efficiency. These models are selected based on their strengths in processing language data, specifically to assess essay structure, coherence, and quality. The approach primarily utilizes supervised learning techniques, relying on labelled data to inform predictions. The models employed include

- **Supervised Learning Models:** Algorithms like regression models and neural networks learn from historical data to generalize assessments for new submissions. With a training dataset comprising essays and corresponding scores, these models attempt to mimic expert grading behaviors by assessing text features aligned with scoring criteria.
- **Support Vector Machines (SVM):** SVMs are particularly effective for classification tasks, where the goal is to categorize essays based on established criteria. SVMs separate different categories within data by identifying optimal hyperplanes, supporting the alignment with predefined scoring rubrics and grading consistency.
- **Neural Networks (e.g., LSTM):** Neural networks, especially long short-term memory (LSTM) networks, are highly effective at capturing complex relationships in sequential data, which is intrinsic to NLP. Their ability to maintain context across long sequences makes them ideal for analyzing the structure, semantics, and flow of essays. This allows for a comprehensive evaluation that includes grammar, vocabulary, and nuanced language patterns.
- **Ensemble Methods:** Techniques like random forest and gradient boosting combine predictions from multiple models to enhance predictive performance. Ensemble methods, which aggregate outputs from SVMs and neural

networks, contribute to more robust predictions and mitigate variability in automated scoring, improving overall scoring reliability.

These machine learning models address specific assessment aspects, such as structure and coherence (SVM), semantic cohesion (LSTM), and holistic scoring accuracy (ensemble methods), creating a system that reflects expert grading patterns.

5.3.3 Dataset Description

The dataset used for AEA includes eight distinct sets of essays, each written in response to a unique prompt. These essays range from an average of 150–550 words and comprise responses that are both independent and source-dependent. The essays were written by students in grades 7–10 and scored manually by multiple raters to ensure grading reliability. Each dataset possesses unique characteristics designed to test the scoring engine's capabilities.

The training data is provided in three formats: a tab-separated value (TSV) file, and two Excel formats. While essay sets 1–6 are currently available, sets 7 and 8 are scheduled for inclusion in the next phase of evaluation. Each file contains 28 columns, including identifiers for each essay (e.g., essay_id, essay_set) and actual essay text. Scores from multiple raters, as well as resolved scores, provide a basis for comparison.

To maintain privacy, the dataset has been anonymized using named entity recognition (NER) from the Stanford NLP toolkit. Identifiable entities such as names and locations are replaced with generic tags (e.g., "@PERSON1," "@LOCATION1"), allowing the dataset to retain its content richness while adhering to ethical data standards.

5.3.4 Data Preprocessing

Data preprocessing is fundamental to AEA and FG, ensuring that the dataset is clean, consistent, and feature-rich. The steps include

- **Data Cleaning:** This process removes irrelevant columns, addresses missing values, and ensures data consistency across the dataset.
- **Feature Extraction:** Raw essays are transformed into numerical representations through:
  - **Word Embeddings:** Techniques like Word2Vec or GloVe convert words into dense vectors that capture semantic meaning, which are essential for understanding essay content and quality.
  - **Term Frequency–Inverse Document Frequency (TF-IDF):** This metric helps represent features by weighting words relative to their importance within each essay, enabling effective content analysis.

- **Dimensionality Reduction:** Principal component analysis (PCA) and similar methods help reduce complexity while retaining essential information, optimizing feature sets for model training.

The FG mechanism, a crucial component of AEA, uses an AI chatbot powered by a generative pre-trained transformer (GPT) model. It analyzes user inputs, such as essays, to provide structured feedback on writing style, grammar, and content clarity, along with targeted suggestions for improvement. By integrating NLP techniques, the chatbot dynamically assesses writing quality and enhances students' understanding and growth.

5.3.5 Model Training

Algorithm Selection: Selecting the appropriate machine learning algorithm is foundational to the success of the model. In AEA, LSTM networks are employed due to their effectiveness in handling sequential data, such as essays, where context and order matter. LSTMs are a type of recurrent neural network (RNN) designed to remember long-term dependencies, making them particularly suited for capturing the intricacies of language. The architecture of an LSTM model typically includes an input layer to accept word embeddings, multiple stacked LSTM layers for processing sequential information, dropout layers to prevent overfitting, and a dense output layer that produces the predicted score, usually using a linear activation function for regression tasks.

Data Preparation for Model Training: Proper data preparation is crucial for effective model training and involves several steps. First, the dataset is split into training and testing sets, allowing the model to be trained on one portion and validated on another to assess performance. Next, text vectorization is performed using Word2Vec, which converts words into dense vectors that capture their semantic relationships. Key parameters for Word2Vec—such as vector size, window size, minimum word count, and down sampling—are essential for accurately representing the vocabulary of the essays. Once the Word2Vec model is trained, each essay is transformed into a fixed-size feature vector by averaging the word vectors it contains. This feature of vector encapsulates the overall semantic meaning of the essay, providing the LSTM model with a comprehensive understanding of the text before training begins.

Model Training Process: The model training process begins with configuring the LSTM architecture. This includes model initialization, where the LSTM is set up with appropriate architecture settings, including input shapes that match the size of the feature vectors. The model is then compiled with a loss function, mean squared error (MSE) for regression tasks, and an optimizer RMSprop, which adapts the learning rate based on recent gradient magnitudes. Metrics such as mean absolute error (MAE) are also included to monitor performance during training.

Over several epochs, the model iteratively learns to predict scores from input feature vectors, refining its predictions with each data pass. This iterative process allows the model to learn to associate the input feature vectors (essay representations) with their corresponding scores, gradually improving its predictions as it processes more data.

Model Evaluation: Once the model has been trained, it must be evaluated to determine its effectiveness. The trained model is used to predict scores on the unseen test set, providing insights into its performance. Key performance metrics include MSE, which measures the average squared difference between actual and predicted scores, and MAE, which indicates the average absolute difference. Additionally, Cohen's kappa is employed to evaluate the level of agreement between predicted and actual scores beyond what would be expected by chance, adding a layer of validation for categorical agreements.

Model Fine-Tuning and Optimization: After the initial evaluation, further refinements can be made to enhance model performance. Hyperparameter tuning techniques, such as grid search or random search, can be employed to find the optimal values for parameters like learning rate, batch size, and the number of LSTM units. Regularization techniques, including early stopping or additional dropout layers, can also be applied to prevent overfitting. Furthermore, implementing cross-validation techniques provides a more robust assessment of model performance by evaluating it on multiple train-test splits.

5.3.6 Evaluation Metrics

For the essay assessment system, key metrics include

- **Mean Squared Error (MSE):** Measures average squared differences between predicted and actual scores, indicating accuracy.
- **Mean Absolute Error (MAE):** Represents average absolute differences, providing straightforward error interpretations.
- **Cohen's Kappa:** Measures the agreement between predicted and actual scores, accounting for chance.

For the FG system, metrics include

- **Response Time:** Measures the system's response duration, with lower times enhancing user experience.
- **Error Rate:** Reflects the percentage of failed user requests, critical for maintaining system reliability.

- **Throughput:** Measures the number of successful responses per second, indicating system efficiency.
- **Memory Usage:** Assesses average memory usage, essential for operational efficiency in limited-resource environments.

5.4 Results

This section outlines findings from empirical analyses of the automated essay scoring (AES) and FG systems, demonstrating their effectiveness through performance metrics and comparisons with traditional grading.

5.4.1 Performance of AES Model

To evaluate the performance of the AES, several key metrics were analyzed (Table 5.1):

- **Mean Squared Error (MSE):** The AES achieved a mean squared error of approximately **3.25**, indicating a moderate level of scoring accuracy, as it represents the average squared difference between predicted and actual essay scores. Although this shows some variability, further optimization could reduce this error.
- **Cohen's Kappa:** A Cohen's kappa score of **0.13** suggests slight agreement beyond chance between the model's predictions and human scores, with room for improvement to better align with human rater patterns. This score reflects the challenge in achieving strong human–model agreement, given the subjective elements in human scoring.
- **Mean Absolute Error (MAE):** With a mean absolute error of **1.34**, the system's predictions display some deviation from actual scores, though this metric highlights the need for refinement to achieve a lower average prediction error.

Table 5.1 Metrics of Assessment System

Metric	Value	Interpretation
Mean squared error (MSE)	3.25	Indicates moderate accuracy; variability in predictions
Cohen's kappa	0.13	Slight agreement beyond chance; needs improvement
Mean absolute error (MAE)	1.34	Some deviation from actual scores; room for refinement
Root mean squared error (RMSE)	1.80	Reflects overall error margin in scoring predictions

- **Root Mean Squared Error (RMSE):** An RMSE of **1.80** reinforces the findings from MSE and MAE, reflecting the overall error margin in essay scoring predictions and emphasizing the system's baseline accuracy.

These metrics collectively highlight the strengths of the AES while also indicating areas for enhancement, particularly in improving alignment with human raters.

5.4.2 Performance of FG System

To assess the efficiency and reliability of the FG system, several key metrics were analyzed (Table 5.2):

- **Response Time:** The system's average response time was **5.66** seconds, indicating reasonable performance but also suggesting room for optimization to meet a target response time of under 3 seconds, improving user experience through faster feedback.
- **Error Rate:** The FG system achieved an impressively low error rate of **0.001%**, signaling high reliability and successful processing of nearly all user requests without issues. This low error rate supports consistent system performance and user trust.
- **Throughput:** With a throughput of approximately **0.114** responses per second, the system demonstrates capacity for handling real-time requests. Increasing throughput further could allow for better handling of high-demand scenarios, enhancing scalability.
- **Memory Usage:** The system maintained an average memory usage of **27.5%**, indicating efficient resource management and potential for scalability. Efficient memory usage is essential for maintaining system performance, particularly in resource-limited environments.

These metrics provide a clear overview of the FG system's effectiveness, with particular attention to optimizing response time and enhancing throughput while maintaining reliability and low error rates.

Table 5.2 Metrics of Feedback Generation System

Metric	Value	Interpretation
Response time	5.66 s	Reasonable performance, room for optimization
Error rate	0.001%	High reliability, near-perfect performance
Throughput	0.114/s	Capacity to handle real-time requests
Memory usage	27.5%	Efficient resource management, potential for scaling

5.4.3 Comparison with Traditional Grading

The comparison between automated grading systems and traditional human grading reveals significant insights regarding speed, consistency, and objectivity. The NLP system demonstrated remarkable efficiency scoring essays in an average of 5.66 seconds per essay, whereas human raters typically required 10–15 minutes for the same task, highlighting the speed advantage of automated systems. In terms of consistency, the automated grading system exhibited high reliability, with low variability in scores for similar content and an error rate of just 0.001%. In contrast, human grading often suffers from variability, as different raters may score the same essay differently, leading to inconsistencies and potential bias. Objectivity is another area where automated systems excel; the use of defined algorithms and models minimizes subjective bias, ensuring that each essay is evaluated based on the same criteria. On the other hand, human raters can be influenced by personal preferences and biases, which may affect their scoring decisions. Empirical studies have shown that advanced NLP models align closely with human evaluators, and the feedback generated is perceived as meaningful and constructive by students. Overall, the automated grading system outperforms traditional methods in terms of speed, consistency, and objectivity, making it a valuable tool for educational settings focused on enhancing writing skills. These findings underscore the transformative potential of NLP technologies in the assessment landscape, providing timely and constructive feedback to learners.

5.5 Discussion

5.5.1 Efficacy of NLP in Automating Assessment

NLP models have proven effective in automating the assessment of writing by evaluating essential elements such as content, grammar, structure, and style. Their advantages lie in their ability to provide rapid analysis and consistent feedback, particularly in identifying grammatical errors and assessing coherence. However, these models also encounter limitations in grasping nuanced writing elements like intent and context, which can lead to misinterpretations, especially in creative or complex texts. While NLP excels in structural assessments, capturing the stylistic richness of writing remains a significant challenge. Consequently, while NLP offers valuable tools for writing evaluation, it is crucial to acknowledge its limitations, particularly in educational settings where understanding subtleties and fostering creativity are paramount.

5.5.2 Comparative Analysis: Human Grading versus NLP Assessment

Educational researchers are increasingly exploring the balance between accuracy and efficiency in grading by examining the relationship between human grading and NLP-based assessment. While human grading offers extensive contextual understanding and can analyze complex writing, it often faces criticism for its subjectivity, inconsistencies, and bias. In contrast, NLP-based assessment provides an objective and standardized approach, evaluating all student work according to the same criteria. However, it struggles to capture the nuances of human language, such as metaphor, irony, and creativity. This analysis investigates how to integrate human and NLP-based grading to create a more reliable and equitable evaluation system by highlighting their respective strengths and weaknesses. It also considers the implications of using NLP tools in the classroom, focusing on issues of equity, the educational experiences of students, and the potential for developing these technologies to better align with human evaluative capabilities.

5.5.2.1 Advantages of Human Grading

1 **Contextual Understanding:** Human graders can interpret complex language, metaphors, and nuanced arguments that may be difficult for NLP systems to fully understand.
2 **Flexibility:** Human graders can adapt to diverse writing styles and unconventional expressions, providing feedback that is tailored to the individual student.
3 **Holistic Evaluation:** Human graders can assess not only the content and structure but also the creativity, originality, and emotional impact of the writing.

5.5.2.2 Limitations of Human Grading

1 **Subjectivity:** Human grading can be inconsistent, with different graders potentially giving different marks for the same piece of writing.
2 **Bias:** Human graders may be influenced by unconscious biases related to the student's background, writing style, or even handwriting.
3 **Time-Consuming:** Manual grading is labor-intensive and can lead to delays in providing feedback to students.

5.5.2.3 Advantages of NLP-Based Assessment

1 **Objectivity:** NLP-based assessment applies the same criteria to all students, ensuring consistency in grading.
2 **Efficiency:** NLP systems can evaluate large volumes of essays quickly, providing immediate feedback to students.
3 **Scalability:** NLP tools can handle large numbers of students, making them ideal for use in large classes or standardized testing environments.

5.5.2.4 Limitations of NLP-Based Assessment

1 **Limited Language Understanding:** NLP systems may struggle with complex language constructs, such as sarcasm, irony, or culturally specific references.

2 **Lack of Creativity Assessment:** NLP tools may focus more on structure and grammar rather than the creative and original aspects of writing.
3 **Dependence on Training Data:** The accuracy of NLP assessment is dependent on the quality and diversity of the data used to train the system.

Both human grading and NLP-based assessment offer distinct advantages and face specific challenges. Human grading shines in its ability to interpret complex language and provide nuanced feedback, while NLP-based assessment excels in consistency and efficiency. By understanding the strengths and limitations of each approach, educators can make informed decisions about when to use one over the other, or how to combine them to create a balanced and effective evaluation system that meets diverse educational needs.

5.5.3 Impact on Educational Practices

The incorporation of AEA and FG into the educational system is revolutionizing traditional teaching and learning methods, with significant consequences for educators and learners alike.

For Teachers: AEA and FG streamline the grading process, making it less time-consuming and labor-intensive. By eliminating the monotonous task of manually grading essays, teachers can focus more on higher-order responsibilities, such as curriculum development and personalized student engagement. AEA's impartiality and consistency reduce grading biases, ensuring more equitable evaluations of student work. Additionally, automated feedback tools allow teachers to provide quick, comprehensive, and actionable insights, which can be challenging in large classrooms.

For Students: The prompt, personalized feedback offered by AEA and FG is crucial for student growth and learning. Objective evaluations help students identify their strengths and areas for improvement without the frustration of manual grading. Real-time feedback fosters an iterative learning process, encouraging students to refine their work continuously. This rapid, formative feedback can lead to significant improvements in writing skills and greater engagement with the writing process. Furthermore, customized feedback accommodates diverse learning rates, allowing students to progress according to their unique needs and abilities, which is particularly beneficial in varied classrooms.

In conclusion, the efficacy and efficiency of teaching and learning are improved when AEA and FG are incorporated into the educational process. Teachers gain the ability to support their students more effectively, while students benefit from immediate, constructive, and individualized feedback that improves learning outcomes and creates a more engaging learning environment.

5.5.4 Ethical Considerations

The implementation of NLP-based essay assessment systems requires careful attention to ethical considerations, particularly concerning fairness, bias, and data privacy. These systems risk perpetuating existing biases in training data, which can disproportionately impact underrepresented student groups and undermine equity in education. It is essential to rigorously test algorithms for bias and continuously update them to reflect diverse linguistic and cultural backgrounds.

Additionally, handling student data raises significant privacy concerns; robust measures must be implemented to protect sensitive information and comply with regulations like GDPR. Human oversight is crucial to maintain accountability and transparency in the assessment process. Educators should be involved in designing and implementing these systems to ensure they align with pedagogical goals and ethical standards, mitigating the risk of over-reliance on automated assessments.

By addressing these ethical, practical, and equity-related issues, we can develop NLP-based assessment tools that enhance educational outcomes while respecting the rights and dignity of all learners.

5.5.5 Case Studies and Real-World Applications

This section explores real-world applications of NLP-based systems in educational institutions and corporate training, highlighting their impact, user interactions, and efficacy. A notable example is Turnitin, which has enhanced its plagiarism-detection platform with NLP-driven feedback mechanisms that provide insights into students' writing. This feature not only identifies potential academic dishonesty but also offers constructive feedback on grammar, style, and coherence, helping students improve their writing skills over time. Educators report that these feedback mechanisms are valuable for targeted instruction and fostering collaborative learning environments.

Another significant application is found in adaptive learning platforms like Grammarly and QuillBot, which provide personalized writing feedback. These tools analyze submissions in real time, offering suggestions and encouraging self-reflection. Empirical evidence shows that students using these platforms often experience improved understanding of writing mechanics and increased confidence. For example, a university study indicated that students who regularly used Grammarly saw significant improvement in their writing scores compared with their peers.

Next, we will explore case studies that illustrate the effectiveness of these NLP systems in educational settings.

Case Study 1: e-rater (ETS)

e-rater, developed by the Educational Testing Service (ETS), is a well-known automated essay scoring system that leverages NLP techniques to evaluate student writing. The system utilizes a combination of machine learning algorithms and linguistic analysis to assess various components of an essay, including content, organization, language use, and mechanics.

The scoring mechanism involves the comparison of student essays to a set of pre-scored essays, allowing the e-rater to assign scores based on multiple dimensions of writing quality. The system is trained on a vast dataset of essays and their associated scores, enabling it to recognize patterns and features indicative of higher-quality writing. Additionally, e-rater provides detailed feedback on specific areas for improvement, such as coherence, grammatical correctness, and the use of vocabulary. This feedback mechanism not only helps students understand their performance but also guides them in refining their writing skills. Studies have shown that essays scored by e-rater correlate strongly with human scores, validating its efficacy as a reliable assessment tool in educational settings.

Case Study 2: Grammarly

Grammarly serves as a prominent example of an NLP-based writing assistance tool that offers real-time feedback on writing quality. Utilizing advanced NLP algorithms, Grammarly analyses text for various aspects of writing, including grammar, punctuation, style, and coherence. The system provides immediate suggestions as users compose their texts, allowing them to see corrections and improvements in real time.

Grammarly employs a multifaceted scoring mechanism that considers the context of the writing, assessing elements such as tone, clarity, and engagement. This contextual understanding allows it to provide personalized recommendations tailored to the user's writing style and goals. Users can receive detailed explanations of suggested changes, enhancing their understanding of writing conventions and improving their overall writing quality. User studies indicate that many Grammarly users report enhanced writing skills and greater confidence in their abilities, showcasing its effectiveness as a writing aid in both academic and professional settings.

Case Study 3: Writing Pal or IntelliMetric

Writing Pal and IntelliMetric are notable examples of systems designed to score essays while providing detailed feedback to help students improve their writing. Both systems utilize sophisticated NLP methodologies, including statistical modelling and linguistic analysis, to evaluate various components of writing, such as argument structure, clarity, and grammar.

Writing Pal, for instance, not only assesses the overall quality of an essay but also generates feedback on specific elements, including thesis statements, supporting arguments, and conclusion effectiveness. The system guides students through the writing process by offering suggestions on how to enhance clarity and coherence, promoting self-directed learning.

IntelliMetric, developed by Vantage Learning, employs a similar approach, utilizing a combination of machine learning techniques and expert-validated scoring rubrics. The system analyses essays based on factors such as content relevance, organization, and language use, providing a score that reflects the essay's overall quality. IntelliMetric also offers actionable feedback, highlighting areas where students can improve their writing.

However, the effectiveness of these systems is often influenced by students' perceptions of the feedback. While many appreciate the instant nature of automated feedback, some express concerns about its depth and the absence of nuanced understanding that human evaluators provide. This feedback gap highlights the importance of integrating human oversight into NLP systems to ensure comprehensive support for students' learning journeys. Overall, these case studies underscore the transformative potential of NLP-based assessment tools in enhancing educational outcomes while also emphasizing the need for ongoing evaluation of their efficacy and user experiences to optimize their implementation.

5.5.6 Limitations and Challenges

Achieving fairness and accuracy in automated writing assessment is challenging, especially for creative or non-standard writing. Bias in training data can skew results, and current systems often struggle with nuanced language, idioms, and cultural references, limiting their ability to fairly assess diverse writing styles. Standard feedback can overlook individual expression, while unconventional styles—like poetry or slang—often fall outside typical algorithms, risking the underrepresentation of marginalized voices.

Emerging solutions, such as few-shot learning and multimodal approaches incorporating audio and video, show promise for enhancing NLP applications in education. These technologies can help algorithms grasp content context and adapt feedback more precisely, supporting inclusivity and better tailored, nuanced evaluations.

5.6 Conclusion

Incorporating NLP systems into educational settings presents a promising pathway toward efficient, scalable, and objective assessment and FG. Through AES and FG, NLP models streamline the grading process, delivering consistent feedback and rapid responses that align well with the needs of modern educational practices. Results indicate that while AES models provide a reliable structure-focused assessment with measurable accuracy metrics such as MSE and Cohen's kappa, they still encounter challenges in aligning with nuanced human judgments, particularly in contexts requiring interpretation of intent or creativity. Additionally, FG systems demonstrated impressive efficiency, with low error rates and manageable resource usage, enabling real-time, formative feedback that supports iterative learning. However, the results also underscore that automated systems still fall short in fully capturing the depth and stylistic diversity of human language, highlighting the ongoing need for human oversight and a balanced, hybrid approach to assessment. Together, the integration of NLP-driven systems and traditional human evaluation methods offers an enriched framework for assessment that balances consistency and depth, making the educational process more inclusive, efficient, and adaptable to diverse learning needs.

5.7 Future Directions

Future advancements in AES should prioritize enhancing the depth of semantic understanding in NLP systems to better interpret complex arguments and nuanced meanings in student writing. Current systems, while effective at assessing structural and grammatical elements, often fall short in comprehending context-rich or creative content. Integrating advanced NLP architectures, such as those based on GPT models, may provide more personalized and meaningful feedback, promoting deeper learning outcomes. Addressing fairness and bias in AES systems is also essential, as disparities in training data and algorithmic biases can disproportionately affect diverse student populations. Future research should focus on identifying and mitigating these biases to support more equitable assessments. Additionally, expanding AES systems to support multimodal assessment—including analysis of text, speech, and video—could offer a richer, more comprehensive view of student skills, accommodating diverse expression forms and learning styles. These future directions underscore a commitment to making AEE systems not only more accurate and informative but also more inclusive and adaptable to the varied needs of educational settings.

To achieve these goals, educators, policymakers, and researchers should collaborate on developing and refining NLP technologies in education. A joint effort is essential to create more inclusive, adaptive, and equitable assessment systems, aligning technological innovation with educational values and goals.

References

Alqahtani, T., Badreldin, H. A., Alrashed, M., Alshaya, A. I., Alghamdi, S. S., Bin Saleh, K., ... Albekairy, A. M. (2023). The emergent role of artificial intelligence, natural learning processing, and large language models in higher education and research. *Research in Social & Administrative Pharmacy: RSAP, 19*(8), 1236–1242. doi:10.1016/j.sapharm.2023.05.016

Amanda, F. D., Dewi, U. P., Mufit, F., & Festiyed, F. (2023). Influence of essay assessment on student competency achievement in science learning: Literature review. *Journal Penelitian Pendidikan IPA, 9*(9), 539–549. doi:10.29303/jppipa.v9i9.4994

Bauer, E., Greisel, M., Kuznetsov, I., Berndt, M., Kollar, I., Dresel, M., ... Fischer, F. (2023). Using natural language processing to support peer-feedback in the age of artificial intelligence: A cross-disciplinary framework and a research agenda. *British Journal of Educational Technology: Journal of the Council for Educational Technology, 54*(5), 1222–1245. doi:10.1111/bjet.13336

Botelho, A., Baral, S., Erickson, J. A., Benachamardi, P., & Heffernan, N. T. (2023). Leveraging natural language processing to support automated assessment and feedback for student open responses in mathematics. *Journal of Computer Assisted Learning, 39*(3), 823–840. doi:10.1111/jcal.12793

Gombert, S., Fink, A., Giorgashvili, T., Jivet, I., Di Mitri, D., Yau, J., ... Drachsler, H. (2024). From the automated assessment of student essay content to highly informative feedback: A case study. *International Journal of Artificial Intelligence in Education, 34*, 1378–1416. doi:10.1007/s40593-023-00387-6

Lagakis, P., & Demetriadis, S. (2022). Automated essay feedback generation in the learning of writing: A review of the field. In *Lecture Notes in Networks and Systems. New Realities, Mobile Systems and Applications* (pp. 443–453). doi:10.1007/978-3-030-96296-8_40

Lemantara, J., Hariadi, B., Sunarto, M. J. D., Amelia, T., & Sagirani, T. (2023). An innovative strategy to anticipate students' cheating: The development of automatic essay assessment on the "MoLearn" learning management system. *IEEE Transactions on Learning Technologies, 16*(5), 748–758. doi:10.1109/tlt.2023.3267518

Susanti, M. N. I., Ramadhan, A., & Warnars, H. L. H. S. (2023). Automatic essay exam scoring system: a systematic literature review. *Procedia Computer Science, 216*, 531–538. doi:10.1016/j.procs.2022.12.166

Yan, L., Sha, L., Zhao, L., Li, Y., Martinez-Maldonado, R., Chen, G., Li, X., Jin, Y. & Gašević, D. (2024). Practical and ethical challenges of large language models in education: A systematic scoping review. *British Journal of Educational Technology: Journal of the Council for Educational Technology, 55*(1), 90–112. doi:10.1111/bjet.13370

Yang, H., He, Y., Bu, X., Xu, H., & Guo, W. (2023). Automatic essay evaluation technologies in Chinese writing—A systematic literature review. *Applied Sciences (Basel, Switzerland), 13*(19), 10737. doi:10.3390/app131910737

6 Enhancing Learning Outcomes for the Dyslexic Students Using AI-Powered Assistants

Anjali Mathur

6.1 Introduction

One of the parameter to observe the student's learning is assessments. Assessments are useful to check the progress. There are multiple methods for assessments like diagnostic assessment – to detect the misconceptions and to evaluating the existing knowledge, Formative assessment for collect and analyzing data on the learning of student, Summative assessments – to evaluate the overall achievement of students. When a combined group of dyslexic and non dyslexic students are in a common study platform, then the dyslexic students are usually not able to achieve the higher scores in assessments as compare to non-dyslexic students. There is a need to provide equal opportunities to such students and encourage them in higher education by offering some tailored assessments or by offering some virtual assistants. In the proposed research work we are using AI-powered approach that is based on assessments to find the academic learning progress in the dyslexic students. Multiple AI-algorithms are used on diagnostic, formative and the summative assessments. The framework begins with the diagnosis of dyslexic students and ends with the enhanced learning outcomes.

Keywords: Adaptive learning, Associate mining, Virtual assistants, Classification.

6.2 Adaptive Learning

The adaptive learning environments can be described as facilitating the learning process of each individual with appropriate learning conditions. Francois (2011) defines adaptive learning as a usage of technology to help the students in their learning process. It provides content and services to meet the needs of individuals or groups (Martinez, 2003). The first step in that direction was the teaching machines. The teaching machines made possible the individualizing instructions. Teaching machines were the first technological step in the instructional programs. Teaching machines promoted computer-assisted instruction and system approach to instruction. It was discussed by Nguyen and Do (2008) that the learning environment is a complex structure

DOI: 10.1201/9781003470304-6

that includes many students who have different characteristics. The difference in physical and mental status of each individual impacts the performance individually. Thus, adaptation to these differences in educational environment is a necessity (Nguyen & Do, 2008), and adaptive learning environments provide systems to achieve this. In a statement by Paramythis and Loidl Reisinger (2004) it was discussed there are four major categories necessary for all adaptive learning environments; namely, adaptive interaction, adaptive course delivery, content discovery and assembly, and adaptive collaboration support. They define adaptive interaction as providing semantic interactions between the user and the system. In adaptive learning systems the technology helps the stakeholders to share their knowledge with the system. The system keeps the student's personal profiles, and based on them, adjusts course to the student by providing different levels and presenting each topic as a series of skills and building blocks to master the concepts (Fischman, 2011). Adaptive learning systems can provide adaptive learning materials like animation, videos, interactive diagrams, and other web-based features as per the requirement by students.

Intelligent tutors are one of the special features of adaptive learning that support the collaborative learning. Interactive tutors help the students to gain the skills in depth, as the system assesses each individual by multiple quizzes. Monitoring the knowledge of each learner and providing the feedback accordingly is another feature of adaptive learning systems. The technology supports the students with various pedagogical activities to construct their own knowledge and check the progress at any time. Students can access the resources as per their need and study them at their pace, in this way the students have a full control on their learning process. The adaptive system provides benefits to the instructors also. Teachers can use various methods to provide the instructions, like problem-based instructions or case reasoning or any other method. They can assess the students and give the assignments on the basis of the student's learning capabilities. Instructors can decide the proficiency level and students do not move forward until they achieve that level. The adaptive learning system provides the student's feedback to help the instructors in analyzing the content's difficulty level.

6.3 Leveraging AI for Enhanced Teaching Efficiency and Effectiveness

6.3.1 Effects of AI on Personalized Learning Experiences

a **Adaptive Learning Platform:** Artificial intelligence (AI)-powered adaptive learning platforms analyze vast amounts of student data, including preference metrics, learning preferences, and cognitive abilities, to deliver customized learning experiences. These platforms dynamically adjust the content, pace, and difficulty level of instructional materials based on individual learner progress, ensuring that each student receives targeted support and challenges aligned with their specific learning needs. Adaptive learning platforms empower students to learn at their own pace, allowing for remediation when necessary and acceleration when mastery is demonstrated, fostering a sense of autonomy and self-directed learning.

b **Personalized Content Recommendations:** AI algorithms can analyze learner's interactions with educational content, such as textbooks, videos, and digital resources, to generate personalized recommendations tailored to their interests and proficiency levels. By leveraging data analytics materials, enrichment activities or relevant learning resources are aligned with individual learning goals and preferences. Personalized content recommendations not only enhance engagement but also facilitate understanding and retention of key concepts.

c **Individualized Assessments:** Traditional assessments often provide limited insights into student's understanding and progress. AI-enabled assessment tools leverage adaptive testing algorithms to generate individualized assessments that dynamically adjust the difficulty level and content based on student's responses in real time. By tailoring assessments to each learner's proficiency level, AI can provide more accurate and comprehensive evaluations of their knowledge and skills, identifying areas of strength and weakness more effectively. Moreover, individualized assessments promote formative feedback, allowing educators to offer targeted interventions and support to address learning gaps.

d **Intelligent Tutoring Systems:** AI-powered intelligent tutoring systems emulate the role of human tutors by providing personalized instruction, feedback, and guidance to learners in real time. These systems utilize cognitive models and natural language processing (NLP) techniques to adaptively scaffold learning experiences, responding to student's actions and misconceptions with targeted hints, explanations, and remediation strategies. Intelligent tutoring systems offer individualized support across various subject areas and learning domains, fostering mastery in learning and meta-cognitive skills development.

e **Data-Driven Insights:** AI analytics tools enable educators to gain actionable insights into student's learning behaviors, preferences, and performance patterns. By analyzing data collected from learning management systems, digital assessments, and online interactions, AI algorithms can identify trends, predict future outcomes, and recommend instructional strategies tailored to individual and group needs. Data-driven insights empower educators to make informed decisions about curriculum design, instructional delivery, and intervention strategies, optimizing the learning experience for all students.

6.3.2 *Enhancing Classroom Engagement*

Incorporation of interactive elements and immersive learning experiences provided by AI enhances the classroom engagement. AI-based technologies like virtual reality and augmented reality enables the students to explore complex concepts in a simulated environment, fostering experiential learning and critical thinking skills.

Virtual Reality and Augmented Reality Applications: Additionally, chatbots and virtual assistants can facilitate instant communication between students and teachers, providing on-demand support and guidance outside of traditional classroom hours. By incorporating AI-driven technologies, educators can create dynamic and interactive learning environments that captivate student's interest and promote active participation.

a **Interactive Learning Tools:** AI-powered interactive learning tools, such as educational games, simulations, and virtual laboratories, provide hands-on experiences that engage students in active learning. These tools leverage gamification techniques, augmented reality, and virtual reality to create immersive learning environments where students can explore complex concepts, conduct experiments, and solve real-world problems in a safe environment. These tools also captivate student's attention and promote deeper engagement with course material.

b **Personalized Learning Pathways:** AI-driven adaptive learning platforms tailor instructional content and activities to suit each student's individual learning preferences, pace, and proficiency level. By presenting students with personalized learning pathways, educators can cater to diverse learning styles and interests, empowering students to take ownership of their learning journey. Personalized learning experiences not only increase motivation and engagement but also enhance retention and comprehension of key concepts.

c **Real-Time Feedback and Assessment:** AI-powered assessment tools provide instant feedback on student responses, allowing educators to gauge understanding, identify misconceptions, and address learning gaps in real time. These tools use NLP algorithms to analyze written or verbal responses and provide personalized feedback tailored to each student's individual needs. By offering immediate feedback, educators can guide student learning more effectively and promote active engagement with course material.

d **Collaborative Learning Platforms:** AI-driven collaborative learning platforms facilitate peer-to-peer interaction, group collaboration, and knowledge-sharing among students. These platforms utilize AI algorithms to match students with compatible peers based on learning knowledge construction. By promoting social interaction and collaboration, AI-driven collaborative learning platforms create a supportive learning community where students can learn from each other and co-create new knowledge.

e **Intelligent Classroom Assistants:** AI-powered classroom assistants, such as chatbots and virtual teaching assistants, provide on-demand support and guidance to students during lectures and independent study session. These assistants use NLP capabilities to understand student's questions and provide instant responses, explanations, and clarifications. By offering personalized assistance and scaffolding, AI-driven classroom assistants enhance student's learning experiences and promote engagement with course material.

6.3.3 Advantages of AI-Driven Technologies

By leveraging AI-driven technologies, educators can gain insights into individual learner and collective learning gaps. They can tailor instructional strategies to target specific areas of need and provide personalized support to students. The ultimate goal is to fostering academic growth and success. Some of the advantages of AI-driven technologies are as follows:

a **Data Analysis and Identification:** AI algorithms can analyze large datasets of student performance metrics, including assessment scores, quiz results, and learning behaviors, to identify patterns and trends indicative of learning gaps. By examining variations, analytics tools enable educators to pinpoint areas where students may be struggling or experiencing difficulty.

b **Personalized Remediation:** Once learning gaps have been identified, AI-powered adaptive learning platforms can deliver targeted remedial instruction and practice activities tailored to each student's individual needs. These platforms dynamically adjust the content, difficulty level, and pace of instruction based on ongoing assessment data, providing additional support and scaffolding to help students master challenging concepts or skills.

c **Intelligent Tutoring Systems:** AI-driven intelligent tutoring systems emulate the role of human tutors by providing personalized guidance, feedback, and assistance to students in real time. These systems use cognitive models and machine learning algorithms to adaptively scaffold learning experiences, offering customized explanations, hints, and examples to address specific learning gaps or misconceptions.

d **Formative Assessment and Feedback:** AI-powered assessment tools can generate formative feedback on student responses, allowing educators to provide targeted interventions and support to address learning gaps as they arise. By offering immediate feedback on quizzes, assignments, and activities, AI-driven assessment tools enable students to identify areas of weakness and take proactive steps to improve their understanding and mastery of key concepts.

e **Data-Driven Intervention Strategies:** AI analytics tools enable educators to track student progress, monitor the effectiveness of intervention strategies, and adjust instructional approaches as needed based on real-time data insights. By leveraging data-driven decision-making, educators can implement evidence-based intervention strategies that target specific learning gaps and promote academic growth among all students.

In conclusion, AI-driven technologies offer diverse opportunities to address learning gaps by leveraging data analytics and providing adaptive learning platforms, intelligent tutoring systems, and formative assessment tools. By identifying areas of weakness, providing personalized remediation, and offering targeted support to students, educators can create inclusive learning environments that promote academic success and empower every learner to reach their full potential.

6.4 Educational Applications of Artificial Intelligence

To support the self-regulated learning, various approaches are available. Open learning model (OLM) is one of the approaches (Gandedkar et al., 2021; Nussbaumer et al., 2015) that can employ machine learning techniques, Bayesian networks, fuzzy logic, and item response theory to make learners perform in real time. It is "open" to students so that the learners can plan, monitor, and reflect on their own learning for self-guided decision-making. Graesser and McNamara (2010) suggested that OLM in self-regulated learning can be achieved through natural language interactions between the learners and virtual agents.

One of the most popular AI-powered virtual agents is guidebots that support productive inquiry. These guidebots maintain multiple learner–agent interactions, including hints and feedback as cognitive assistance. They guide the learners to be aware of, reflect on, and correct their misconceptions during the learning processes. A Bayesian networks–based AI-powered virtual agent was introduced in 2003 that could automatically update the dialogs based on the learner's performance and guide learners' reasoning processes for knowledge construction. In same way, de Freitas and Neumann (2009) represent the exploratory learning as a theoretical base for immersive simulation-based learning. They supported the AI-based approach that helps the students to develop problem-solving skills with the iterative cycles of experience, exploration, reflection, abstraction, and testing. In the comparative study of guidebots and teachable agents, it's clear that the guidebots benefit the learners with lower prior knowledge, while the teachable agents benefit the students with higher prior knowledge as they require complex problem-solving skills and deeper domain knowledge. Affective-sensitive AI systems in simulation-based learning can track students' affective states. D'Mello and Graesser (2012) introduced affective AutoTutor using state-of-the-art sensing technologies and machine learning techniques to address and regulate students' boredom, confusion, and frustration by capturing and mining their conversational cues, body language, and facial features. Another aspect of affective computing in AI-powered learning simulations is using emotion-expressive virtual agents. Embodied agents in simulation-based learning can cue learners via virtual motor actions, gaze, and gesture to direct students' attention and convey verbal and non-verbal communications. Meta-analysis found that AI-powered affective agents had a significant and moderate effect on motivation to learn, and yielded a small effect on knowledge retention and knowledge transfer. Lawson et al. (2021) revealed that learners were able to attend to virtual agents' emotional expressions (positive or negative), and self-reported that virtual agents with positive emotions promoted learning. In their experiments, Craig and Schroeder (2017) compared virtual agents with voices using classic speech engine, contemporary speech engine, and human voice. They found a voice effect for science learning (i.e., the formation of lightning). Participants in the contemporary TTS engine group outperformed in the transfer test.

Assessment is regarded as a key component in AI-integrated simulation-based learning (Castillo-Segura et al., 2021; Dalinger et al., 2020). The authors argued that assessment facilitated participants to reflect on their gap in teaching performance. Real-time feedback and multimodal interactions facilitated the teaching performance assessment (Dalinger et al., 2020). Current practice of AI assessments for supporting student learning involves the use of data-driven prediction. Modern machine learning algorithms used to support the assessment for learning are support vector machines (SVMs), neural networks (Castillo-Segura et al., 2021; Moon et al., 2020; Yang et al., 2021), and latent semantic analysis combined with regular expressions (Graesser et al., 2010). Castillo-Segura et al.'s (2021) systematic literature review on surgical technical skills assessment revealed four aspects to be considered—(1) sensors; (2) multimodal data collection (i.e., body movements, eyes tracking, and/or the combinations), including baseline indicators; (3) machine learning algorithms (i.e., SVMs and neural networks); and (4) feedback mechanism (i.e., real-time and delayed feedback). Likewise, hidden Markov models (HMMs) were used for assessing, classifying, and providing feedback on dental skills in simulation (Rhienmora et al., 2011). In-simulation data were mined to afford the automatic tracking of users' actions. The assessment afforded by HMMs was then used to generate tutoring feedback for dental operations. Yang et al. (2021) built artificial neural network (ANN) computational models to assess learners' cognitive abilities in English language learning. ANNs simulate human brains by interconnecting neurons to process information simultaneously. The three-layer ANN model results can be used to predict performance or to map features for the prediction. Yang et al.'s (2021) ANN model results were applied in a user-friendly online platform to predict learners' cognitive performance and assess learners' verb and past tense performance. Yang et al. (2021) suggested that the generated reports helped teachers and instructional designers identify learners' learning progress to adapt teaching. In practice, large transformer-based natural language models based on deep learning have been developed to be leveraged to solve local educational problems with customization and contextualization. We can conclude that the AI-based virtual agents can do human-like conversations and can demonstrate affective states with verbal, voice, text, or facial expressions.

6.5 Students with Dyslexia

A sort of learning disorder is called dyslexia in which the brain shows malfunctioning related to sounds and their corresponding letters. Brain functions like hearing, storing, remembering, and producing different speech sounds does not respond quickly and accurately, which makes a candidate to struggle with reading, writing, and spelling. The dyslexic students usually take a longer time to decode words when reading and may have limited comprehension of what they've read. This affects the academic progress and learning skills of dyslexic students. The analysis skills, word reading, and reading comprehension can fall below grade level for the dyslexic students. Such learning deficits build up over time, making it more and more challenging for students with dyslexia to experience academic success. The struggles for dyslexic students are not only limited to academics, it impacts their social and emotional behaviors also. Such students can't express themselves properly and usually loose the better job opportunities. In conclusion, dyslexic students generally suffer from following issues:

a **Phonological Awareness Deficits:** The ability to identify and manipulate the sounds of languages is considered as phonological awareness. Deficits of this causes the difficulties in reading, writing, and learning processes.
b **Reading Difficulties:** The students can't read fluently, feel difficult to understand what they read, and struggle to decode the words.
c **Writing Difficulties:** The students can't frame the sentence structure, struggle with punctuation, spelling and grammar, and find it difficult to write coherently.
d **Executive Functioning Difficulties:** All types of cognitive processes come under the executive functioning, like planning, organizing, completing tasks, etc. Usually, dyslexia-suffering students find it challenging to stay organized and manage with the academic tasks.
e **Social–Emotional Challenges:** Individuals with dyslexia may feel frustrated, anxious, or ashamed about their difficulties and may struggle to keep up with their peers academically.

6.5.1 Age-Wise Symptoms for Dyslexic Students

a **In Grades K–5:** The dyslexic students suffer with blending letter sounds, sounding out unfamiliar words, recognizing words that rhyme, skipping smaller words such as *at*, *as*, *so* while reading aloud. The students struggle with spelling the same word consistently and remembering important details from readings. Usually, the students with dyslexia avoid reading as much as possible.
b **Students in Grades 6–12:** It's difficult for the students with dyslexia to recall the common abbreviations and acronyms. Finding the right words while speaking is also a major difficulty for such students. Generally,

they use some substitute words in place of the correct one. Taking notes and copying material from the board; following multistep instructions; spelling all words phonetically; summarizing stories; making sense of jokes, idioms, and puns; reading at a normal or quick pace are some of the common signs of dyslexia students.

c **Dyslexia Students in STEM:** When any of the dyslexic student opts for science, technology, engineering, or mathematics fields for the higher studies, then the situation becomes more difficult for them. The very first hurdle is understanding the new scientific and technical terminology and notations. The reading, remembering, and reproducing the notations are troublous tasks for such students. The students with dyslexia struggles with visual stress and usually finds the digits appear to move or overlap with each other, in such situation working with calculators and reading superscripts, subscripts, fractional values, data present inside the tables are a big hurdle for them. While studying with any textbook if by chance the figure/graph comes on one page and the details about them are on another page, then the dyslexic students become confused and they go back and forth between several pages.

d For the STEM area, there is always an essential activity to work at laboratory or to complete the field work. Where, the students have to listen to and remember instructions, take accurate notes, organize their time appropriately, work in groups, record data, and make on-the-spot mathematical calculations. Students with dyslexia find this a bit difficult due to lesser understanding, not able to balance the time and make careful observations on the practical. While doing group activities, the students with dyslexia get more stressful, and due to reading, writing, and phonetic difficulties they feel inferior and frustrated.

6.5.2 *Possible Helps for Dyslexia Students*

a A separate module glossary would be beneficial for them that can provide technical vocabulary, notations, taxonomy, and scientific terms at a one place, where they can access easily. Providing a visual diagram for new technical words would be a big help for them.

b Refer the good books for study, where the general accessibility guidelines are offered inside the book.

c For the "to-do" task list or the reading list, mention the most essential reading at the top of the list so that the students should not miss any important information.

d When interspersing notation into notes, texts, and slides, ensure that they are in a logical order and that the notation relates directly to the text around it, in order to create a logical flow through the material.

e When presenting data on spreadsheets, use alternate coloring of columns, rows, and/or cells in data tables and spreadsheets to make them easier to read.

f Ensure that feedback on assignments is detailed and clearly written so that there is no misunderstanding, particularly if it is handwritten.

6.6 AI-Powered Virtual Assistants for Dyslexic Students

Various research works were conducted to support the dyslexic children and to enhance their language skills. Speech recognition, text to speech, dictation of texts, converting voice message into written text are few of the technologies based on AI. The researchers used multiple AI-based algorithms to find new directions for the enhancement in learning skills. Adaptive reinforcement learning framework was proposed to support the teaching of dyslexic students, where the difficulty levels of tasks were get adjusted. In another research work, NLP and machine learning techniques were used to identify and highlight difficult word or phrases for dyslexic readers. The system provides real-time assistance by providing the reader with definitions, synonyms, and pronunciation guides for difficult words.

6.6.1 AI-Assisted Language Learning Models

The models that utilize AI technology to enhance language acquisition come under this category. These models can offer personalized support and adapt to the specific needs of dyslexic students. Two most common language learning models are as follows:

a **Adaptive Learning Model:** To analyze the learning patterns and academic progress of students with dyslexia, the model was generated. The model has capabilities to tailor the lessons, exercises, and materials that focus on areas where a student needs more assistance. One such example is language learning platform—Duolingo. It utilizes machine learning algorithms to personalize language learning experiences. Mathspace is also an example of adaptive learning model that provides a mix of video modules and interactive activities personalized to each user. It is leveraged with quizzes and practice problems that provide a more interactive experience to the learners.

b **Multisensory Instruction Model:** It is a way of teaching that engages more than one sense of the student at a time. A teacher makes the students to use sight, hear, movements, and touch to connect letters and their sounds. Air writing, sand paper letters, word building, tapping out sounds, story sticks are few of the popular methods to implement this learning. AI-powered multisensory learning enhances the teaching experiences by providing dynamic simulations, 3D models, generating captivating images, or short videos. A new open source AI-model is announced by Meta that links together multiple streams of data, including text, audio, visual data, temperature, and movement readings.

6.6.2 *Digital Tools for Dyslexic Students*

a **Text-to-Speech Tools:** Natural Reader is a text-to-speech tool that can convert any written text, such as MS Word, a website, PDF files, and emails, into spoken words. It offers a range of natural-sounding voices, allowing dyslexic students to listen to content rather than solely relying on reading.

b **ReachDeck Toolbar:** It is web page navigation software available for most versions of Windows that is designed to help those with dyslexia and second-language learners browsing the internet. The software strips the web page down to its essential text, so the user can focus on the text alone. Its text-to-speech feature also comes with a magnifying glass icon that follows the text as it is read aloud.

c **Speech-to-Text Tools:** Google Docs has a feature called "voice typing." To use voice typing, your computer microphone needs to be on and working. Open a document in Google Docs. Click Tools and then Voice typing. A microphone box appears. When you're ready to speak, click the microphone. Speechnotes is a web-based speech-to-text tool that allows students to quickly dictate their notes instead of typing them. This will save them time and effort. Some additional features of the tool include transcribing and adding punctuation.

d **Dyslexia-Friendly Fonts:** OpenDyslexic for Chrome is a chrome extension that overrides all fonts on web pages with the OpenDyslexic font. It formats pages to make them more readable. It was created to increase readability for students with dyslexia. BeeLine Reader is a tool that uses color gradients to guide the student's eyes from one line to the next. This can help with reading speed and comprehension. BeeLine Reader also includes a setting option for an Open Dyslexic Font, allowing students with dyslexia to read in an adjusted font.

e **Mind Mapping Tools:** MindMeister is an online tool that enables collaborative mind mapping. It's excellent for group projects or brainstorming sessions. For dyslexic students, visualizing information can be an effective way of understanding and retaining what they are learning. Google Drawings is one of my favorite tools. It's so easy to create a mind map in Google Drawing. Google Drawing allows you to draw shapes, write text, and then connect them. You can add color, images, and even share your mind map.

f **Audio Books and Bookshare Services:** Bookshare is a site that offers text-to-speech audiobooks for students with dyslexia. Students can listen to books, follow along with highlighting, read in braille or large font, and customize their reading experience. Learning Ally is another resource that offers text-to-speech audio books for students with dyslexia. It offers a plethora of educational texts and literature.

g **Note-Taking Apps with Audio Integration:** OneNote with Learning Tools offers an "Immersive Reader" mode, which reads out text and highlights it simultaneously, aiding comprehension. Notability is an app that is beneficial for iPad users. Students can take notes, annotate PDFs, and even record lectures for playback.

6.7 Proposed Methodology

The AI-powered virtual assistants are generally used for speeding up the communications, increase the outcome, and to improve the working level. Basically, these assistants make a person to do a work individually without showing dependencies on others. When we talk about students, they are directly dependent on a teacher for their learning. Nowadays, lot of tools are available that can work as a virtual teacher. Most of the virtual teacher tools are helpful for normal students. There are rarely any tools available that can work with a combined group of normal and dyslexic students. In this regards, we are proposing a framework that works as follows (Figure 6.1 shows diagrammatical representation of the proposed model):

1 The proposed AI-powered virtual assistant is developed in Python language with GUI mode.
2 The very first phase is the diagnosis assessment to diagnose any dyslexic student. It takes the output generated by item adaptive testing as the input and with the help of binary classification generates output for two values: dyslexic or non-dyslexic.
3 For the dyslexic classified students, the next step is formative assessments. That are used to collect and analyze data on the learning of students. Home

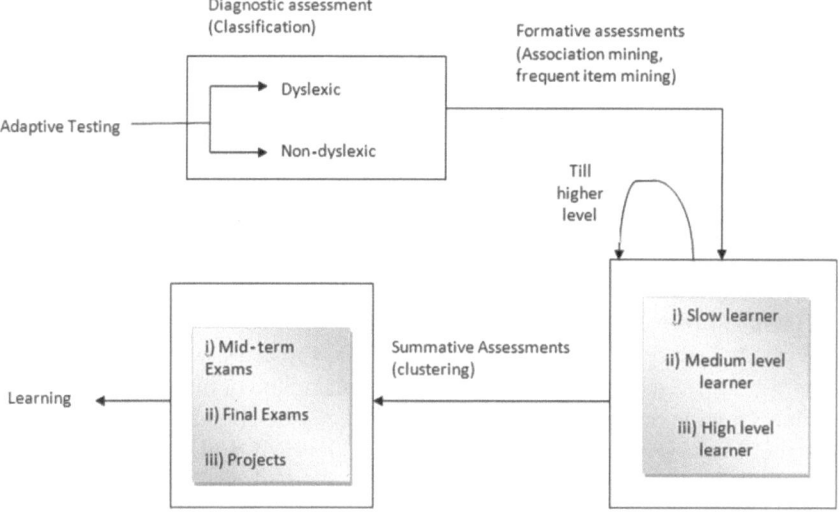

Figure 6.1 Proposed Methodology.

assignments, in-class activities, quizzes are some of the activities that come under these assessments. We scheduled the formative assessments for three categories: slow learners, medium-level learners, and high-level learners.

4 As the formative assessments are considered as continuous assessments, so a student has to practice till the learning level reaches to the high level.

5 As shown in Figure 6.1, the details of the high-level learners will be move to the next step that is summative assessment. The step will measure the learning in one-time mode: during the mid-term exams or the term-end exams or the final evaluation of a project. The students who can pass the summative assessments are considered as learned students.

6.7.1 *Diagnostic Assessments*

The diagnostic assessments are used to detect the misconceptions and to evaluate the existing knowledge. The diagnostic assessments can classify the students on certain measurement scales on the basis of existing knowledge. In this research work, we are using adaptive testing to classify the dyslexic and non-dyslexic students with diagnostic assessments.

a **Item Adaptive Testing:**
   The item adaptive assessment checks for the student's response to an individual item and selects the next question presented in the test based on difficulty level. For example, a teacher may ask students to list the characteristics of any certain term, if the student can do this correctly, a more challenging test item will be given, like differentiate the term with the other closer terms. If the student is not able to do the task correctly, then a lesser challenging item will be presented, like define the term. As we are working for the dyslexic students at the higher education level, we are ignoring the basic difficulties related to reading and writing. The STEM students need to be more focused on remembrance, understanding, analysis, and decision-making. These parameters are checked on the metrics of time, accuracy of response, and the range of questions attended by the student. Figure 6.2 shows the GUI representation of item adaptive testing. In Figure 6.2, three core topics are given. A student can choose any one of them for assessment. Each topic further contains a list of items, students can go with any one item and face the questions related to that.

b **Classification:**
   With the help of item adaptive testing, it's easy to classify the students. The item adaptive model can be used with any discipline of higher education. It covers a wide range of topics and various levels of difficulty. Classification is the first step for identifying the learning level of dyslexic students. For the classification models, AI provides multiple methods, like Bay's classification, decision tree, rule-based classification, etc. The process is to predict the correct label of a given input data. Training a machine learning model on historical student's data can help the teachers to accurately analyze

Figure 6.2 Item Adaptive Testing.

their learning level. In this work, the binary logistic regression model is used for the classification purpose. The model is well suitable for the binary dependent variables where the output has only two values; here the values are dyslexic or non-dyslexic. We are using three major independent variables: "assessment completion time," "accuracy of response," and the "total number of questions attended" to train the model. The threshold value can be set by the evaluator accordingly.

The binary classifier evaluates with following parameters: confusion matrix, precision, recall, and F1 Score.

a **Confusion Matrix:** It works with four parameters:

True Positive (TP): The student is dyslexic and the model also predicts the same.
False Positive (FP): The student is non-dyslexic but the model predicts "dyslexic."
True Negative (TN): The student is non-dyslexic and the model also predicts the same.
False Positive (FN): The student is dyslexic but the model predicts "non-dyslexic."
After obtaining the values of TN, FP, TN, and FN, the accuracy score is calculated as follows:

$$\text{Accuracy} = \frac{TP + TN}{TP + FP + TN + FN} \tag{1}$$

In case any of the values from TP, TN, FP, and FN comes as zero, then the accuracy value will not be considered as a correct result. In such cases, we have to go with other evaluating methods.

b **Precision:** The method is used to find out all the true values from the predicted positive values.

$$Precision = \frac{TP}{FP + TP} \tag{2}$$

When a model makes few false positive predictions, then the precision value is high. Higher precision indicates that the model is good and rarely doing any misclassifications.

c **Recall:** It calculates the total true positive predictions.

$$Recall = \frac{TP}{FN + TP} \tag{3}$$

Higher recall indicates that the model is good and rarely doing any misclassifications.

As the precision and the recall are highly connected, the F1 score is used to provide the harmonic mean of both of them.

d **F1 Score:** For any imbalanced datasets, where there may be a chance that recall and the precision would be skewed, the F1 score is used. It combines both the recall and the precision to a single number to provide an overall measure of the model.

$$F1 score = \frac{2 \times Recall \times Precision}{Recall + Precision} \tag{4}$$

6.7.2 Formative Assessments

In this research work, we are categorizing the formative assessment in three parts: slow learners, medium-level learners, and high-level learners. Again the measuring parameters are same: completion time, accuracy of response, and total number of questions attended. The branching assessments from the adaptive testing will help to find the level of learners. The AI-based association mining models will monitor the level of learning. By using frequent item mining, it would be easy to track the weak areas of a student. It helps to find out the frequent items where a student shows low level of learning like differentiation in the mathematics, debugging errors in programming language, establishment of server connection in database connectivity, etc. The learning level is increased by minimizing the frequent patterns of weaker points. The frequent and associated item sets from higher-level learners are measured as the learning rate and the details of the students along with their learning rate is passed to the next level of the proposed model.

a **Branching Adaptive Testing:**
   Another type of adaptive assessment is branching adaptive testing where the test questions are presented based on a pre-configured path depending on how the student answered the previous question (i.e., their score). For example, a science assessment may begin by having students attempt a lower-level, fact-based question. Depending on how a student answers that question the test may move into more complex question type that uses higher-order thinking skills and require a more in-depth understanding of the topic.

b **Association Rule Mining:**
   This is a data mining technique used for discovering frequent patterns or associations between variables in large datasets. The process works on the idea to find rules that predict the occurrence of an item based on the occurrences of other items in the transaction. As we are working on students with dyslexia, that we received from the above step, for each student we have to find out the core weaker points that appear as an association for the student. The strength and reliability of association rule mining are measured using three key metrics:

   If an item X shows its frequency with item Y, then

   1   $$\text{Support} = \frac{\text{Frequency}(X,Y)}{N} \tag{5}$$

   2   $$\text{Confidence} = \frac{\text{Frequency}(X,Y)}{\text{Frequency}(X)} \tag{6}$$

   3   $$\text{Lift} = \frac{\text{Support}}{\text{Support}(X) \times \text{Support}(Y)} \tag{7}$$

6.7.3 Summative Assessments

The summative assessments are usually conducted after certain time of the teaching-learning process, whether after the completion of half of the course, or after the completion of the full course. It can be conducted in the mode of mid-term exams, final exams, projects, etc. When any of the students passes the summative assessments, then it will be considered as the learned. By using clustering algorithms, the groups of learned students can be maintained.

a **Clustering Algorithms:**
   Clustering is an unsupervised machine learning approach that works on the unlabeled data. A group of such unlabeled data points, that are similar to each other based on their relation to the surrounding data points, are considered as a cluster. Various clustering algorithms are available, for this research work we are using density-based cluster algorithm. The algorithm identifies core points with a minimum number of neighboring points within a specified distance. The cluster expands by connecting these core points to their neighboring points until the density falls below a certain threshold. If there are any points that do not come under any cluster, they are considered as outliers or noise. The two must-required parameters for density-based algorithm are the minimum point number needed to form the cluster, and the threshold of radius distance, defined as the neighborhood of every point.

6.8 Conclusion

One of the parameters to check the learning progress of a student is assessments. Diagnostic, formative, and summative are the most common methods of assessments. Usually, dyslexic students can't get higher score in the assessments as compared with the non-dyslexic students. The students with dyslexia may be progressing in learning but they should not be equally compared with the non-dyslexic students. There should be some AI-powered virtual assistant for real-time adaptive assessments to enhance learning outcomes for dyslexic students. The proposed research work is carried out in this direction. The proposed methodology is based on various AI-based algorithms that separate dyslexic with non-dyslexic students and then measure their learning progress using assessments and adaptive testing.

References

Castillo-Segura, P., Fernández-Panadero, C., Alario-Hoyos, C., Muñoz-Merino, P.J., & Kloos, C.D. (2021). Objective and automated assessment of surgical technical skills with IoT systems: A systematic literature review. *Artificial Intelligence in Medicine, 112,* 1–17, 10.1016/j.artmed.2020.102007.

Craig, S. & Schroeder, N. (2017). Reconsidering the voice effect when learning from a virtual human. *Computers & Education, 114.* 193–205. 10.1016/j.compedu.2017.07.003.

Dalinger, T., Thomas, K. B., Stansberry, S., & Xiu, Y. (2020). A mixed reality simulation offers strategic practice for pre-service teachers. *Computers & Education, 144,* 103696.

de Freitas, S. & Neumann, T. (2009). The use of 'exploratory learning' for supporting immersive learning in virtual environments. *Computers & Education*, 52(2), 343–352. ISSN 0360- 1315, https://doi.org/10.1016/j.compedu.2008.09.010.

Fischman, J. (2011, May 8). The rise of teaching machines. The Chronicle of Higher Education. Retrieved from http://chronicle.com/article/The-Rise-of-TeachingMachines/127389/

Francois, C. (2011). What is adaptive learning? Retrieved on 24 May 2011 from www. wisegeek.com/what-is-adaptive-learning.htm

Gandedkar, N., Wong, M., & Darendeliler, M. (2021). Role of virtual reality (VR), augmented reality (AR) and artificial intelligence (AI) in tertiary education and research of orthodontics: An insight. *Seminars in Orthodontics, 27*. 10.1053/j.sodo.2021.05.003.

Graesser, A. C., & D'Mello, S. (2012). Emotions during the learning of difficult material. In B. H. Ross (Ed.), The psychology of learning and motivation (pp. 183–225). Elsevier Academic Press. https://doi.org/10.1016/B978-0-12-394293-7.00005-4.

Graesser, A., McNamara, D., & Graesser, A. (2010). Self-regulated learning in learning environments with pedagogical agents that interact in natural language. *Educational Psychologist, 45*. 10.1080/00461520.2010.515933.

Lawson, A. P. & Mayer, R. E. (2022). Does the emotional stance of human and virtual instructors in instructional videos affect learning processes and outcomes? *Contemporary Educational Psychology*, 70, 102080, ISSN 0361-476X, https://doi.org/10.1016/j.cedpsych.2022.102080.

Martinez, M. (2003). Adaptive learning. Retrieved on May 24, 2011 from www. trainingplace.com/source/research/adaptivelearning.htm

Moon, T., Brighton, C., & Tomlinson, C. (2020). Using differentiated classroom assessment to enhance student learning. 10.4324/9780429452994.

Nguyen, L., & Do, P. (2008). Learner model in adaptive learning. *Proceedings of World Academy of Science, Engineering And Technology*, 35, 396–401.

Nussbaumer, A., Kravcik, M., Renzel, D., Klamma, R., Berthold, M., & Albert, D. (2014). A framework for facilitating self-regulation in responsive open learning environments. *arXiv preprint arXiv:1407.5891*.

Paramythis, A., & Loidl-Reisinger, S. (2003). Adaptive learning environments and e-learning standards. In *Second European Conference on e-learning* (Vol. 1, No. 2003, pp. 369–379). Chicago.

Rhienmora, P., Haddawy, P., Dailey, M. N., Khanal, P., & Suebnukarn, S. (2008). Development of a dental skills training simulator using virtual reality and haptic device. *NECTEC Technical Journal*, 8(20), 140–147.

Yang, X. S., Zhou, J. J., & Wen, D. Q. (2021, Jan 1). An optimized BP neural network model for teaching management evaluation. *Journal of Intelligent & Fuzzy Systems*, 40(2), 3215–3221.

7 Transforming Education through AI-Powered Personalized Assessment Models

S. Kanthimathi, Prayasha Nanda,
Shravan Venkatraman,
Varsana Renganayagan, and
Sivaraman Eswaran

7.1 Introduction

7.1.1 Importance of AI in Education

Education today is undergoing a rapid transformation, driven by technological advancements and a deeper understanding of students' diverse needs and learning styles. Traditional teaching and assessment methods, which rely heavily on standardized tests and rigid rubrics, have exposed significant shortcomings in addressing individual differences among learners. These conventional approaches often use a one-size-fits-all strategy, failing to accommodate the broad spectrum of student abilities and learning preferences.

AI has emerged as a revolutionary force in this evolving landscape. As educational institutions increasingly adopt digital tools, AI stands out as a technology with the potential to address many of the limitations inherent in traditional assessment models. By leveraging AI-driven personalized assessment models, educators can tailor feedback and support to meet the unique needs of each student. This customization not only enriches student engagement but also enhances learning outcomes by aligning assessments more closely with individual learning styles and needs. By integrating personalized assessments, AI transforms education by offering tailored evaluation strategies that maximize learning potential and address individual student needs (Bozkurt et al., 2021).

One of the primary benefits of AI in education is personalization. AI-powered chatbots and virtual assistants can provide immediate academic assistance. An AI model can analyze a student's strength, weakness, and learning style based on the capacity of information that can be grasped by the student and whether the student is understanding or memorizing a certain subject. With this information, AI-powered systems can tailor learning paths to pace with individual needs, helping in better and focused learning. In fact, the model may identify patterns and knowledge gaps that may go unnoticed by the educators! The model can also adapt real time based on the

DOI: 10.1201/9781003470304-7

student's performance and engagement. As the student learns at their own pace and time, this creates a flexible learning environment and allows them to efficiently use their most productive hours, regardless of the place or time.

AI in education can also tackle non-educational tasks, such as automating repetitive tasks, administrative work to free up educators' schedules (Bredberg, 2024), and automatically grade certain types of questions, such as MCQs and fill in the blanks. This can save teachers countless hours of work. As per the World Economic Forum, implementation of AI in administrative tasks could reduce the time spent on these routine duties by 20%, allowing teachers to focus more on interacting and mentoring their students (Chopra, 2023).

National Testing Agency (NTA) has started implementing AI to help reduce malpractices (Gupta, 2024). The model is fed a certain pattern and can flag a student if they display any suspicious or unusual activity, in real time. Potential impersonators, such as previous toppers, have been mapped into it as well. In India, the student–teacher ratio is often high. Incorporating AI in the classroom can be a game-changer. It can help bridge the gap between teachers and students by providing personalized support. Additionally, AI can assist in eliminating language barriers by offering multilingual learning resources and real-time translation services (Pangotra, 2024). These tools can help in levelling the playing field to give all students an equal chance to succeed. By integrating personalized assessments, AI transforms education by offering tailored evaluation strategies that maximize learning potential and address individual student needs.

7.1.2 *The Need for Personalized Assessments*

The importance of personalized assessments is underscored by several key factors. Personalized assessments align with individual learning styles, providing a more accurate picture of a student's understanding and abilities by focusing on critical thinking and problem-solving skills rather than rote memorization. This alignment is crucial as it goes beyond traditional tests, which often fail to capture the full range of student capabilities.

Moreover, personalized assessments contribute to an improved learning experience by offering feedback specifically designed to meet each student's needs. This approach creates a more engaging and motivating learning environment, allowing students to leverage their strengths and address their weaknesses, which in turn leads to enhanced academic performance and reduced test anxiety (Hubalovsky et al., 2019). Timely and relevant feedback, essential for effective learning, is another advantage of personalized assessments. By providing ongoing and constructive feedback, these assessments help students track their progress and identify areas for improvement, supporting targeted growth and development.

7.1.3 Objectives of the Chapter

The chapter aims to explore several facets of assessment in the context of educational transformation. First, it examines the shortcomings of traditional assessment models, shedding light on their limitations and the need for innovative solutions. This exploration sets the stage for a deeper understanding of how advanced technologies can offer improvements.

Next, the chapter scrutinizes the potential of modern, adaptive evaluation tools powered by advanced technologies. It delves into how these technologies can revolutionize assessment practices by enhancing feedback systems, creating customized assessments, and providing valuable insights into student learning.

To illustrate the practical application of these concepts, the chapter features a case study of the dynamic feedback-driven learning optimization framework (DFDLOF). This case study demonstrates how AI-enhanced models can be effectively implemented in digital learning environments.

Finally, the chapter discusses the creation of AI-powered assessment models, outlining the key aspects and requirements for developing effective and equitable AI-based systems. It concludes by addressing the limitations and challenges associated with integrating advanced technologies in education, such as technological constraints, algorithmic biases, and the need for alignment with course syllabi.

Section 7.1 presents the introduction, covering the background and context of the chapter, the importance of personalized assessments, and the objectives that the chapter aims to achieve. Section 7.2 provides a thorough assessment of the literature including an analysis of pertinent research and current frameworks that serve as the basis for the analysis that follows in this chapter. Section 7.3 discusses traditional assessment models, focusing on standardized assessments, marking rubrics, and the limitations of these methods in addressing individual student needs. It also explores the gap between teacher expectations and learner understanding. Section 7.4 discusses in detail about the proposed methodology including the adoption of enhanced DFDLOF for the Indian education system. Section 7.5 provides a case study of the DFDLOF, illustrating its applications in Assessment and Learning in Knowledge Spaces (ALEKS), NTA, TalentLMS. Section 7.6 examines the limitations and challenges of AI in education, including syllabus constraints and bias in AI algorithms. It also suggests solutions to address these challenges. Section 7.7 concludes the chapter, summarizing key points and suggesting future directions for AI-driven assessments in education.

7.2 Related Work

González-Calatayud et al. (2021) proposed an analysis of AI's role in student assessment by conducting a systematic review of research. The problem identified in the paper is the limited reflection on the pedagogical aspects in

AI-based educational assessments, particularly in formative evaluation. The authors' primary contribution is identifying AI's use in automatic grading and the need for teacher training to maximize the benefits of AI in educational assessment across various educational levels, not just higher education.

Aditi Bhutoria (2022) proposed a review of AI-driven personalization in education, focusing on addressing the limitations of the traditional "one-size-fits-all" approach. The problem centers on the need to cater to individual student needs, which current education systems struggle with. The paper's contribution lies in highlighting AI's success in tailoring educational content to individual students' requirements, emphasizing the structural changes AI brings to education, while also acknowledging challenges such as data privacy and accessibility to digital resources.

Maher (2023) proposed an exploration of AI's integration in education, specifically targeting personalized learning experiences. The problem statement revolves around the need to individualize education in a digital age where students have diverse learning preferences and paces. The authors contribute by discussing AI's potential in enhancing e-learning through personalized content delivery and virtual tutors while also raising concerns regarding the ethical implications of AI in education.

Comesaña et al. (2023) proposed a review of AI's impact on primary and secondary student assessments, focusing on improving performance prediction and evaluation processes. The problem tackled is the lack of objective and efficient assessment methods at lower educational levels. The paper's key contribution is identifying the application of AI tools, such as neural networks and educational robots, to automate evaluations and enhance engagement, demonstrating the benefits AI can bring to student performance evaluation in early education.

Murtaza et al. (2022) proposed a framework for a personalized e-learning system to overcome the limitations of conventional e-learning that delivers the same content to all learners. The problem is the lack of tailored content delivery that adapts to individual learner needs and preferences. Their contribution includes presenting a comprehensive review of current AI-based personalized learning solutions and proposing a modular framework that addresses the requirements and challenges of personalization, emphasizing the importance of adaptable learning models and future research directions.

Ouyang et al. (2022) conducted a systematic review of AI applications in online higher education from 2011 to 2020. They found that AI is used for predicting learning outcomes, recommending resources, automatic assessments, and enhancing learning experiences. Traditional AI technologies were common, while advanced methods like deep learning were less utilized. The study highlighted the need for integrating educational theories into AI and recommended more empirical research to assess the effectiveness of AI in online higher education.

Zawacki-Richter et al. (2019) conducted a systematic review of AI applications in higher education, analyzing 146 articles published between

2007 and 2018. They found that AI in education is primarily explored in computer science and STEM fields, focusing on profiling, prediction, assessment, adaptive systems, and intelligent tutoring. The study noted a lack of critical discussion on the challenges and risks of AI, as well as a weak connection to pedagogical theories, highlighting the need for more ethical and educational exploration in AI's application in higher education.

Popovici and Mironov (2015) explored the effectiveness of personalized e-learning systems, which tailor content and assessments to individual learners using AI techniques. The study identified key factors and challenges in personalized education, reviewed existing research, and proposed a framework with five modules for delivering personalized e-learning. The paper emphasized the importance of different learning models and theories in enhancing personalization and provided insights into future research directions, benefiting academicians and researchers interested in the development and implementation of such systems.

Momin (2023) examined the transformative impact of AI on education, with a focus on personalized learning and adaptive assessment. The paper discusses the historical evolution of education and the integration of AI, highlighting the significance of customized learning experiences. It also explores how AI-driven adaptive assessments offer advantages over traditional testing methods. The study synthesizes existing research, case studies, and trends to provide a comprehensive understanding of how AI is revolutionizing education.

Finally, Pardamean et al. (2022) demonstrate how AI models, specifically collaborative-filtering models in their case, can improve learning outcomes and eliminate the need for human-driven assessments in online environments. Maher (2023) further supports AI's benefits, showing that AI-driven personalized learning tools lead to statistically significant improvements in student grades and consistent performance, while also making learning more appealing. However, educators express concerns over over-reliance on AI, emphasizing the importance of retaining human interaction in teaching. Falsk (2023) expands on these findings while also urging the need for ethical considerations around data privacy and algorithmic bias. Arslan et al. (2024) underscore the promising role of generative AI in creating personalized assessments, which could lead to more engaging and relevant test materials, though it calls for cautious exploration to ensure assessments remain valid, reliable, and aligned with educational goals.

7.3 Traditional Assessment Models

7.3.1 The Limitations of Standardized Assessments, Marking Rubrics

Standardized assessments have long been a cornerstone of educational evaluation, aiming to measure student performance against consistent benchmarks

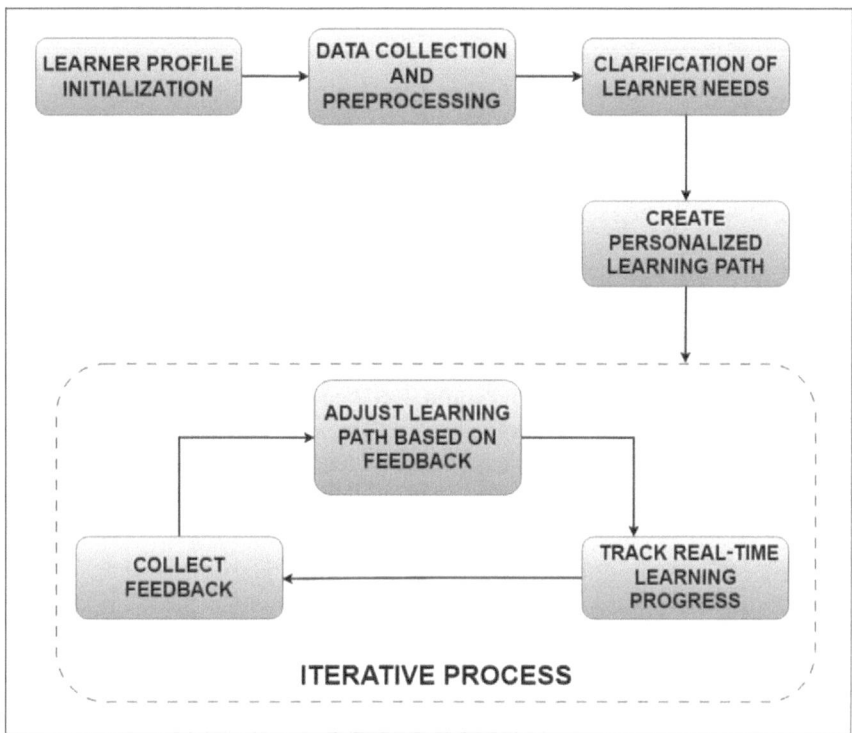

Figure 7.1 Overall framework of AI-powered Personalized Assessments.

(Figure 7.1). While they offer a level of consistency and comparability, they also present notable drawbacks. One significant limitation is their lack of flexibility. Standardized tests typically focus on specific content areas and ignore the different learning styles or paces, providing an incomplete view of a student's skills and understanding.

These tests often emphasize basic problem-solving and factual recall, sometimes at the expense of deeper comprehension and critical thinking. Eventually these assessments do not fully capture a student's capabilities. Additionally, the high-pressure nature of standardized testing can induce anxiety and stress, which may skew results and negatively impact student performance.

Marking rubrics, which provides a structured framework for evaluation, also comes with challenges (Chen and Wang, 2021). One issue is the potential for subjectivity and bias, especially when assessing complex or subjective tasks. Though rubrics offer a general overview of strengths and weaknesses, they often fall short in providing detailed feedback necessary for comprehensive improvement. Moreover, rubrics can be rigid, failing to account for the various ways students can demonstrate their knowledge and skills, similar to standardized tests.

7.3.2 *Bridging the Gap between Teacher Expectations and Learner Understanding*

A significant concern with traditional assessment models is the gap between teacher expectations and learner understanding. Assessments that are created based on educators' expectations may not align with how students actually process and understand information. This misalignment can lead to an inaccurate representation of students' true abilities and comprehension.

Traditional assessments often overlook the diverse backgrounds, prior knowledge, and learning preferences of students, resulting in evaluations that may not accurately reflect each student's progress or skills. Furthermore, these assessments may lack timely and specific feedback, which is crucial for students to understand their mistakes and improve. This deficit in feedback can hinder students' learning and development, underscoring the need for more flexible and responsive assessment models.

7.4 Proposed Methodology

7.4.1 *AI-Enhanced Personalized Assessments and Dynamic Question Generation*

There is a growing recognition of the need for advanced, technology-driven personalized assessments that offer a more nuanced approach, which aligns better with individual learning needs and provides actionable feedback to support ongoing development (Peng et al., 2019). By leveraging AI and other advanced technologies, educational assessments can become more adaptable and effective, addressing many of the limitations of traditional methods and paving the way for a more personalized and equitable learning experience.

AI's ability to assess students' previous performance and generate dynamic questions creates a personalized and adaptive learning environment to achieve that. By analyzing the student's historical data, AI algorithms can build a comprehensive profile of each student's strengths, weaknesses, and learning style. This data-driven approach enables educators to tailor instruction to meet individual needs. The algorithm can pinpoint areas where the student is struggling and recommend targeted interventions.

With this information, AI can generate questions that are tailored to their level of understanding and can adapt the difficulty of questions such that the questions are challenging enough to promote learning but not too difficult so as to discourage students. This approach can help prevent boredom and frustration while maximizing learning gains. The process can also be gamified, to make learning not only more enjoyable but also retainable.

AI can create a variety of question types, such as multiple-choice, fill-in-the-blank, and short answers, to assess different cognitive skills. This can also help ensure that assessments are fair and unbiased by eliminating human error and reducing the potential for discriminatory practices.

In conclusion, AI is reforming the educational landscape through automation, personalization, and effective feedback. This technology holds the power to revolutionize educational outcomes globally, benefitting both teachers and students.

7.4.2 Enhanced Dynamic Feedback-Driven Learning Optimization Framework (DFDLOF)

7.4.2.1 Overview of DFDLOF

Historically, education methods were static and had a one-size-fits-all approach because of logistical constraints and resource limitations. But now, in the digital era, personalized education has become a new normal and does not try to fit every learner into a box. With every technological advance, new solutions to help a student blossom come into play, and DFDLOF is no exception.

The DFDLOF is a novel framework created to offer educators with a new tool to support the learner's journey in a personalized learning environment.

The model integrates various components, including data collection mechanisms, machine learning algorithms, and a dynamic feedback system, to create a comprehensive learning pathway. This framework specializes in creating detailed student profiles by collecting and analyzing vast quantities of learner data, such as demographics, learning styles, performance metrics, and engagement to discern patterns and insights that are imperceptible to the human eye (Mccutcheon et al., 2015).

7.4.2.2 Adaptation of Enhanced DFDLOF for the Indian Education System

The DFDLOF is well-suited for an all-round development of the learner in academics, and thus provides a good base that can be built upon to suit different socioeconomic environments. This chapter focuses on optimizing it to be suited for assessment models in the Indian context.

The framework can serve as a transformative assessment model by providing a dynamic and personalized approach. Rather than the usual traditional and summative assessments, it shifts the focus to a continuous and formative evaluation. The assessments are also customized according to the student's current knowledge level and the topics learnt. It tracks student progress by their interaction and responses in real time, and the feedback systems are most crucial in nurturing growth with timely interventions and adjustments.

An important question type in the Indian education system is higher-order thinking skills (HOTS) type, and the algorithm can assess the student's ability to examine given information and apply their learnings in a real-world scenario and help heighten their critical thinking skills (Christudas et al., 2018).

In addition to this, existing framework can restructure the model for the Indian education system, and that is the involvement of required algorithms that can analyze paragraph answers, such as short answer questions and long answer questions.

In India, education is more focused on the wording and structure of students' long answers, and teachers scan the answer for several keywords and appropriately give marks. The shortcoming of this traditional method is that understanding doesn't fetch good grades. A student may have understood a topic well and formed their answer in their own words, but this response may not be given marks if they have not included the appropriate words and phrases.

The demographic impacted by this the most is in middle and high school, in the age group 11–17 years old. The board exams, the final examination of the academic year conducted at the end of 10th and 12th grades, evaluate with this keyword approach and the results stay with a student for their entire lives, and even serve as a metric that colleges and jobs assess them with, later in life.

There is a research gap in this area, as digitalized learning isn't prevalent in the country yet, and many students do not have access to the internet. But the times are changing, and there is a need to create personalized pathways for this answer type as well.

And thus, to further optimize the framework for the Indian context, this chapter introduces two novel evaluation criteria: *articulation* and *cognitive abilities apart from the existing parameter critical thinking*. These criteria will focus on the structuring of answers in assessments and provide feedback on the same to aid the student to write just as well as they understand (Peng et al., 2019).

7.4.2.2.1 CRITICAL THINKING

Critical thinking is the ability to analyze information and make thoughtful decisions. In AI-powered assessments, this involves creating questions that require students to think beyond rote memorization. The AI system can generate scenarios or problems that prompt students to apply their knowledge in new ways, encouraging them to think critically about the subject matter.

For example, instead of merely asking a student to recall a definition, the AI could present a real-life situation where the student must apply that concept to solve a problem. The system evaluates the response based on how well the student identifies the issue, analyzes it, and proposes a logical solution. This approach helps students develop critical thinking skills that are crucial not just for exams but for real-world problem-solving as well.

7.4.2.2.2 ARTICULATION

Articulation refers to how well a student expresses their understanding of a topic. Traditionally, in the Indian education system, articulation has often been judged by the use of specific textbook keywords and phrases. While this method aims to ensure that students are learning the correct information, it can limit their ability to express ideas creatively in their own words. Students may feel compelled to focus more on memorizing these keywords rather than truly understanding the concepts behind them (Popovici & Mironov, 2015).

AI-powered assessment models have the potential to change this approach by encouraging students to express their understanding more naturally. Instead of solely rewarding the use of specific keywords, the AI can evaluate how well the student articulates their ideas, regardless of whether they use the exact terms from the textbook.

For instance, if a student explains a scientific concept using their own words but demonstrates a clear understanding, the AI can recognize and reward this effort. By shifting the focus from memorization to comprehension, students are encouraged to engage more deeply with the material and develop a genuine understanding, which is likely to benefit them beyond the classroom.

To bridge the gap between traditional expectations and this new approach, the AI can provide suggestions or alternative ways to articulate ideas that still align with the syllabus. For example, the AI could suggest how to use certain key terms effectively within a broader, more personalized explanation. Over time, this helps students learn to balance the need for precise language with the freedom to express their own understanding.

7.4.2.2.3 COGNITIVE ABILITIES

Cognitive abilities refer to the mental skills that help a student process information, remember facts, and solve problems. In an AI-powered assessment system, this parameter is crucial for evaluating a student's understanding of concepts and their ability to apply knowledge (Yang & Zhang, 2023).

AI can test cognitive abilities by asking questions that range from remembering facts to solving complex problems. For example, a basic question might ask a student to remember a fact, while a more complex question could require them to analyze a situation and make a decision based on the information provided. By varying the difficulty and type of questions, the AI can get a better sense of each student's cognitive strengths and areas that need improvement.

Furthermore, the AI can track a student's progress over time, identifying patterns in their learning. If a student consistently struggles with a certain type of question, the AI can adjust the difficulty level or provide additional resources to help them improve. This personalized approach ensures that each student receives the support they need to develop their cognitive abilities effectively.

AI-powered automated grading systems are designed to quickly and accurately assess students' work. These systems can evaluate answers based on the earlier mentioned criteria: critical thinking, articulation, and cognitive abilities, providing a complete assessment of each student's performance.

7.4.3 Automated Marking Systems

In an education system where exams are crucial, timely and fair evaluation is essential. AI-powered automated marking systems can grade exams quickly, reducing the workload on teachers and ensuring consistency in marking. These systems can be trained to recognize patterns in student responses, such as the logical flow of arguments, the clarity of explanations, and how well students articulate their understanding (Wang, 2022; Chen and Wenlan (2019).

For instance, in a history exam, the AI could assess whether the student provided an accurate and coherent explanation of an event, even if they didn't use the exact textbook language. By focusing on the clarity and depth of understanding, the system can assign scores that reflect the student's true knowledge and ability to express it.

7.4.4 Constructive Feedback Mechanisms

One of the significant advantages of AI-powered assessment models is their ability to provide instant, constructive feedback. Instead of simply marking an answer as right or wrong, the AI can explain why a particular answer was correct or where the student went wrong. This feedback is crucial for helping students understand their mistakes and learn from them. For example, if a student articulates an idea well but misses a key concept, the AI can point it out and suggest how the response could be improved. If the answer lacks depth, the AI might offer tips on how to enhance the explanation (Bozkurt et al., 2021). This type of detailed feedback helps students refine their skills and better prepare for future assessments. To further engage students, the AI can incorporate a gamified feedback system. After receiving feedback, students could be challenged to revise their answers or tackle similar questions to earn points or unlock new levels. This approach not only reinforces learning but also makes the process more enjoyable, encouraging students to keep improving.

7.4.4.1 Applications of Enhanced DFDLOF

DFDLOF employs several algorithms to predict learner needs and dynamically generate personal learning paths (U.S. Department of Education, Press release, 2023). These paths are carefully paced such that the content is challenging but not difficult, and the algorithm continually adjusts to support the user and reinforce previous learning to ensure knowledge retention. Additionally, it ensures that the content remains relevant and aligned with the learner's current understanding and learning objectives. Sentiment analysis is also integrated into the framework to understand student feedback, emotions, attitude, and interaction toward topics.

This framework provides real-time feedback for immediate correction, and long-term feedback for a comprehensive report that guides the learner (Liang & Chen, 2018). These valuable insights can be used by educators to gauge their students and help them with weak points. In addition, providing constructive feedback significantly enhances student motivation and engagement.

The framework's efficacy is evaluated based on certain criteria, which includes improvements in learner performance, enhanced knowledge retention, active participation and engagement, and reduced dropout rates. A user-friendly interface that is easy to interact and navigate with enhances the learning experience. Biases and ethical implications have also been considered in this framework to ensure smooth and fair learning conditions.

Teacher facilitation in personalized learning environments is little researched. Adaptive systems concern only the learner and do not take into consideration the role of an educator as a guide who can provide contextual understanding, which cannot be substituted by technological advancements (Xing & Guan, 2022). And therefore, the best utilization of technology lies in enhancing, not replacing the human aspects of instruction – and the framework aims to achieve this.

Table 7.1 summarizes different machine learning algorithms, some of their datasets, and their roles in enhancing personalized learning. It highlights how supervised learning helps predict student performance and those in need of additional support, while neural networks manage complex data to analyze patterns in student interaction. Unsupervised learning algorithms, like clustering, are useful for scaling with growing data for targeted instruction, and reinforcement learning allows the system to adapt and optimize the learning process in real time. Finally, deep learning techniques, such as sentiment analysis, are used for analyzing student emotions and engagement to establish a positive and motivating learning environment.

7.5 Case Study of Successful AI Adoption in Learning Platform

A real-world example of this is the adaptive learning platforms of ALEKS and NTA.

7.5.1 ALEKS

As a web-based learning and assessment system that uses AI to personalize studying for students, ALEKS can chart a student's knowledge by using

Table 7.1 Machine Learning Algorithms in Personalized Learning

Criteria	Algorithm used	Dataset	Contribution to personalization
Accuracy and efficiency	Supervised learning algorithms 1. Decision tree algorithm (DTA) 2. K-nearest neighbors and naïve Bayes	1. Manav Rachna college dataset 2. Educational dataset of secondary school in Gaza Strip (2015)	Has a record of high accuracy in educational contexts and predictive analytics; essential for forecasting student performance and identifying those in need of additional support
Complex data handling	Layered neural networks 1. Self-attentive neural knowledge tracing + (SAINT+) 2. Self-attentive knowledge tracing (SAKT)	1. EdNet 2. ASSISTments2015	Can process and learn from large, diverse datasets; proficient in analyzing unstructured data
Scalability	Unsupervised learning algorithms 1. Density-based spatial clustering 2. K-means	Synthetic data of 57 students	Algorithms like clustering can efficiently scale growing dataset sizes of content and personalization
Real-time adaptation	Reinforcement learning 1. Bi-graph contrastive learning-based knowledge tracing (Bi-CLKT) 2. Deep knowledge tracing (DKT, DKT+, DKT+ forget) 3. Bayesian knowledge tracing (BKT)	1. ASSISTments, STATICS 2011 2. Junyi, Algebra 2005–2006 3. Algebra I	Can continuously adapt to the environment and optimizes the learning experience
Sentiment analysis	Deep learning algorithms like deep item response theory (Deep-IRT)	ASSIST2009	Helps to capture learning behaviors and emotions to measure engagement and satisfaction

open-ended questions and reliably evaluating the answers. This obliges the students to genuinely solve the problem; they cannot merely try out different proposed solutions (in question types like MCQs). ALEKS generates questions based on the student's performance, creating a customized learning path that adjusts to their progress and improves student outcomes (Harati et al., 2021).

7.5.2 NTA

In India, the National Testing Agency (NTA) is the body in charge of holding different entrance examinations for universities. The NTA adopted AI-driven technologies to improve the fairness of competitive exams and reduce cheating. The NTA-developed AI system attempts to identify and stop exam cheating in real time. NTA has implemented this using real-time surveillance, pattern recognition, face recognition, and anomaly detection (Gupta, 2024).

7.5.3 TalentLMS

A learning management system called TalentLMS is dedicated to providing individualized e-learning experiences. In e-learning, personalization means adjusting the course material to each student's unique needs, interests, and skill level. TalentLMS gained its success through adaptive learning path, interactive and engaging content, learning analytics, and effective real-time feedback and assessment (Kraleva et al., 2019).

7.6 Navigating the Complexities of AI in Education

7.6.1 Integration of AI with Course Syllabus Constraints

One of the primary challenges in implementing AI-powered personalized assessment models is ensuring they align with the structured course syllabus. The Indian education system often operates within a well-defined syllabus that dictates what students need to learn at each grade level. While this structure provides a clear path for student learning, it also presents challenges for AI systems that must operate within these boundaries.

AI systems are powerful tools that can analyze vast amounts of data and provide insights tailored to individual learning needs. However, these systems rely heavily on the data they are fed and without clear guidance, these systems can go beyond the intended scope of the curriculum. For instance, if an AI system is not correctly aligned with the syllabus for a 10th-grade science course, it might introduce topics that are too advanced, such as university-level physics concepts, which are beyond the student's current level of understanding. This phenomenon, often referred to as "AI hallucination," occurs when the AI generates content that is outside the scope of the required learning. This not only risks confusing the student but also shifts their focus away from the main learning goals of the course.

To prevent such issues, it is essential to ensure that the AI system is provided with a clearly defined and up-to-date syllabus. This requires close collaboration between educators, curriculum developers, and AI engineers. Educators must clearly outline the scope of what students need to learn, and AI developers must ensure that the system adheres strictly to these boundaries. For example, if the syllabus for a history course focuses on modern Indian history, the AI should be programmed to generate content and assessments that reflect this focus, without introducing irrelevant topics from ancient history or unrelated regions (Chopra, 2023).

Furthermore, the dynamic nature of educational syllabi presents another challenge. In many education systems, syllabi are periodically revised to reflect new knowledge, educational priorities, or changes in societal needs. For an AI system to remain effective, it must be able to quickly adapt to these changes. This requires an ongoing process where updates to the syllabus are communicated to the AI system and integrated into its algorithms. Without such updates, the AI risks becoming outdated, providing students with information that is no longer relevant or aligned with the current curriculum.

To address these challenges, it is recommended that educators regularly review the AI-generated content and assessments to ensure they align with the syllabus. This collaborative approach ensures that the AI remains a valuable tool that enhances, rather than complicates, the learning process. By working together, educators and AI developers can create a system that supports student learning in a targeted and effective manner.

7.6.2 *Addressing Bias in AI Algorithms and Technical Considerations*

Another significant challenge in implementing AI-powered personalized assessment models is the potential for bias in AI algorithms. AI systems learn from the data they are trained on and if this data is not representative of the diverse student population, the resulting assessments may be biased. Bias in AI can manifest in various ways, from the type of questions generated to how student responses are evaluated.

For example, if an AI system is trained primarily on data from urban schools, it may not accurately reflect the learning needs and challenges faced by students in rural areas. This could result in assessments that are more difficult or less relevant for certain groups of students, leading to unfair evaluations. In diverse educational settings, it is crucial that AI systems are trained on a broad and representative data set that includes students from various backgrounds, regions, and learning environments.

To mitigate bias, it is essential that AI developers and educators take a proactive approach. One way to address this is by ensuring that the data used to train the AI is diverse and inclusive. This includes data from students across different socioeconomic backgrounds, linguistic groups, and geographic regions. By training the AI on a wide range of data, the system can develop a more balanced understanding of student needs, resulting in more accurate assessments (Chopra, 2023).

While this framework offers many benefits, there are some challenges that need to be addressed. One of the biggest hurdles is the difficulty of integrating this system into existing educational setups. It requires a lot of data collection and processing, and some institutions might struggle with the need for advanced expertise in machine learning. Another important concern is the privacy and security of student data. Since the framework relies heavily on this data, it's crucial to ensure it is protected and used ethically.

There's also the risk of becoming too dependent on technology, which could overshadow the essential human aspects of teaching and learning. Although the framework is designed to adapt to different learning environments, its effectiveness in various cultural and socioeconomic settings still needs to be explored further. It's vital to make sure that the system works well and is accessible to students from all backgrounds to be widely adopted.

Additionally, teachers play a crucial role in addressing potential bias in AI systems. While AI can provide valuable insights and assessments, it is ultimately the teacher who understands the individual needs and context of their students. Teachers can provide feedback to the AI system, helping to fine-tune its assessments and ensuring that they are fair and appropriate for all students. For instance, if a teacher notices that the AI is consistently generating assessments that are too difficult for a particular group of students, they can adjust the system to better match the students' abilities and needs (Bredberg, 2024).

From a technical perspective, AI developers can employ various techniques to reduce bias in AI algorithms. One approach is fairness-aware machine learning, which involves actively identifying and correcting bias during the model development process. This might include techniques such as re-weighting data samples to ensure that underrepresented groups are adequately represented or implementing algorithms that detect and mitigate bias in real time.

Transparency in AI decision-making is critical for building trust and ensuring fairness in educational assessments. By providing insights into how AI systems arrive at their conclusions, educators and students can better understand, evaluate, and address potential biases. Techniques such as explainable AI play a key role in this process by offering clear explanations of the AI's reasoning, enabling both educators and students to assess the fairness, accuracy, and reliability of its decisions.

7.7 Conclusion

AI is rapidly changing the landscape of education, offering numerous benefits for both teachers and students. By automating mundane tasks, personalizing learning, and providing valuable feedback, AI has the potential to revolutionize education systems worldwide. The chapter has discussed the potential benefits of AI-based personalized assessments and enhanced DFDLOF by looking at the gaps in the traditional assessment models.

By tailoring assessments to each student's needs, these technologies support a more holistic approach to education, one that moves beyond rigid standardized testing. This transformation not only enriches the learning experience but also empowers students to build on their strengths and address areas needing improvement.

The proposed model is also complemented with case studies of existing platforms like NTA in India, TalentLMS, and ALEKS. While these platforms already enhance learning with adaptive testing and efficient content delivery, the AI model goes a step further by adjusting question difficulty and topics in real time based on each student's performance, providing a clearer and more precise picture of their competencies and learning gaps. Students who struggle with certain topics can be presented with questions that gradually increase in difficulty by giving them a path to improve, reducing the anxiety that often accompanies standardized tests. The real-time feedback loop fosters deeper engagement, making the learning process more interactive and motivating.

The chapter also addressed issues with syllabus limitations while highlighting the significance of adding crucial factors like critical thinking, articulation, and cognitive capacities into AI-powered evaluation models. Subsequently, the use of sophisticated AI methodologies is anticipated to augment educational evaluations even more, providing customized feedback and stimulating more profound student involvement. Looking ahead, the possibilities for AI in education are vast. Future research must concentrate on enhancing these technologies in order to alleviate current constraints, such as syllabus alignment and fairness in evaluations, to guarantee fair and efficient evaluation procedures. As this technology continues to advance, we can expect to see even more innovative and impactful applications in the classroom that seamlessly integrate into diverse educational contexts, offering personalized support to students from all backgrounds.

References

B. Arslan, B. Lehman, C. Tenison, J. R. Sparks, A. A. López, L. Gu and D. Zapata-Rivera, "Opportunities and challenges of using generative AI to personalize educational assessment", *Front. Artif. Intell.*, vol. 7, Article 1460651, 2024, DOI: 10.3389/frai.2024.1460651.

A. Bhutoria, "Personalized education and artificial intelligence in the United States, China, and India: A systematic review using a human-in-the-loop model", *Comput. Educ. Art. Intel.*, vol. 3, 2022, 100068, DOI: 10.1016/j.caeai.2022.100068.

A. Bozkurt, A. Karadeniz, D. Baneres, A. E. Guerrero-Roldán and M. E. Rodríguez, "Artificial intelligence and reflections from educational landscape: A review of AI studies in half a century", *Sustainability*, vol. 13, no. 2, pp. 800, Jan. 2021.

L. Bredberg, "Using AI in education use case 7:10 —Administrative task automation", July 11, 2024.

S. Y. Chen and J.-H. Wang, "Individual differences and personalized learning: A review and appraisal", *Universal Access Inf. Soc.*, vol. 20, no. 4, pp. 833–849, Nov. 2021.

D. Chopra, "How AI is being deployed to safeguard integrity in competitive exams", Dec. 18, 2023.

B. C. L. Christudas, E. Kirubakaran and P. R. J. Thangaiah, "An evolutionary approach for personalization of content delivery in e-learning systems based on learner behavior forcing compatibility of learning materials", *Telematics Inform.*, vol. 35, no. 3, pp. 520–533, 2018.

V. González-Calatayud, J. M. Fernández, F. J. García-Peñalvo, and T. García-Serrano "Artificial intelligence for student assessment: A systematic review, application of technologies in e-learning assessment", *Appl. Sci.*, vol. 11, no. 12, p. 5467, 2021, DOI:10.3390/app11125467.

P. Gupta, "How AI is being deployed to safeguard integrity in competitive exams", May 2, 2024.

H. Harati, L. Sujo-Montes, C.-H. Tu and S. Armfield, "Assessment and learning in knowledge spaces (ALEKS) adaptive system impact on students' perception and self-regulated learning skills", *Edu. Sci.*, vol. 11, no. 10, p. 603, Oct. 2021, DOI: 10.3390/educsci11100603.

S. Hubalovsky, M. Hubalovska and M. Musilek, "Assessment of the influence of adaptive e-learning on learning effectiveness of primary school pupils", *Comput. Hum. Behav.*, vol. 92, pp. 691–705, Mar. 2019.

M. Iqbal, "AI in education: Personalized learning and adaptive assessment". *Cosmic Bull. Bus. Manag.*, 2023.

M. J. K. O. Jian, "Personalized learning through AI", *Adv. Eng. Innovation.*, vol. 5, pp. 16–19, 2023, DOI:10.54254/2977-3903/5/2023039.

R. S. Kraleva, V. Kralev and M. Sabani, "An analysis of some learning management systems", *Inter. J. Adv. Sci. Eng. Inform. Technol.*, vol. 9, no. 4, pp. 1190–1198, Aug. 2019, DOI: 10.18517/ijaseit.9.4.9437.

M. Martínez-Comesaña, X. Rigueira-Díaz, A. Larrañaga-Janeiro, J. Martínez-Torres, I. Ocarranza-Prado, and D. Kreibel, "Impact of artificial intelligence on assessment methods in primary and secondary education: Systematic literature review", vol. 28, no. 2, pp. 93–103, July–December, 2023, DOI: 10.1016/j.psicoe.2023.06.002.

K. McCutcheon, M. Lohan, M. Traynor and D. Martin, "A systematic review evaluating the impact of online or blended learning vs. face-to-face learning of clinical skills in undergraduate nurse education", *J. Adv. Nursing*, vol. 71, no. 2, pp. 255–270, Feb. 2015.

M. Murtaza, I. Sarwar, M. Shafiq, A. Ahmad, Z. Halim, H. Anwar, and K. Munir, "AI-based personalized e-Learning systems: Issues, challenges, and solutions", *IEEE Access*, vol. 10, 2022, DOI: 10.1109/ACCESS.2022.3193938.

F. Ouyang, L. Zheng and P. Jiao, "Artificial intelligence in online higher education: A systematic review of empirical research from 2011 to 2020", *Educ. Inf. Technol.*, vol. 27, pp. 1–33, Feb. 2022.

A. Pangotra, "AI's role in addressing the language barriers", Sep. 20, 2024.

B. Pardamean, T. Suparyanto, T. W. Cenggoro, D. Sudigyo and A. Anugrahana, "AI-based learning style prediction in online learning for primary education", *IEEE Access*, vol. 10, pp. 35725–35735, 2022, DOI: 10.1109/ACCESS.2022.3160177.

H. Peng, S. Ma and J. M. Spector, "Personalized adaptive learning: An emerging pedagogical approach enabled by a smart learning environment", *Smart Learn. Environ.*, vol. 6, no. 1, pp. 1–14, Dec. 2019.

A. Popovici and C. Mironov, "Students' perception on using e-learning technologies", *Proc.-Social Behav. Sci.*, vol. 180, pp. 1514–1519, May 2015.

F. Raza, "AI in Education: Personalized Learning and Adaptive Assessment", 2023. 10.13140/RG.2.2.24796.77446.

Y. Rui and Z. Suyin. "Exploration of AI smart teaching based on computer and information technology means", *Comput. Inform. Technol.*, vol. 31, no. 02, pp. 115–118, 2023.

U.S. Department of Education, Office of Educational Technology, Artificial Intelligence and Future of Teaching and Learning: Insights and Recommendations, Washington, DC, 2023.

Z. Wang, "Current situation and hotspot analysis of "artificial intelligence + education" research in China", *Technol. Horizon*, vol. 25, pp. 28–30, 2022.

C. Yinbo and Z. Wenlan, "Research hotspots, trends and implications of foreign education artificial intelligence", *Open Edu. Res.*, vol. 25, no. 4, pp. 43–58, 2019.

L. Yinli and L. Chen, "Analysis of the status quo, typical characteristics and development trend of AI education applications", *China E-edu.*, vol. 3, pp. 24–30, 2018.

O. Zawacki-Richter, V. I. Marín, M. Bond and F. Gouverneur, "Systematic review of research on artificial intelligence applications in higher education—Where are the educators?", *Int. J. Educ. Technol. Higher Educ.*, vol. 16, no. 1, pp. 1–27, Oct. 2019.

8 Enhancing Student Engagement and Success in Post-COVID-19 through AI Technologies

A. Peter Soosai Anandaraj, V. Murugananthan,
A. Judith Arockiya Gladies, S. Sridevi,
V. Vijayalakshmi, and B. Senthilkumaran

8.1 Introduction

The COVID-19 pandemic has acted as a significant driver for the swift adoption and development of digital technologies in education. This shift from traditional in-person teaching to remote and hybrid learning environments has been crucial for sustaining educational activities during lockdowns and social-distancing measures. While this transition has highlighted the benefits of new educational technologies, it has also revealed their limitations. In this setting, artificial intelligence (AI) has emerged as a key resource, offering potential solutions to the numerous challenges encountered by educational institutions. AI encompasses various technologies such as machine learning, natural language processing (NLP), and data analytics. These technologies collectively provide novel approaches to improve student engagement and achievement in the aftermath of the pandemic (Russell & Norvig, 2020). By leveraging these advanced tools, educators can address some of the critical issues exacerbated by the pandemic and work toward more effective and equitable educational practices.

AI's potential to transform education is particularly evident in its ability to improve student engagement. Engagement, defined as the extent of students' involvement, enthusiasm, and commitment to their learning activities, is a key determinant of academic success (Fredricks et al., 2004). The shift to online learning during the pandemic highlighted the limitations of traditional educational approaches in maintaining high levels of engagement.

Many students experienced decreased motivation and involvement due to the challenges of remote learning environments, such as lack of direct interaction with peers and instructors, and difficulties in accessing and navigating online platforms (Murphy, 2020). AI technologies can tackle these challenges by fostering more interactive and customized learning experiences. For instance, intelligent tutoring systems powered by AI can offer immediate feedback and adjust instructional material to fit each student's unique needs, thus boosting engagement by presenting content that is both suitably challenging and relevant (VanLehn, 2011).

DOI: 10.1201/9781003470304-8

Similarly, adaptive learning platforms, such as those provided by Carnegie Learning and DreamBox Learning, use advanced algorithms to modify educational content and adjust exercise difficulty based on student performance, thereby improving engagement and motivation. Furthermore, AI's role in enhancing academic success cannot be overstated. AI technologies enable the implementation of predictive analytics, which involves analyzing data to forecast student outcomes and identify those at risk of academic difficulties. Predictive analytics tools can help educators monitor student performance in real time and provide early interventions to support students before they fall behind (Siemens, 2013). For instance, AI-driven early warning systems can track various indicators such as attendance, assignment completion, and participation, alerting educators to students who may need additional support. This proactive approach is crucial for addressing academic challenges promptly and effectively, leading to improved retention rates and academic performance (Arnold & Pistilli, 2012). Additionally, AI can support curriculum design by providing insights into which teaching methods and materials are most effective for different groups of students, thereby allowing educators to refine their strategies and resources based on evidence (Hattie, 2009). AI also holds promise for addressing educational disparities, which have been exacerbated by the pandemic. Students from marginalized backgrounds have faced greater disruptions to their learning, highlighting the need for equitable access to educational resources and support (García & Weiss, 2020). AI technologies can help bridge these gaps by offering tailored learning experiences that accommodate diverse cultural and linguistic backgrounds. For example, AI-powered language translation tools and culturally adaptive content can help ensure that all students have access to relevant and understandable educational materials (Kumar & Rosé, 2020). Moreover, assistive technologies driven by AI can support students with disabilities by providing accessible learning solutions such as speech recognition, text-to-speech systems, and personalized learning aids, thus promoting a more inclusive educational environment (Scherer, 2012).

In summary, the COVID-19 pandemic has accelerated the integration of digital technologies into education, with AI emerging as a significant tool for enhancing student engagement and success in the post-pandemic landscape. By offering personalized learning experiences, supporting academic achievement, and addressing educational disparities, AI holds the potential to revolutionize education and address key challenges faced by institutions. Nonetheless, addressing ethical and privacy concerns is essential to ensure that AI technologies are utilized in a fair, transparent, and responsible manner. Continued exploration and development in AI will be crucial for unlocking its full potential and achieving substantial improvements in educational outcomes. The integration of AI into education represents a paradigm shift with profound implications for how teaching and learning are conducted. AI technologies, which include machine learning, NLP, and data analytics, offer a host of advantages that can significantly enhance the educational experience, particularly in the context of the post-COVID-19 era. The pandemic highlighted critical gaps in educational delivery and equity, making the need for innovative solutions more pressing than ever.

8.1.1 Customized Learning Experiences

A key advantage of AI in education is its capacity to provide highly customized learning experiences. Traditional educational approaches often use a uniform method that may not account for the diverse needs, strengths, and weaknesses of individual students (Fredricks et al., 2004). AI-driven adaptive learning systems overcome this limitation by tailoring educational content to fit each student's unique requirements. For example, platforms like Carnegie Learning and DreamBox Learning employ advanced algorithms to modify the difficulty and delivery of instructional materials in real time based on a student's performance (Carnegie Learning, 2022; DreamBox Learning, 2022). Such customization not only increases student engagement but also enhances comprehension and retention by offering challenges that align with their current knowledge level (VanLehn, 2011).

8.1.2 Efficiency and Administrative Relief

AI technologies also contribute significantly to the efficiency of educational institutions by automating routine tasks and administrative functions. Traditional grading and assessment methods can be time-consuming and labor-intensive, often detracting from the time educators can spend on direct instruction and student support.

8.1.3 Enhancing Access and Inclusivity

AI technologies are instrumental in advancing accessibility and inclusivity in education. The pandemic has highlighted significant gaps in educational access,

Especially for students with disabilities and those from various linguistic and cultural backgrounds (García & Weiss, 2020). AI-driven assistive technologies, such as speech recognition and text-to-speech systems, offer crucial support for students with visual or auditory impairments, making learning materials more accessible and equitable (Scherer, 2012). Additionally, AI-based translation tools can overcome language barriers, allowing non-native speakers to access quality educational content and engage fully in learning activities (Kumar & Rosé, 2020). These innovations contribute to a more inclusive educational environment, ensuring that all students have the chance to succeed.

8.1.4 Leveraging Data for Enhanced Decision-Making

AI in education provides valuable data-driven insights that can significantly enhance decision-making and improve educational outcomes. Predictive analytics tools process extensive amounts of data to uncover trends and patterns related to student performance, engagement, and progress (Siemens, 2013). This functionality allows educators to make well-informed decisions regarding instructional strategies, identify students who may be at risk of falling behind, and implement timely interventions.

8.1.5 Scalability and Reach

AI technologies offer scalable solutions that can be implemented across diverse educational settings, from individual classrooms to large-scale institutions. AI-powered platforms can accommodate large numbers of students simultaneously, providing consistent and high-quality educational experiences regardless of class size or geographical location (Baker, 2018). This scalability is particularly advantageous for reaching students in remote or underserved areas, expanding access to quality education, and bridging gaps in educational equity. For example, AI-driven online courses and virtual tutoring systems can offer personalized support to students in locations where traditional educational resources may be limited, thereby addressing disparities and enhancing educational opportunities on a broader scale (Chui et al., 2016).

8.1.6 Support for Lifelong Learning

Finally, AI technologies support lifelong learning by providing flexible and adaptive learning opportunities for learners at all stages of life. As the demands of the workforce and society evolve, continuous learning and up skilling become increasingly important. AI-powered platforms can offer personalized learning paths and resources for adult learners seeking to acquire new skills or advance their careers (Chui et al., 2016). By providing on-demand access to learning materials and tailored support, AI facilitates ongoing education and skill development, helping individuals stay current with industry trends and maintain relevant competencies throughout their lives.

In conclusion, integrating decision-making into education provides a range of significant benefits, including tailored learning experiences, improved efficiency, greater accessibility, and enhanced data-driven decision-making. These advantages are especially pertinent in the post-COVID-19 educational environment, where innovative solutions are crucial for overcoming existing challenges and enhancing educational outcomes. As educational institutions adapt to the evolving needs of students and the modern world, AI technologies will be essential in shaping the future of education.

8.2 Related Works

The integration of AI into education has resulted in the creation of numerous systems and tools designed to improve teaching and learning processes. These AI-driven systems tackle various educational challenges, including personalized learning, student engagement, administrative efficiency, and accessibility. This section offers an overview of notable AI systems in education, highlighting their benefits and drawbacks to provide a thorough understanding of their effectiveness and promises.

8.2.1 Intelligent Tutoring Systems (ITS)

Intelligent tutoring systems (ITS) are AI-driven systems designed to provide personalized instruction and feedback to students. Notable examples include Carnegie Learning's MATHia and Pearson's MyLab. These platforms utilize machine learning algorithms to evaluate individual student performance and tailor instructional content accordingly (Carnegie Learning, 2022).

Advantages: ITS provide numerous advantages, including immediate feedback, customized learning pathways, and the capacity to accommodate various learning styles and speeds. By examining student interactions and performance data, these platforms can pinpoint knowledge gaps and offer targeted support, thereby enriching the overall learning experience (VanLehn, 2011).

Disadvantages: Despite their benefits, adaptive learning platforms face several limitations. A significant challenge is their reliance on high-quality, well-labeled data to effectively train the algorithms. Inaccurate or biased data can result in less effective or unfair learning experiences.

8.2.2 Adaptive Learning Platforms

Adaptive learning platforms, such as DreamBox Learning and Knewton, use AI to tailor educational content to the individual needs of students. These platforms analyze data from student interactions to adjust the difficulty of tasks, recommend resources, and provide personalized learning experiences (DreamBox Learning, 2022; Conklin, 2016).

Advantages: Adaptive learning platforms excel in delivering customized learning experiences that address each student's unique strengths and weaknesses. They can help bridge learning gaps by adjusting instructional content in real time, which enhances student engagement and learning outcomes.

Disadvantages: One of the main challenges of adaptive learning platforms is the potential for data privacy concerns. The extensive data collection required for personalization raises questions about how student data is managed and protected. Additionally, the effectiveness of adaptive learning systems can be limited by the quality of the underlying algorithms and the breadth of the content they support.

8.2.3 AI-Powered Analytics Tools

AI-powered analytics tools, such as those developed by Blackboard and Canvas, provide educators with insights into student performance and engagement. These tools use data analytics to track metrics like attendance, participation, and assessment scores, offering predictive insights that can help identify at-risk students and inform instructional strategies.

Advantages: The primary advantage of AI-powered analytics tools is their ability to offer data-driven insights that can enhance decision-making and improve educational outcomes. By identifying trends and patterns, these tools enable educators to intervene early and support students before they face significant challenges. The predictive capabilities of these systems help in allocating resources more effectively and addressing potential issues pro-actively (Siemens, 2013).

Disadvantages: One notable disadvantage is the potential for misinterpret-ation of data, which can lead to inappropriate interventions or misplaced resources. Additionally, the reliance on data analytics requires accurate and comprehensive data collection, which can be challenging to achieve consist-ently. There is also a risk that the focus on quantitative metrics might over-shadow qualitative aspects of learning, such as student well-being and the development of critical thinking skills (Baker et al., 2014a).

8.2.4 Virtual and Augmented Reality (VR/AR) Systems

Virtual and augmented reality (VR/AR) systems such as those created by zSpace and Google Expeditions provide immersive learning experiences that can significantly boost engagement and comprehension. These technolo-gies employ AI to develop interactive simulations and virtual environments, allowing students to explore and interact with educational content in innova-tive ways.

Advantages: VR/AR systems provide highly engaging and interactive learning experiences that can make complex concepts more accessible and under-standable. By immersing students in virtual environments, these systems can enhance experiential learning and foster deeper comprehension of sub-ject matter. They also offer opportunities for remote or distance learning, allowing students to engage with content in a more dynamic and interactive manner (Chiu et al., 2016).

Disadvantages: The main challenges associated with VR/AR systems include high implementation costs and the need for specialized hardware and software. These systems may also face technical limitations, such as latency issues or limited content availability, which can affect the quality of the learning experience.

8.2.5 Chatbots and Virtual Assistants

AI-driven chatbots and virtual assistants, such as IBM Watson Tutor and Duolingo, offer support and guidance to students by providing instant answers to questions, facilitating learning activities, and assisting with language acquisition (Afzal, 2019; Duolingo, 2023).

Advantages: Chatbots and virtual assistants offer 24/7 support, enabling students to receive help and engage with educational content outside of regular class hours. These tools also reduce the workload on educators by handling routine queries and administrative tasks.

Disadvantages: The effectiveness of chatbots and virtual assistants is contingent upon the quality of their NLP capabilities. Poorly designed chatbots may struggle to understand and address complex or nuanced student queries, leading to frustration and disengagement. There is also a risk of students becoming overly reliant on automated support, which might diminish their development of critical thinking and problem-solving skills.

8.2.6 AI-Enhanced Content Creation Tools

AI-enhanced content creation tools, such as Grammarly and Copy.ai, assist educators and students in generating and refining written content. These tools use AI algorithms to provide grammar and style suggestions, generate content ideas, and improve writing quality.

Advantages: These tools improve the quality of written communication by offering real-time feedback on grammar, punctuation, and style. They can help students develop better writing skills and produce polished, professional-quality content. For educators, AI-enhanced content creation tools streamline the process of creating instructional materials and assessments.

Disadvantages: While these tools offer valuable assistance, they may not always provide contextually appropriate suggestions, which can lead to inaccuracies or misunderstandings. There is also a risk that overreliance on these tools might hinder the development of students' independent writing and critical thinking skills. Additionally, AI-enhanced content creation tools can be expensive, which may limit their accessibility for some users.

8.2.7 AI-Based Assessment and Evaluation Systems

AI-based assessment and evaluation systems, such as those developed by Turnitin and Gradescope, use AI to evaluate student work and provide feedback. These systems analyze assignments and exams for originality, adherence to criteria, and overall quality.

Advantages: AI-based assessment systems can enhance the accuracy and consistency of evaluations by applying objective criteria and reducing the potential for human bias. For educators, these systems offer streamlined grading processes and insights into student performance.

Disadvantages: The reliance on AI for assessment may lead to concerns about fairness and transparency. Algorithms may not fully capture the nuances of student work, potentially resulting in inaccurate evaluations. Additionally, there may be issues with the security and privacy of student data, as well as the need for ongoing updates and maintenance to ensure the system remains effective and relevant.

8.2.8 AI-Driven Learning Management Systems (LMS)

AI-driven learning management systems (LMSs), such as Moodle and Canvas, incorporate AI features to enhance course management and delivery. These systems provide tools for tracking student progress, facilitating communication, and managing educational content.

Advantages: AI-driven LMSs offer a range of benefits, including automated administrative tasks, AI-powered systems experiences, and data-driven insights into student performance. By integrating AI, LMSs can offer enhanced features such as predictive analytics, adaptive learning paths, and intelligent content recommendations.

Disadvantages: There is also a risk of technology dependence, where the focus on automated systems might overshadow the importance of human interaction and support.

In conclusion, the existing AI systems in education offer a variety of advantages, including personalized learning, enhanced efficiency, and improved data insights. Understanding these advantages and disadvantages is crucial for developing effective AI-driven educational solutions and ensuring that they are implemented in ways that maximize their benefits while addressing potential drawbacks. As AI technology continues to evolve, ongoing research and development will be essential in refining these systems and addressing the complexities associated with their use in education. The chapter emphasizes ethical AI deployment in education by addressing data privacy through measures such as anonymization of student data, secure storage protocols, adherence to consent-based data collection practices, and alignment with frameworks like General Data Protection Regulation (GDPR) to ensure compliance with international data protection standards.

8.3 Impact of AI on Student Engagement

Student engagement is a vital element in achieving academic success and enhancing overall learning experiences. It is defined as the extent of enthusiasm, involvement, and dedication that students demonstrate toward their educational activities. Engagement plays a crucial role in influencing academic performance and retention rates (Fredricks et al., 2004). The COVID-19 pandemic highlighted the challenges of maintaining high levels of engagement in remote and hybrid learning environments, prompting educators and researchers to explore innovative solutions.

8.3.1 Personalized Learning Experiences

A study by K12 Inc. (2021) found that students using adaptive learning technologies demonstrated increased engagement levels and improved academic outcomes compared with their peers in traditional learning environments. The study highlighted that personalized learning experiences facilitated by AI tools could help students stay motivated and engaged by providing appropriate challenges and feedback.

8.3.2 Immediate Feedback and Interaction

AI technologies facilitate immediate feedback and interaction, which are crucial for sustaining student engagement. AI-powered feedback systems and intelligent tutoring platforms offer prompt responses to student inquiries and performance, enabling swift adjustments to learning strategies. For instance, platforms like Pearson's MyLab provide real-time, personalized feedback on assignments and assessments, allowing students to understand and correct their mistakes as they occur. Research by Baker and Siemens (2014b) highlights that real-time feedback from AI systems can boost student engagement by fostering a more interactive and responsive learning environment. Their study revealed that students receiving immediate feedback were more likely to stay engaged and motivated, as they could quickly address and rectify their misunderstandings.

8.3.3 Gamification and Interactive Learning

Gamification, the integration of game-like elements into educational contexts, is another way AI enhances student engagement. AI technologies can support gamified learning environments by providing personalized challenges, rewards, and progress tracking. Platforms like Classcraft and Kahoot! use AI to create interactive and engaging learning experiences that motivate students through game mechanics and competition.

8.3.4 Adaptive Learning Pathways

AI-driven adaptive learning platforms offer customized learning pathways that adjust based on student performance and engagement levels. These platforms analyze data on student interactions and progress to modify the difficulty and type of content presented. For instance, DreamBox Learning's adaptive math program adjusts the complexity of problems based on real-time student performance, ensuring that students are consistently challenged without becoming overwhelmed.

The study found that students using adaptive platforms were more engaged and motivated, as the content was aligned with their individual learning needs and progress.

8.3.5 Increased Accessibility and Inclusivity

AI technologies also contribute to increased accessibility and inclusivity in education, which can positively impact student engagement. AI-powered tools, such as language translation services and assistive technologies, help bridge gaps for students from diverse linguistic and cultural backgrounds (Kumar & Rosé, 2020). For example, AI-driven translation tools can make educational content accessible to non-native speakers, while assistive technologies support students with disabilities by providing tailored learning aids (Scherer, 2012). The study highlighted that students who have access to supportive technologies are more likely to participate actively in their learning activities and feel valued within the educational setting.

8.4 Improving Academic Success with AI

Academic success, defined as the achievement of educational goals such as high grades, skill acquisition, and graduation, is a central aim of educational institutions. AI technologies offer innovative solutions to traditional educational challenges, providing personalized, efficient, and effective learning experiences. This section explores how AI contributes to improving academic success through personalized learning, predictive analytics, enhanced accessibility, and supporting teachers in their instructional roles.

8.4.1 Tailored Learning Experiences

AI significantly improves academic success through tailored learning experiences. Unlike traditional education's one-size-fits-all model, which may not address the diverse needs of individual students, AI-driven adaptive learning platforms—such as those from Carnegie Learning and DreamBox Learning—use advanced algorithms to customize educational content according to each student's unique strengths, weaknesses, and learning pace. These platforms continuously analyze student performance data to adjust task difficulty and provide personalized recommendations, ensuring that students engage with material that is appropriately challenging. This tailored approach not only maintains student engagement but also enhances their mastery of concepts. For example, AI systems can pinpoint areas where a student is struggling and offer targeted practice exercises or resources to bridge these gaps. Such individualized learning strategies contribute to better retention and comprehension of material, ultimately boosting academic performance.

8.4.2 Predictive Analytics

Predictive analytics is another powerful application of AI in education, significantly contributing to academic success. AI-driven predictive analytics tools analyze vast amounts of data to forecast student outcomes and identify those at risk of academic difficulties. These tools can track various indicators, such as attendance, assignment completion, and participation, providing real-time insights that enable educators to intervene early (Siemens, 2013). For example, AI-powered early warning systems can alert educators when a student exhibits signs of disengagement or poor performance, prompting timely support and interventions. This proactive approach allows educators to address potential issues before they escalate, thereby improving student retention and success rates (Arnold & Pistilli, 2012). Moreover, predictive analytics can help institutions allocate resources more effectively, ensuring that support services are directed to students who need them the most.

8.4.3 Enhanced Accessibility

AI technologies also play a crucial role in enhancing accessibility, which is essential for ensuring academic success for all students. The COVID-19 pandemic highlighted significant disparities in educational access, particularly for students with disabilities or those from diverse linguistic and cultural backgrounds (García & Weiss, 2020).

8.4.4 Supporting Teachers

AI does not replace teachers but rather complements their instructional roles, enhancing their ability to improve student outcomes. AI-driven tools can automate routine tasks, such as grading and attendance tracking, allowing educators to dedicate more time to direct instruction and student support. Furthermore, AI provides teachers with data-driven insights into student performance, enabling them to refine their teaching strategies to better address their students' needs.

8.5 AI and Remote Learning During COVID-19

The COVID-19 pandemic compelled educational institutions around the globe to rapidly transition to remote learning. This sudden shift presented numerous challenges, from ensuring equitable access to maintaining student engagement and academic integrity. AI played a crucial role in addressing these challenges, providing innovative solutions that facilitated the continuity of education during this unprecedented time.

This section explores how AI has supported remote learning during the COVID-19 pandemic through enhanced online learning platforms, personalized instruction, monitoring student engagement, and ensuring academic integrity. AI has significantly enhanced online learning platforms, making them more interactive and responsive to student needs.

AI-powered platforms such as Coursera, EdX, and Khan Academy utilize machine learning algorithms to customize the learning experience for each student. These platforms examine student interactions, performance data, and preferences to suggest personalized learning paths and resources.

8.5.1 Personalized Instruction

Personalized instruction is critical in a remote learning environment where students may not have direct access to their teachers. AI-powered tutoring systems like Squirrel AI and Carnegie Learning's provide one-on-one tutoring that mimics the benefits of human tutoring. These systems use NLP and machine learning to understand student queries and provide detailed, context-aware explanations and feedback. AI tutoring systems can identify individual learning gaps and offer targeted practice to address them.

8.5.2 Monitoring Student Engagement

Maintaining student engagement in a remote learning environment is challenging, but AI technologies have provided effective solutions. AI-powered analytics tools like Zoom's attention tracking feature and ProctorU's engagement monitoring use facial recognition and behavioral analysis to assess student engagement during online classes.

8.5.3 Ensuring Academic Integrity

Academic integrity is a significant concern in remote learning environments, where traditional supervision methods are less effective. AI technologies have addressed this issue by providing robust proctoring solutions that ensure fair assessments. AI-driven proctoring tools like ProctorU and ExamSoft use machine learning algorithms to monitor students during exams, detecting behaviors that indicate potential cheating.

8.6 Future Directions in AI for Education

As AI technologies advance, their role in education is expected to grow significantly, offering innovative solutions to long-standing challenges and enhancing learning experiences.

Future intelligent tutoring systems will become increasingly sophisticated, using advanced NLP and machine learning algorithms to deliver highly personalized and responsive instruction. These systems will be capable of understanding and adapting to individual student needs in real time, providing tailored feedback and support similar to one-on-one human tutoring. The future of AI in education promises substantial transformation, driven by key advancements. Improved data analytics will allow educators to gain deeper insights into student performance and learning patterns, facilitating early identification of students at risk and enabling timely, data-driven interventions to boost retention and academic success. Predictive analytics will further enhance curriculum design and instructional strategies by analyzing extensive performance data to tailor educational content and teaching methods to individual needs. This study utilizes a mixed-methods approach to thoroughly examine the effects of AI-powered adaptive learning platforms on student engagement and academic performance in higher education. By integrating quantitative data analysis with qualitative insights, the research seeks to offer a detailed understanding of the impact of AI technologies on educational results.

8.6.1 *System Design*

The system design of the proposed AI-driven solution for enhancing student engagement is structured into three core stages: data acquisition, AI model development, and result interpretation (Figure 8.1).

Proposed System Architecture
The system comprises three main components:

Data Collection Layer: This layer captures student data from multiple sources, including LMSs, student feedback forms, and assessment results. These data points reflect engagement levels, performance metrics, and learning preferences.

Processing and Analysis Layer: Preprocessing of raw data ensures consistency and removes noise. The processed data is then analyzed using AI models to identify patterns and generate insights.

Output and Recommendation Layer: Based on the analysis, personalized learning strategies are suggested, such as tailored content delivery and adaptive quizzes, ensuring alignment with individual student needs.

Implementation steps:

Data Pre-processing: Data collected is cleaned by removing redundant or incomplete entries. For numerical data, normalization techniques are applied, ensuring values fall within a common scale.

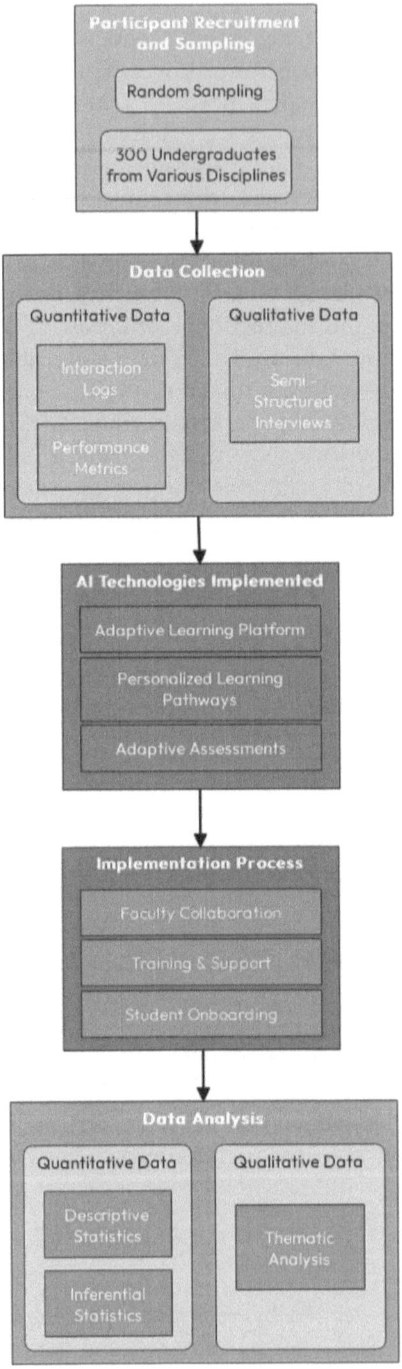

Figure 8.1 Proposed System Design.

AI Model Integration: Algorithms like random forests for decision-making or neural networks for adaptive recommendations are trained on historical data. This ensures the system predicts optimal learning paths and engagement strategies for each student.

Evaluation Metrics: The system is evaluated using precision, recall, and F1-score to measure its accuracy in predicting student outcomes and providing recommendations.

8.6.2 Participants and Sampling

8.6.2.1 Participants

The study targets 300 undergraduate students from a large urban university, ensuring a broad representation across various academic disciplines. This diverse participant pool allows for a detailed examination of the AI platform's impact on students from different fields, including humanities, sciences, engineering, and social sciences. The diversity in academic backgrounds also helps in assessing whether the AI technology's effectiveness varies across different disciplines.

8.6.2.2 Sampling Method

The random sampling technique is utilized to select participants from course rosters. This method involves generating random numbers to choose students from each course list, thereby reducing selection bias and enhancing the representativeness of the sample. Random sampling ensures that the results are not skewed by any particular group and that every student has an equal opportunity to participate, which increases the validity of the research findings.

8.6.2.3 Justification for Sampling Size

The sample size of 300 students is strategically chosen to ensure both statistical power and manageability. This number provides a robust dataset for detecting statistically significant effects while being feasible for in-depth qualitative analysis. A sample of this size allows for meaningful subgroup analyses, such as comparing the impact of AI on students in different disciplines or academic years.

8.6.3 Data Collection

Quantitative Data Collection:
Quantitative data is gathered through the AI-powered adaptive learning platform, which tracks a range of student interactions and performance metrics. The data collected includes

Student Interaction Logs: These logs record various aspects of student engagement, such as the duration of sessions, the frequency of logins, and the types of resources accessed. Interaction logs offer insights into how students use the platform and how their engagement patterns correlate with academic performance.

Performance Metrics: This includes data on assessment scores, assignment grades, and progress through personalized learning pathways. Performance metrics provide a direct measure of academic outcomes and allow for the evaluation of the AI platform's impact on students' learning achievements.

Qualitative Data Collection:
Qualitative data is collected through semi-structured interviews with a subset of students. These interviews aim to explore students' subjective experiences and perceptions of the adaptive learning platform. Key aspects of the interview process include

Interview Questions: Questions are designed to elicit detailed responses about students' experiences with the AI platform, including their perceptions of its usability, effectiveness, and impact on their learning. Questions also address students' attitudes toward AI in education and any challenges they encountered.

Interview Procedure: Interviews are conducted either in person or via videoconferencing platforms, depending on participants' preferences and availability. Each interview is designed to be conversational and open-ended, allowing participants to express their thoughts freely. Interviews are recorded, transcribed, and analyzed to ensure that participants' voices are accurately represented.

Rationale for Mixed-Methods Approach:
Combining quantitative and qualitative methods offers a nuanced perspective on the impact of AI technologies. Quantitative data provides objective measures of engagement and performance, while qualitative data offers deeper insights into students' personal experiences and attitudes. This mixed-methods approach allows for a more comprehensive analysis of how AI-driven adaptive learning platforms affect student outcomes.

8.6.4 AI Technologies Implemented

Adaptive Learning Platform:
The study integrates an advanced AI-powered adaptive learning platform designed to personalize the educational experience for each student. Key features of the platform include

Personalized Learning Pathways: The platform employs advanced machine learning algorithms to evaluate individual student data and generate customized learning pathways. These pathways adjust in real time according to students' progress and performance, ensuring that each learner receives content and assessments tailored to their unique educational needs.

Recommendation Engine: The recommendation engine offers personalized suggestions for additional learning materials, practice exercises, and supplementary resources. By analyzing students' interaction patterns and performance data, the engine helps students access relevant content that enhances their understanding and retention of the subject matter.

Adaptive Assessments: The platform's adaptive assessments adjust the difficulty level based on students' responses. This dynamic approach helps maintain an appropriate level of challenge, encourages continuous learning, and provides immediate feedback to support student improvement.

Adaptive Learning System Algorithm: This pseudocode illustrates the process of dynamically adjusting learning content based on student performance metrics, ensuring personalized learning experiences.

Algorithm: AdaptiveLearningSystem
Input: Student Profile, Learning Content, Performance_Metrics
Output: Personalized_Content

```
1 Initialize Learning Path based on Student_Profile
2 For each Module in Learning Content:
   a  Deliver Module to Student
   b  Collect Feedback and Performance_Metrics
   c  If Performance_Metrics < Threshold:
       i   Provide Additional_Resources
       ii  Reassess Performance
   d  Update Learning_Path based on new Performance_Metrics
3 Return Personalized Content
```

Technology Integration:
To ensure seamless integration of the adaptive learning platform into existing course structures, the implementation process includes

Alignment with Course Objectives: The platform's features are aligned with course goals and learning outcomes to ensure that the AI-driven content complements traditional instructional methods. Faculty members collaborate with the implementation team to integrate the platform into the curriculum effectively.

Customization and Flexibility: The platform offers customization options for educators to tailor its features according to specific course requirements and teaching styles. This flexibility allows for the accommodation of diverse pedagogical approaches and ensures that the AI technology enhances rather than disrupts existing teaching practices.

8.6.5 Implementation Process

Collaboration with Faculty:
Successful implementation of the adaptive learning platform requires close collaboration with faculty members. Key aspects of this collaboration include

Curriculum Integration: Faculty members work with the implementation team to ensure that the AI platform's features are integrated into the curriculum in a way that supports and enhances course content. This collaboration involves mapping the platform's capabilities to course objectives and ensuring that it aligns with instructional strategies.

Training and Professional Development: Training sessions are conducted for educators to familiarize them with the platform's functionalities and best practices for using it in their teaching. Professional development opportunities include workshops, webinars, and hands-on training to ensure that faculty members are confident and competent in using the AI technology.

Technical Support:
Technical support is provided throughout the implementation process to address any issues and ensure smooth operation of the platform. Support services include

Helpdesk and Troubleshooting: A dedicated helpdesk is available to assist both students and educators with technical problems and questions related to the platform. Troubleshooting support ensures that any issues are resolved promptly, minimizing disruptions to the learning experience.

User Guides and Resources: Comprehensive user guides, tutorials, and FAQs are provided to help users navigate the platform and utilize its features effectively. These resources are designed to be user-friendly and accessible, supporting users in their adoption of the AI technology.

Student Onboarding:
To facilitate students' adoption of the adaptive learning platform, onboarding activities include

Orientation Sessions: Orientation sessions introduce students to the platform, its features, and how it will be used in their courses. These sessions help students understand the purpose and benefits of the AI technology and set expectations for its role in their learning.

Instructional Materials: Students receive instructional materials, including guides and video tutorials, to help them become familiar with the platform's functionalities and features. These materials provide step-by-step instructions for using the platform effectively.

8.6.6 Data Analysis

Quantitative Data Analysis:

Quantitative data analysis employs statistical methods to explore the connection between AI platform usage and academic outcomes. Key analyses include

Descriptive Statistics: These statistics summarize and characterize the main features of the quantitative data. Measures of central tendency (mean, median) and dispersion (standard deviation) are calculated to provide a comprehensive overview of student engagement and performance.

Inferential Statistics: Inferential statistical methods, such as correlation and regression analysis, are used to investigate the relationships between AI usage metrics and academic performance. Correlation analysis identifies the strength and direction of associations between variables, while regression analysis evaluates the effect of AI usage on academic outcomes, accounting for potential confounding factors.

Qualitative Data Analysis:

Qualitative data from interviews is analyzed using thematic analysis to identify and interpret patterns and themes. The analysis process includes

Transcription and Coding: Interview recordings are transcribed verbatim to create a detailed record of participants' responses. Codes are applied to segments of text to identify key themes and concepts. This process helps organize the data and highlights recurring patterns in students' experiences and perceptions.

Thematic Analysis: Thematic analysis involves examining the coded data to identify overarching themes and insights. This analysis provides a deeper understanding of students' subjective experiences with the AI platform, including their perceptions of its impact on engagement and academic success (Table 8.1).

The integration of AI into post-secondary education has led to notable advancements in both student engagement and academic success, as revealed by the mixed-methods study conducted. The research, involving 300 undergraduate students at a large urban university, aimed to evaluate the effectiveness of AI-driven adaptive learning platforms. Through quantitative analysis of interaction logs and performance metrics alongside qualitative interviews, the study provided a holistic view of AI's impact on the learning experience. The findings indicate a substantial increase in student engagement attributed to AI technologies. Specifically, students utilizing adaptive learning platforms demonstrated higher average interaction times with learning materials compared with their counterparts using traditional educational methods. This was evident from the data collected, which showed

Table 8.1 Key Themes from Student Interviews

Theme	Description	Example quotes
Ease of use	Students found the platform user-friendly.	"The interface is intuitive and easy to navigate."
Personalization	The adaptive features helped tailor learning.	"I appreciated the customized learning materials."
Engagement	Increased motivation and engagement were reported.	"The platform kept me more engaged in my studies."
Challenges	Some technical issues were noted.	"There were occasional glitches during exams."
Feedback	Immediate feedback was valued.	"The instant feedback on quizzes was very helpful."

a significant rise in the hours students spent engaging with course content after the implementation of AI tools. The AI platforms offered personalized learning pathways, which tailored educational resources and assessments to individual student needs, thereby fostering a more engaging learning environment. This increase in engagement was corroborated by qualitative feedback from student interviews, where participants expressed a positive shift in their motivation and interest in the subject matter, largely due to the tailored and interactive nature of the AI tools.

Sentiment Analysis in Educational Discussions: This pseudo code demonstrates how AI can analyze student text inputs to gauge engagement and emotional states.

```
Algorithm: SentimentAnalysis
Input: Student_Text
Output: Sentiment_Score

1 Preprocess Student_Text:
    a Remove special characters and stop words
    b Tokenize words
2 Load Sentiment_Model (trained on educational data)
3 For each word in Tokenized_Text:
    a Retrieve Sentiment_Score from Sentiment_Model
    b Aggregate scores
4 Normalize Sentiment_Score
5 Return Sentiment_Score
```

Moreover, the impact of AI on academic success was also significant. The analysis of academic performance metrics revealed that students who actively used AI-driven platforms saw marked improvements in their grades and retention rates. This can be attributed to the adaptive learning features of the AI systems, which provided real-time feedback and customized learning experiences. The study's quantitative data highlighted a correlation between the frequency of AI tool usage and higher academic achievement, suggesting that personalized learning interventions facilitated by AI contribute to better academic outcomes. This finding was further supported by qualitative data from student interviews, where students reported that the AI tools helped them better understand complex concepts and perform well in their assessments. The role of AI in supporting remote learning during the COVID-19 pandemic was another key focus of the study. The pandemic posed significant challenges for education, necessitating a shift to online learning environments.

AI technologies played a pivotal role in bridging the gap created by this sudden transition.

The study found that AI-driven platforms were instrumental in maintaining student engagement and providing effective learning experiences despite the physical separation from traditional classroom settings. The personalized support and resources offered by AI were crucial in adapting to the new learning environment, highlighting the technology's flexibility and effectiveness in various educational contexts. Looking ahead, the study suggests several future directions for AI in education. The evolving nature of AI technologies presents opportunities for further refinement of adaptive learning systems. Future research should explore advancements in AI algorithms and their application across diverse learning contexts to enhance educational outcomes.

8.7 Conclusion

The integration of AI technologies into post-COVID-19 education marks a significant shift toward more personalized and adaptive learning environments. This chapter examined how AI is transforming educational practices, with a particular focus on its effects on student engagement and academic achievement. Through a rigorous mixed-methods approach, quantitative data revealed significant improvements in student participation and academic performance with AI-driven adaptive learning systems. Qualitative insights underscored positive student perceptions toward AI technologies, highlighting their efficacy in tailoring learning experiences to individual needs while addressing ethical considerations such as data privacy and algorithmic bias. The discussion synthesized empirical findings with existing literature, emphasizing AI's potential to foster inclusive and effective educational ecosystems. Looking forward, future research should focus on scaling AI technologies across diverse educational contexts and exploring long-term effects on student learning outcomes. By leveraging AI's capabilities to personalize learning experiences and support educators in navigating evolving educational landscapes, stakeholders can harness technology to create resilient and equitable educational environments post-pandemic. Looking ahead, future research should explore scaling AI technologies across diverse educational contexts, developing strategies to integrate qualitative assessments with quantitative metrics, and evaluating the long-term effects on critical thinking and student well-being. Furthermore, the integration of AI with emerging technologies such as augmented and virtual reality (AR/VR) holds promise for enhancing interactive and immersive learning experiences, paving the way for innovative educational paradigms.

References

Afzal, S., Dempsey, B., D'Helon, C., Mukhi, N., Pribic, M., Sickler, A., Strong, P., Vanchiswar, M. and Wilde, L. The personality of AI systems in education: experiences with the Watson tutor, a one-on-one virtual tutoring system. *Childhood Education*, 95(1), 44–52, 2019. https://iaied.org/showcase/6hRMxzuPi8sYwCw6YiU8YS

Arnold, K. E., and Pistilli, M. D. "Course signals at Purdue: Using learning analytics to increase student success," in *Proc. 2nd Int. Conf. Learning Analytics and Knowledge*, 2012, pp. 267–270.

Baker, R. S., "Big data and education," in *Handbook of Learning Analytics*, 2018, pp. 11–24.

Baker, R. S., and Siemens, G., "Educational data mining and learning analytics," in *Learning Analytics: Building Bridges between Data and Learning*, Springer, 2014a, pp. 13–24.

Baker, R. S. J. d., and Inventado, P. S. "Educational data mining and learning analytics," in *Learning Analytics: From Research to Practice*, J. A. Larusson and B. White, Eds. Springer, 2014b, pp. 61–75. doi:10.1007/978-1-4614-3305-7_4.

Carnegie Learning, "*Carnegie Learning: Personalized Math Programs*," 2022.

Chui, M., Manyika, J., and Miremadi, M. Where Machines could Replace Humans—and Where They Can't (Yet). *McKinsey Quarterly*, 2016.

Conklin, T. A. (2016). Knewton (An adaptive learning platform available at www.knewton.com/).

DreamBox Learning, "*DreamBox Learning: Adaptive Math Solutions*," 2022.

Fredricks, J. A., Blumenfeld, P. C., and Paris, A. H. "School engagement: Potential of the concept, state of the evidence," *Rev. Educ. Res.*, vol. 74, no. 1, pp. 59–109, 2004.

García, E., and Weiss, E. *The Impact of the COVID-19 Pandemic on Education Equity*. Economic Policy Institute, 2020.

Hattie, J. *Visible Learning: A Synthesis of Over 800 Meta-Analyses Relating to Achievement*. Routledge, 2009.

Kumar, R., and Rosé, C. P. "AI for social good in education: A research agenda," *AI Open*, vol. 1, pp. 10–24, 2020.

Murphy, M. P. A. "The pandemic and the pivot to online learning: Insights and recommendations," *Educ. Technol. Res. Dev.*, vol. 68, no. 4, pp. 2191–2201, 2020.

Roberts, B. K12 Inc.: Virtually Failing our Students. Chicago. 2021. www.k12.com/

Russell, S. J., and Norvig, P. *Artificial Intelligence: A Modern Approach*, 4th ed. Pearson, 2020.

Scherer, D. *Assistive Technology: Access for All Students*. Routledge, 2012.

Siemens, G. "Learning analytics: The emergence of a discipline," *Am. Behav. Sci.*, vol. 57, no. 10, pp. 1380–1400, 2013.

9 AI Tools for Plagiarism Detection and Academic Integrity

S. Baghavathi Priya, B. Kavya Sai, and Tamil Selvi Madeswaran

9.1 Introduction

In this chapter, we focus on the inclusion of artificial intelligence (AI) applications in the education industry while discussing its aim in promoting academic integrity by way of anti-plagiarism tools as well as the ethical concerns that battle such practices. The chapter will highlight relevant issues like how AI makes it easy to detect plagiarism and its different forms to students, what limitations and ethics are provided with the applications of AI in schools, and how ready or what mechanisms are in place to help students and teachers adapt to these technology changes.

Adopting AI in education plays a pivotal role in curbing academic dishonesty owing to the sophisticated impostor detection methods constructed by such AI systems. AI systems, for instance Turnitin and Grammarly, go beyond designing submission comparison systems with the help of daunting collections of printed and internet material by encompassing natural language processing (NLP) which serves the purpose of identifying shifts in writing patterns and possible cheating. Additionally, these tools help in enhancing "original" work by assessing student efforts and encouraging them to work on their submissions before resubmission. With the tendency of educational establishments to embrace AI-powered systems, their ethical implications such as respect for privacy, justice, and accountability must also be dealt with to avoid these technologies enhancing learning in an unbalanced and unfair manner.

There is a great urgency that calls for the need to ensure that AI will be used in a competent and constructive manner. The chapter ends with recommendations for teachers and educational institutions regarding the usage of AI tools while also inspiring ethical behaviour and addressing the upcoming era of AI in education.

The progressive incorporation of AI in education began from the very first clever pedagogical systems constructed way back in the 1970s. As the machine learning (ML) revolution in the 2000s arrived, AI-based platforms were capable of offering valuable insights to instructors regarding how the

DOI: 10.1201/9781003470304-9

students were performing, hence providing personalized education at scale. The term *artificial intelligence* refers to all computer systems designed to perform tasks that typically require human intelligence. ML is one of the subsets of AI and relates to algorithms that learn from past data and use that to predict outcomes or execute some kind of action. *Natural language processing* (NLP) is the term for another area in which AI research has gained recognition.

Plagiarism detection and writing improvement are two prominent uses of AI tools like Turnitin and Grammarly. Using chemical fingerprinting, text-matching algorithms, and semantic parsing, Turnitin checks every student submission against various academic sources for similarity and provides originality reports. In the same vein, Grammarly also examines the writing for grammar mistakes using NLP technology, and checks documents for plagiarism based on the writing styles, text structures, and contents. Notwithstanding, these two systems are not perfect; Turnitin's algorithms could be ineffective in tackling paraphrasing and irrelevant domain text appropriations, while the capabilities of Grammarly in detecting plagiarism do not perform well where complex syntax and closure plagiarism are in use. Notwithstanding, the advantages that such tools confer are not of a hundred percent guarantee and there is need for constant enhancements as newer forms of academic cheating keep emerging over time.

AI is revolutionizing education in several innovative ways that promote learning experiences as well as supporting teachers. An example is Carnegie Learning's MATHia, a tutoring AI that gives learners personalized feedback on math-related topics among others. Institutions like Georgia State even employ AI chatbots for student concerns over admissions and other financial aid issues. The implementation of AI systems such as Turnitin and Grammarly to deter academic dishonesty has been successfully carried out by several institutions including the University of Melbourne and Georgia State University.

9.1.1 Available Free Tools

Among such free tools would be facilitators for educational institutions that might integrate AI smoothly, some of which might be mentioned as follows, which facilitate teaching and enhance the experience in learning: they range from Grammarly or assistance for writing, from personalized learning on Khan Academy to actual hands-on Google AI experiments for AI idea testing, or from coming up with ideas to responding to a question with resources such as ChatGPT.

Educational technology has witnessed the development of AI systems, which have moved from purely automation systems in the early days to complicated systems in use today. In the past, simple tasks like computer-based tutoring or giving feedback were considered "AI". The rapid advancement of technology and the growth of AI in education exposes the potential in improving academic performances of learners. However, there are potential challenges raised concerning ethics of use, privacy, and academic integrity among others.

9.1.2 *The Rise of Plagiarism in the Digital Age*

The rise of plagiarism in the digital age is closely associated with experiences and perceptions of students born long after the digital revolution. Today's students who grew up surrounded by fast internet connection, smart cell phones, and highly sophisticated digital gadgets approach academic integrity differently compared with their predecessors.

Plagiarism has become rampant among scholars because of easy access to academic information through the internet which allows them to copy essays or even other types of writing that have been already executed (Gotterbarn, et al., 2006). This allows students who lack originality find their course mates' essays and pass them off as theirs because they do not understand how authentic pieces are written (Harris, 2001.

9.1.3 *The Role of AI in Upholding Academic Integrity*

The role of AI in supporting the transition into a digital age where everything is readily available online, it has become increasingly challenging for researchers to maintain academic integrity. This is because sophisticated tools used for both research and writing can be a boon or bane depending on their intended purpose.

AI tools are revolutionizing the preservation of academic integrity by using sophisticated algorithms to detect even the slightest forms of plagiarism and data fabrication. Tools like Turnitin and Grammarly do not only compare submissions against vast databases of academic work but also analyse writing patterns to identify potential dishonesty.

9.1.3.1 *Leveraging AI Tools to Uphold Academic Integrity*

AI tools have been increasingly applied in the learning environment to promote academic integrity and responsible student behaviour. Some of the widely used tools include Turnitin and Grammarly, whose efficiency in detecting plagiarism and writing aid has been unparalleled. For example, Turnitin searches through a vast database of academic works and online resources to match a student's submission against other similar pieces that may indicate plagiarism.

Besides detecting plagiarism, the quality and coherence of the writing that leads to improved academic integrity is enhanced in AI tools. Grammarly uses sophisticated algorithms that alert students about grammar, punctuation errors, style, even tone to ensure that they present quality work that was originally theirs.

In many empirical studies, it has been proven that AI tools can really enhance educational output and promote academic integrity. For example, Sutherland-Smith and Bansal (2015) found that Turnitin significantly reduced plagiarism cases in students, thus showing that awareness of plagiarism-detection mechanisms encourages originality in student work.

Intelligent tutoring systems (ITSs) also have shown promising potential in personalizing learning experiences. According to a meta-analysis conducted by Koedinger et al. (2015), ITSs can really enhance academic performance based on the individual learning needs of students. Automated essay scoring (AES) tools, according to Burstein et al. (2003), have been proven to provide feedback similar to that of human graders in maintaining high standards in writing assessments.

9.1.4 Public Interest in AI Technologies and Their Impact on Education

The rapid rise of AI technologies is generating a lot of public interest, especially with regard to their application in different sectors such as education. Rather, understanding the burdens and ethical challenges that come with the use of AI tools in educational institutions tends to tame the excitement. One area that has received quite some attention is the use of AI in maintaining academic integrity through, for example plagiarism detection. (Aler Tubella et al. (2024))

The use of AI has been a topic of debate with people taking sides for its use as a means of enhancing education and its use for academic dishonesty. The incorporation of AI technologies in education has brought ethical issues in the society about the fairness and transparency of the system as well as people's privacy.

9.1.4.1 Challenges and Restrictions to Implement AI in Education

Implementing AI in the education sector has quite a few challenges and constraints that have to be fulfilled for proper implementation. Many of these revolve around educator resistance, which often arises due to a lack of knowledge about AI or fear of being replaced. Rapid technological change may fear many educators, and the educators will become unwilling to try new tools. (Ali & Graepel, 2024)

Another potential chance is of over-reliance on technology in the teaching process. While AI tools will provide insights and support, over-reliance on these technologies can result in the dwindling of critical thinking ability among students. Educators may unwittingly shift their emphasis from creating deep learning experiences to using AI-driven methods for assessment or content delivery.

9.2 AI-Based Plagiarism-Detection Tools

9.2.1 *Overview of AI Tools in Plagiarism Detection*

AI tools in plagiarism detection will help to look for to what extent previous studies on the application of AI tools in plagiarism detection compared with the traditional methods available. In fact, research carried out by Chawla et al. (2022) proves that once AI-based system for detection is provided, the results obtained show better performance than conventional systems, achieving 90% accuracy detections against low figures of up to 70% detections with conventional systems.

AI tools, like Turnitin, Grammarly, and Copy leaks also known as internet-based plagiarism-detection systems, employ complex algorithms of NLP in deciphering not just the obvious cases of plagiarism but also its more subtle forms such as rephrasing and ideas misappropriating. Engaging language-related technologies such as Turnitin, Grammarly, and Copy leaks on the other hand entail the use of advanced, natural processing language and ML capabilities. Xian, et al., (2024)

AI tools are now able to understand context better, hence differentiating between commonly used phrases and real plagiarism. Therefore, the false rates are reduced and the level of assurance in the reports for plagiarism is thus enhanced. The major concern in using AI for detecting forms of plagiarism centre on its ethical implications; particularly concerning privacy issues and how likely it is predisposed to biases.

9.2.1.1 *How Machine Learning and NLP Work in Plagiarism Detection*

This makes ML enhance plagiarism detection because it allows models to analyse massive data, where they can learn vocabulary and structure patterns and writing habits through different texts. Through often-supervised learning, the model can identify similarities in plagiarism structure, paraphrasing, or structure-based similarities, as well as direct plagiarism.

NLP further strengthens these tools by breaking down and understanding the syntax, semantics, and context within texts. Techniques like tokenization and syntactic parsing can let the NLP algorithm actually pick up changes in the meaning and style, revealing an attempt at concealment through synonym substitutions or simply changing the sentence.

9.2.2 *The Role of AI Writing Aids in Education: ChatGPT and Others*

AI writing aids such as ChatGPT significantly impact to the changes in writing for students and professionals. This program is based on advanced NLP technology and offers enormous help to the user in creation, correction, and also enhancement of written works.(Xiong et al., 2024)

In addition to education, these AI text generators are employed in numerous industries including scientific writing where there is a high demand for precision and clarity in the written documents. (Roe et al., 2023) However, much of these writing aids help in enhancing one's writing skills and increasing productivity. (Koedinger et al., 2015)

9.2.2.1 Ethical Issues Related to AI's Use in Education

The benefits of academic integrity provided by the use of plagiarism-detection services supplemented by AI technologies come at a price too in terms of several ethical concerns, especially privacy and bias. For example, works produced by certain students are captured in AI systems so that future submissions of that work may be confirmed against that data in the system. This brings about issues on who owns the data and the risks involved in handling such information. (Khalifa & Albadawy, 2024)

A major factor that adds to the complexity of the ethical aspects related to the use of plagiarism-detection devices based on AI technologies entails their lack of transparency and accountability. A number of these tools are what is referred to as black box systems. Most users do not access or understand the algorithms that are used.

Incorporating AI resources in instruction necessitates additional training for the teachers on the tools and their ethical usage, with emphasis on privacy, fairness, and transparency. They have to encourage academic honesty, explaining that AI should exist to enhance learning rather than to monitor it. It is important to connect with the students regarding the education system using AI to gain their trust and help control the use.

When it comes to preserving academic honesty and promoting creativity and critical thinking, it is very important to find the right equilibrium between AI tools and human judgment. For example, AI and information communication technology (ICT) tools should be used by educators to support the work of teachers rather than replacing the teachers, such as the case of a plagiarism detector or a grammar checker. It is important, however, that the delicate balance of student assessment does not shift entirely to emotional interaction, engaging students to think, and providing instead a great deal of work to the teachers, but rather the way student work is evaluated (Roe, et al.,2023)

9.2.2.2 Practical Applications in Universities: Effective Use of AI Tools

For evaluating work at the University of California, Berkeley, a tremendous repository of academic and internet-based sources is examined in Turnitin, while taking advantage of ML and NLP to check on the originality. Academic integrity workshops are held together at Berkeley, where a majority of the focus is kept upon educating students about appropriate and honest practices in research and writing rather than merely imposing penalty on detected cases.

Similarly, Harvard University, among others, has started taking AI tools like Grammarly with NLP capabilities so that students can be mentored to improve their writings and citations to avoid incidental plagiarism. Harvard asks these students to use such assistive tools so that more is learned from mistakes.

9.2.2.3 Broader Impacts on Society and Global Context

Another extension of the discussion on AI in education could encompass the broader social implications, including employability and skills development. With educational institutions currently embracing AI technologies, they play a crucial role in shaping the workforce for the future. Even beyond this, AI changes the skills needed to compete in the job market and challenges learners to become more digitally aware and more thoughtful.

Examples of AI integration into education systems across continents will add value to the discussion as well as emphasize the global trends in AI adoption and the difficulties that come with it. Several countries are trialling AI technologies in education from personalized learning platforms in the United States to AI-powered tools used for management purposes in Finland, which are aimed at easing such burdens improving the efficiency of resource utilization.

To recapitulate, AI presents many advances with significant threats to academic honesty and educational activities. Therefore, when seeking integration techniques, institutions should be cautious and promote high-tech tools' usage with, for instance, creativity, ethics, and simplicity, among others such as the use of critical thinking.

9.2.3 Comparing Traditional versus AI-Driven Detection Methods

In the past, a teacher or an editor would detect if an essay contains plagiarized material, by looking at already known materials like books or other students' previously submitted essays. For instance, some of the methods used in this undertaking include checking printed material by comparing it with several books, other includes simple searches on keywords using databases (Md. Sharafat Chowdhury, 2024).

On the other hand, the use of AI tools employs intricate algorithmic models and NLP with ML techniques to explore and evaluate vast datasets in a very short time and very precisely. For example, these platforms such as Turnitin and Grammarly can be used even as a paper is being submitted to assess the paper against various online information including the journals, books, and other students' papers submitted.

However, it is challenging to develop this kind of technology because with all its merits, it can be invasive and pose implications on privacy and security as well as cause worry about false alarms. Conversely, typical methods are less effective/efficient, but allow for contextual and situational judgement from the reviews by the human in charge of that work.

9.3 Machine Learning Algorithms in Plagiarism Detection

9.3.1 Understanding Machine Learning in Academic Integrity

In the same vein as traditional methods of identifying plagiarism or using machines for that purpose, ML has become an important means highlighting the way academic integrity can be upheld especially in detecting and combating cheating. In algorithms built with ML, structure and misplaced elements are recognized in text, hence tracing copies and pasted materials that might be too hard to detect for traditional systems. This is useful especially in today's world where there are sophisticated devices that enable students to only modify some parts of the work with the help of different anti-plagiarism materials. (Macfarlane, 2021)

ML is a key area of focus for researchers the world over to safeguard academic integrity against unethical practices. The five most common obstacles include lack of validity aka false positives whereby certain original papers are deemed copied from other sources; there has to be a balance between extremes mentioned earlier.

But there are many challenges when it comes to detecting cases of plagiarism. Certain original works might get wrongfully classified under this classification, thus generating false positives; hence it is necessary to establish an equilibrium between these two binomial spectrums that is, a machine and a human if it is struck at a certain moment in time, sometimes resulting in miscommunication or even abuse incidences. (Burstein et al., 2003)

9.3.2 Training Algorithms with Plagiarism Datasets

The process of developing algorithms to detect the existence of plagiarism is a meticulous exercise that builds significantly on the quality and the type of datasets involved. Data preprocessing consists of those actions that are performed in order to prepare raw data for processing, particularly, for running of the algorithms (Parkins, 2024)

Data Augmentation: Among the techniques used to manipulate data sets are the use of synonym or sentence-positioning alteration or any other methods of that nature. This step improves this aspect of identifying and appreciating variations in writing and the various tricks employed in writing to avoid tracing copied works. The performance of any model in practice depends on the training of the model and the input data given, thus making it a critical component in the design of a working plagiarism detector.

9.3.3 Key Algorithms: Support Vector Machines and Neural Networks

Support vector machines (SVMs) find the best hyperplane that can separate different classes in multidimensional space. However, SVMs may fail on noisy datasets, particularly urban environments, where there are mixed pixels for instance the regions where trees grow together with apartments. When classes overlap, SVMs may perform poorly giving rise to wrong predictions and this can be demonstrated by greater proportions of errors between urban vegetation and built-up places. (Chowdhury, 2024)

Since neural networks (NNs) have the ability to learn from data using layers of interconnected neurons, they are much better than others when it comes to intricate classification challenges. In situations where land cover types cannot be easily distinguished by linear boundaries, these representations prove very useful since they can also represent complex relationships hidden in the data. On the other hand, for NNs to succeed, overcoming the misconceptions, integrating with legacy systems and also addressing legal and financial challenges, and establishing impact metrics are key to successfully implementing AI in the academic integrity as shown in Table 9.1.

9.4 Natural Language Processing (NLP) Techniques

9.4.1 Role of NLP in Detecting Content Similarity

Understanding textual overlaps, particularly in academic or scholarly writing, can be challenging, but rather, this is where NLP comes in. Syntactic parsing is one more sophisticated NLP approach which generates a tree that exhibits grammatical constituents of a given sentence. With such techniques, NLP can detect paraphrasing, synonyms, and other complex ways to change contents that simpler systems may miss. (Mohamed Khalifa & Albadawy, 2024)

9.4.2 Semantic Analysis for Plagiarism Detection

The semantic analysis part of linguistics deals with how the content in a piece of text or a code is interpreted rather than merely matching the syntactic surface of texts.

Latent Semantic Analysis (LSA): It is the most widely used and most sophisticated method of semantic analysis when it comes to understanding how different terms relate in the paper or collection of papers based on the word co-occurrence and occurrence patterns.

Advantages of Using LSA in Copied Text Detection: LSA possesses the strength to carry out an analysis and surface changes effectively. Detection of conceptual parallels: LSA is able to locate such codes—even if they have entirely different words and structures—as long as the concepts are the same and as such, it is a more sophisticated detection system.

Table 9.1 Challenges and Solutions in Implementing AI for Academic Integrity

Challenge	Description	Potential solutions
Overcoming misconceptions and lack of knowledge	Misconceptions about AI capabilities due to media representation, anecdotes, and general ignorance	– Develop all-inclusive training programmes for educators, including hands-on workshops and seminars – Provide clear guidelines on AI's capabilities and limitations
Institutionalizing AI in higher education	Legacy systems and LMSs face challenges in integrating AI tools as a result of compatibility problems; this is made worse by the existence of data silos and absence of technical assistance.	– Put your money where it counts by getting adaptable AI solutions integrated into the current systems – Decrease compartmentalization by making data management seamless
Legal and regulatory considerations	Determining accountability on account of decision-making with the usage of AI faces several ethical and legal challenges like automation bias, transparency, informed consent, among others.	– Create ethical regulations and guidelines that are explicit – Make certain that AI instruments are open and allow humans to intervene in decision-making
Resource allocation and financial costs	The high costs involved in AI tool implementation as far as getting them, training, maintaining, and operating are concerned; institutions may be cautious due to limited budget and absence of urgent financial benefits	– Formulate financial strategies that encompass both public and private cooperation – Cost-efficient AI solutions with gradual execution must be given precedence – Utilize, if possible, AI tools that are open-source
Measuring impact and effectiveness	One of the main challenges in evaluating effects of AI tools on education results has been failure to assess what inputs are required for successful implementation	– To evaluate how well AI is performing in education, it is important to create metrics and KPIs – Before the actual implementation, it is essential to do pilot projects and collect information on the effects of AI

Challenges and Limitations: However, there are some limitations as far as the use of LSA for plagiarism detection is concerned:

Dimensionality Problems: These are sentences which need to be steamed as they are long winds. In my opinion instead of steaming, if segmentation is done, it will create a good fluency of ideas and thus better understanding of the passage. (Cosma & Joy, 2012)

Application in Plagiarism-Detection Systems: Although LSA is primarily focused on text analytics, its application to source code plagiarism detection is an emerging challenge.

9.4.3 Analysing Syntactic Parsing and Its Role in Detecting Structure Sensitivity in Texts

For the comprehension and processing of natural language (NL), there is a need to conduct a syntactic analysis of its constructions. In information extraction (IE) and opinion mining tasks, for instance, even slight differences in the syntax of the same information can lead to the correct classification. (Galitsky, 2013)

Moreover, syntactic structure awareness plays an important role when it comes to searching and evaluation of relevance. In layman's terms, syntactic parsing and structure sensitivity mark out an additional level of processing that aids completion of most language-processing tasks by offering more precise ways of deriving meaning contained in the texts.

9.5 Advantages of AI in Academic Integrity

9.5.1 Strategies for Ensuring Originality and Enhancing Quality in Academic Writing with AI Tools

There are programs available today like plagiarism-detection software, for instance Turnitin or Copy scape, which searches through many databases with all the past student projects and is able to identify cases of even accidental cheating among others. All that is required is within reach: the correction of grammatical mistakes or a study of sentence structures and their relevance will allow one to construct a new sentence which conveys the same message as that of another text. Such programs as Grammarly or ChatGPT bring about substantial enhancement in the target languages used while writing thereby promoting clarity or coherence in completing any given task.(Mohamed Khalifa & Mona Albadawy, 2024.)

Furthermore, this also allows AI to be utilized in a more positive light where ethical writing practices are encouraged through more effective and efficient means of monitoring academic dishonesty or misconduct by teachers and institutions. For example, one may identify negative patterns such as excessive dependence on AI to produce written material, which could lead to inadequate academic authenticity. (Gustilo et al., 2024)

9.5.2 Advancements in Plagiarism Detection and AI-Driven Content Feedback for Academic Writing

The system with the aid of GPT-3.5 generates different datasets that include a wide range of texts with plagiarized materials, each covering different types of plagiarism. In order to detect true positives, the system applies BERT, and also SBERT, a variant of BERT that generates sentence embeddings. BERT is a powerful model that can appreciate differences in text variation and complex text editing because it can understand the concept of the text in context.

Besides this, Facebook AI Similarity Search (FAISS) is used in order to facilitate information retrieval so that it is faster than ever before. FAISS speeds up the process by building an index on clusters of text embeddings allowing potentially similar text identification instantly. This helps narrow down what requires deeper analysis and thus save computation power in terms of resources at hand.

The system's content feedback feature gives users particular useful information about their texts. After it finds (the) possible plagiarisms, this program gives feedback about what kind of (plagiarism) it was and how much of it was detected.

9.5.3 The Double-Edged Sword: AI-Generated Text and Its Detection

Plagiarism is the act of using someone else's work as one's own without proper citation. However, the emergence of AI is rapidly changing the understanding of plagiarism. Mainly because AI content detectors are often ineffective, compare-and-contrast essays have been the greatest source of worry for teachers in flagging any signs of copying.(Binglin Chen et al. (2024))

The primary reason for this is the ease and relative effectiveness of concealment. Self-plagiarism refers to the procedure in which a person, without referring to the usage of one's own previously published text, publishes the same or very similar work in multiple places or purposes. AI generated content can still be considered constructive plagiarism even when it doesn't copy someone else's work because it recreates the general message without capturing the specific and distinct expression of the idea. (Perkins (2024))

"Cry, my beloved country ,for the world and the way it has deteriorated in what is truly an exceptional story. Culture continues to revolve, despite all efforts around the biological padding that constitutes professional ethics in any social care- oriented field". Academic lifting and use of copied work, self- or otherwise, still happens under the cloak of ethical behaviour towards nursing. This is as a result of children's natural curiosity to explore everyone's culture, creators included, who paints a picture, fabricates a sculpture, or composes a tune.

However, this is an issue that many students today have no idea of its dimensions or related rights. Offenses include, but are not limited to, purposive reproduction of an artwork, building, or any other creative output by intending to claim as one's own that which one has not created. The culture of cyberspace and most of its contents have become negative, creating a cultural rather than physical, barrier to the study and understanding of rehabilitation as a discipline.

9.6 Navigating Ethical Challenges in AI-Based Plagiarism-Detection Systems

However, incorporating AI into education raises profound ethical issues. Algorithmic prejudice, data security, and responsibility for AI-based decision-making are among the issues. This would typically cite documents such as the AI Ethics Guidelines by UNESCO, as organizations draft robust policies on the application of AI that encourages innovation but safeguards ethics.

It is necessary to take the human stand in order to acquire important skills such as empathy, critical imaginaries, and ethical reasoning. It is therefore argued that justice will be when AI can only act as an assistant to the tutor and not replace him on all fronts. Such ground-breaking educational initiatives, which blend project-based training or cooperative learning methods with AI, are likely to foster creativity in such settings conducive to children's growth and development, and preserve their humanity in the face of current technological advancements.

There may ever be resistance to risk replacing teaching strategies using AI tools amongst educators because of possible concerns over technology reliability, lack of awareness, or fear of losing their job. In order to counter such limitations, it is important for institutions to channel resources towards professional development that trains educators on the use of such tools and on the efficacy of AI tools on academic integrity or student achievement. Educators may also demonstrate engagement to the resistance through participation in the resolution of issues or concerns that they may have over the institution of a given tool. Effective communication and provision of support on a regular basis will promote the willingness of the teachers to embrace the technology and reduce their apprehension.

9.6.1 *Striking a Balance between AI Technology and Academic Freedom*

Making sure that ephemeral advancements cater more towards educational practices than constrain them is not easy, and a thoughtful balancing act between technology and academic freedom would be necessary. The downside here is technology-driven coercions which may push for common ways of doing things in classrooms; thus, jeopardizing teachers' power to select or modify these methods according to their own field specialization and teaching strategies.

The other area is the involvement of the current academic discussion relating to ethical concerns surrounding the adoption of AI in educational environments. For example, Mennella et al., (2024), mentioned the possibility of biases in the AI algorithms, therefore calling for more transparency and accountability through the development and application of these algorithms. (Macfarlane, 2021)

Although technological integration has its advantages to the teaching–learning process, technology integration may also come across as a more managed and organized system where the emphasis is on age norms rather than educational creativity. For instance, there are certain specific computer applications that are made compulsory to the students by the colleges as well as high school, which makes it difficult for the instructors to adapt different styles according to the subject matter or the styles of teaching employed by them. (Currie, 2023)

Education systems must find ways to embrace the rapid technological changes without sacrificing the core values of academic freedom; hence technology should be used to assist in teaching rather than dictating the ways of teaching. This suggests that there should be interaction between the employees of the institution and the administration so that the positive aspects of the technologies and the issues of privacy are combined.

9.6.2 *Addressing Misuse and Potential Pitfalls of AI Tools*

The adverse consequences of generative AI tools when misused call for an integrated approach to manage and reduce the risk factors involved. (Cotton, 2023) Hence the first action in preventing abuse of this technology involves recognizing the range of strategies that are adopted by these evil actors, which go as far as inferring human characteristics to objects and even altering video recordings to create fake images (Mouta, et al., 2024).

In addition, consistent investigations and observations are necessary to keep up with changing scams. Measures such as OECD AI Incidents Monitor and AI Incident Database offer information about latest risks or events which can help make effective mitigating plans. Also, the AI-powered plagiarism-detection process is shown in Figure 9.1.

9.6.3 *Promoting Ethical AI Practices through Stakeholder Education*

The people who have been informed about AI technology can take better decisions about this thing because they know what are its ethical considerations and it leads them to get the techniques that are more ethical in this field. It calls for a qualified person to educate stakeholders on the acceptable and efficient use of these technologies.

One way forward would be implementing training sessions based on scenarios dealing with various ethical dilemmas alongside real-life applications of AI. By doing so before any unethical behaviour occurs, it

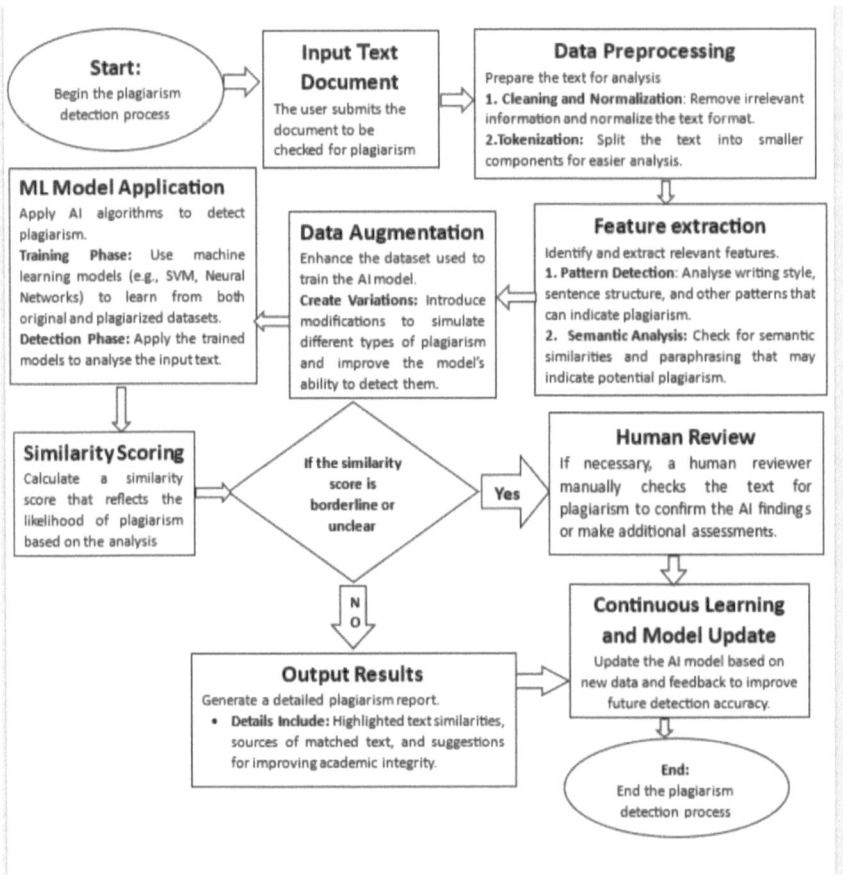

Figure 9.1 AI-Powered Plagiarism Detection Process.

gives stakeholders an opportunity that they can use for purposes of dealing with possible ethical dilemmas. For instance, participants could consider hypothetical cases involving AI. (Redrup Hill et al., 2023)

Through the aforementioned scenarios, stakeholders can create strategies that will help reduce risks and make sure AI tools promote rather than hinder educational equality. Also, continuous professional growth programmes for teachers and other interested parties must be created to keep them abreast of the recent trends in AI as well as ethical standards.

To round off, informing stakeholders about appropriate use of AI requires them to be equipped with both theoretical understanding and practical skills. Stakeholders who have extensive knowledge on the implications of using AI from an ethical perspective can assist with its better integration within educational contexts by provision of materials that address these kinds of issues head-on.

9.7 Challenges in Implementing AI Tools

9.7.1 Overcoming Misconceptions and Lack of Knowledge

The application of AI technology, including generative AI in education is faced with various hindrances including stereotypes and lack of knowledge by different players. There are many factors that account for the misconception of AI, for instance, the portrayal of AI in the media, individual experiences, and the public's understanding of what it really can or cannot do. In effect, the context of learning is assumed to be filled with care, creativity, and critical thinking, and all these attributes only belong to the teachers. Another common dilemma is the so-called mystique. (Mouta et al., 2024)

Yet another obstacle is the gap between the promise of AI and its real-world application. In order for this to happen, targeted educational initiatives should be developed that clarify what AI can and cannot do. Through workshops, seminars, or hands-on training sessions, AI will be demystified as regards both technical issues and pedagogy.

9.7.1.1 Understanding Large Language Models (LLMs) and Hallucinations

Large language models (LLMs) are impacting education in great ways: personalization, instant access to information, and tools that help students be more creative. However, there is this very concerning phenomenon of "hallucinations," or generating false information or really misleading information as if it were factual. Such hallucinations in a learning environment can mislead students, undermine their understanding, and create distrust regarding AI-driven tools. (Asbai, 2024)

However, educators must teach these digital literacy skills to their learners and discuss the critical review of content generated by the AI. Thus, teaching the curriculum with the critical discussion about LLM limitation will enable educators to ensure that the students distinguish correctly between the right information and the wrong one. Learning institutions should develop validation frameworks to test the output from LLMs and stress the fact that fact-checking is the way to go. (Alkaissi & McFarlane, 2023)

9.7.2 Institutionalizing AI in Higher Education

Assisting in Ensuring Integration with Existing Systems: One of the challenges faced while integrating AI technologies into the higher education structure is ensuring their relevance to the current systems in place. Additionally, the issue is exacerbated by the presence of disconnected data repositories within the organization.

Costs of Resources and their Allocation: One more major difficulty introduced by the integration of AI applications into the university system concerns the commercial side of the issue. The incorporation of such technologies in the beginning always means a lot of expenditure, more so in cases where a lot of institutions work on tight budgets.

9.7.3 Legal and Regulatory Considerations

Use of AI in healthcare is rather complex primarily due to digital pathology which is influenced by legal and ethical issues. For example, Barrett's oesophagus poses all these challenges in Gehrung et al. (2021) system which is a semi-automated system for the early detection of Barrett's oesophagus. It is the kind of problem that illustrates the importance of having interdisciplinary conversations about those rules and use so that patients' trust and safety will not be at risk from AI.

One example of this comes from the fear of patients towards an artificially intelligent device (AID) which can be seen in two scenarios: (1) when a human being's input is very crucial, and (2) where other professionals also have their experiences/background to support the decisions they make that may not please the client. It is related to the Gehrung et al. case where there exists a semi-automated system for Barrett's oesophagus with similar issues (Redrup Hill, et al., 2023).

9.8 Preparing for AI Integration in Education

9.8.1 Preparing Educators for AI Integration

There are several dimensions that educators preparing for AI integration encounter that support their appropriate use of tools and technology in teaching and learning.

Understanding AI Technologies: First and foremost, it is crucial to learn about the basics of AI and its technology—its uses, limitations, and how effective it can be in a classroom environment.

Ethics and Responsible Use: One of the greatest challenges that educators are faced with is that of the responsible use of AI in education.

Curriculum Integration: Integrating AI into the education systems also involves gear that proceeds laying a foundation for teaching with AI.

Education in a Dynamic Period Long-Term Aspect: Contemporary technology development is a fast-paced period, therefore these professions should always include an ongoing professional training program. For example, even if one attended relevant conferences or somehow took an online course, they should still be a part of particular communities speaking on the topic so that the content on AI does not get stale.

Institutional Support for Effective AI Integration: The integration of AI in education calls for support from the respective institutions. Schools and colleges should provide materials, facilities, and education policies that will make it possible to use AI technology. As such, among other things, they have to invest in information technology infrastructure, offer technical assistance, and create a culture of experimentation as well as innovation around AI tools.

9.8.2 Promoting Ethical Use of AI Among Students and Developing AI Literacy in Academic Communities

In order to assist teachers in addressing the ethical challenges posed by the use of AI tools in academia, existing ethical principles and guidance can be of great help. (Southworth et al., 2023) For, instance, UNESCO provided AI Ethics Guidelines that promote ideals such as transparency, fair play, accountability, and privacy, for individuals to ensure a comprehensive approach in dealing with the challenges posed by technology in education. Such frameworks allow for the resolution of ethical issues that may arise when AI technologies are applied in practice. (Zhang et al., 2023)

The rapid rise of AI further requires that AI literacy at the K–12 level be promoted, as students have to be informed about not only technical areas but also the ethical and wider social implications of AI.

9.9 The Future of AI in Academic Integrity and Education

9.9.1 Innovations in AI for Academic Integrity and Embracing Traditional Academic Virtues

The newer technologies that are found in AI have contributed to the development of fresh strategies for maintaining academic integrity in higher learning. For instance, Turnitin and Grammarly (plagiarism-detection software) are now more effective than before in spotting complicatedly paraphrased and distorted assignments, as opposed to outright copy-pasted drafts.

In addition, AI helps to improve the online examination proctoring systems which not only help to detect incidents of cheating even during the sessions but also has the capability of detecting cases of plagiarism. For instance, these tools may assess the movement of the camera, the typing pace at the keyboard, and the environment surrounding the user in order to check for any dishonest actions.

9.9.2 The Evolving Landscape of AI in Education

Technology has made great strides and as such the AI in education sector is undergoing great transformations. The integration of AI in education is not only enhancing the availability of teaching resources for teachers, the methods of teaching and the way students learn are also changing. It comes with both promises and constraints, such as devising new curricula, revising educational approaches, and handling ethical dilemmas.

9.9.3 *Responsible and Collaborative AI Integration*

This will be vast and exciting regarding the future of AI in education, which points towards a responsible and collaborative approach that does not jeopardize the virtues of academia but rather enhances the outcome of learning. Predictions show how personal learning pathways will change by being facilitated by AI, responding to the specific needs of the students while maintaining teacher oversight.

By embracing diversified perspectives into a coherent and holistic discussion of AI, one aims to provide for a real understanding in AI in schools. The other reason is that it helps in the recognition of voices of marginalized groups so that AI tools are developed and implemented in ways that are inclusive and equitable for educational settings.

The implications of AI go beyond academic integrity to broader societal issues, such as digital equity and the evolving job market. Ensuring digital equity will allow all students to reap the benefits of AI-driven education, regardless of socio-economic status. Above that, future students need preparation on what the long run shall hold.

9.10 Conclusion

On one hand, the introduction of new AI tools in academia comes with benefits, while, on the other, it has its fair share of drawbacks in so far as it affects academic dishonesty and plagiarism. For example, the University of California, Berkeley, utilized a software named Turnitin which was one of the most prevalent software used for checking plagiarism in order to curb the level of cheating amongst the students.

In addition, this chapter underscores the importance of equipping teachers and students with the necessary training for the effective adoption of AI in the educational norm. Hence, this requires that there are higher expectations for the teachers as regards how they are able to use the technology and more so the ethics of using the technology in a way that encourages the use of AI while fostering academic integrity.

This implies that it is essential for the contemporary education discourse to address the implications of AI technologies. One of the many challenges of integrating AI into academic practice is that the acceptance of the new technology compromises the efficiency of the previous academic standards. Current studies show that AI is enhancing non-plagiarism programs; however, it does incite education paradigm shifts concerning plagiarism, creativity, and learning.

One illustration of this is the technological acceptance model (TAM) which would help explain the usefulness and ease of use of AI tools to the teachers and the students, respectively (Davis, 1989). In research done by (Ghimire et al., 2024), it was suggested that AI is not an issue for educators as they are trained and aware of such technologies so able to use them ethically and for the best reasons.

Along the same lines, the existing discourse on AI has the effect of ethics on academic integrity which is further enriched by the words of scholars like Binns (2018) who argues that there should be accountability and a guarantee of caveats in the systems of AI.

In summary, although AI tools hold much promise in addressing challenges in plagiarism and academic dishonesty, their integration into educational systems should be informed by theoretical frameworks and ethical considerations. There is no doubt that continuous improvement in AI will lead to its wider application in the education sector providing more advanced structures for maintaining academic honesty and individualized learning. Future directions in research should focus on the societal issues surrounding the use of these technologies, the implementation of AI in various learning environments, and how teachers will change to guarantee the appropriate utilization of these technologies.

References

Aler Tubella, A., Mora-Cantallops, M. & Nieves, J.C. (2024). How to teach responsible AI in higher Education: challenges and opportunities. *Ethics Inf. Technol.*, *26*, 3. https://doi.org/10.1007/s10676-023-09733-7

Ali, H. & Graepel, T. (2024). *Educational Revolution: Overcoming Challenges in Generative AI Adoption.* DOI: 10.13140/RG.2.2.26609.29282.

Alkaissi, H. & McFarlane, S. I. (2023). Artificial hallucinations in ChatGPT: Implications in scientific writing. *Cureus*, *15*(2). DOI: 10.7759/cureus.35179

Asbai, A. (2024). Mitigating Hallucination in Large Language Model Code Generation for Higher Education: An Evaluation of Retrieval Augmented Generation. Retrieved from https://urn.kb.se/resolve?urn=urn:nbn:se:kth:diva-351389

Binns, R. (2018). *Fairness in machine learning: Lessons from political philosophy.* In *Proceedings of the 2018 Conference on Fairness, Accountability, and Transparency* (pp. 149–159). Association for Computing Machinery. https://doi.org/10.1145/3287560.3287583

Burstein, J., Chodorow, M., & Leacock, C. (2003). Automated essay scoring using machine learning. In *Proceedings of the 2003 conference of the North American chapter of the Association for Computational Linguistics* (pp. 188–195). Association for Computational Linguistics. https://doi.org/10.3115/1073445.1073475

Chawla, S., Aggarwal, P., & Kaur, R. (2022). An intelligent approach for semantic plagiarism detection in scientific papers. *Proceedings of the 2022 International Conference on Computational Intelligence and Data Science (ICCIDS)*, 1–5. https://doi.org/10.1109/ICCIDS54856.2022.9799070

Chen, B., Lewis, C. M., West, M. & Zilles, C. (2024). Plagiarism in the Age of Generative AI: Cheating Method Change and Learning Loss in an Intro to CS Course. In *Proceedings of the Eleventh ACM Conference on Learning @ Scale (L@S'24)*. Association for Computing Machinery, New York, NY, 75–85. https://doi.org/10.1145/3657604.3662046

Chowdhury, M. S. (2024). Comparison of accuracy and reliability of random forest, support vector machine, artificial neural network and maximum likelihood method in land use/cover classification of urban setting. *Environ. Challenges*, *14*, 100800. ISSN 2667-0100, https://doi.org/10.1016/j.envc.2023.100800

Cosma, G. & Joy, M. (2012). An approach to source-code plagiarism detection and investigation using latent semantic analysis. *IEEE Trans. Comput.*, *61*(3), 379–394. DOI: 10.1109/TC.2011.223

Cotton, D. R. E., Cotton, P. A. & Shipway, J. R. (2023). Chatting and cheating: Ensuring academic integrity in the era of ChatGPT. *Innov. Educ. Teach. Int.*, *61*(2), 228–239. https://doi.org/10.1080/14703297.2023.2190148

Currie, G. M. (2023). Academic integrity and artificial intelligence: Is ChatGPT hype, hero or heresy? *Seminars Nucl. Med.*, *53*(5), 719–730, ISSN 0001-2998, https://doi.org/10.1053/j.semnuclmed.2023.04.008

Davis, F. D. (1989). Perceived usefulness, perceived ease of use, and user acceptance of information technology. *MIS Quarterly, 13*(3), 319–340. https://doi.org/10.2307/249008

Gehrung, M., Crispin-Ortuzar, M., Berman, A.G., O'Donovan, M., Fitzgerald, R.C., & Markowetz, F. (2021, May). Triage-driven diagnosis of Barrett's esophagus for early detection of esophageal adenocarcinoma using deep learning. *Nat. Med.* 27(5), 833–841. doi: 10.1038/s41591-021-01287-9. Epub 2021 Apr 15. PMID: 33859411.

Ghimire, A., Prather, J., & Edwards, J. (2024). Generative AI in education: A study of educators' awareness, sentiments, and influencing factors. *arXiv preprint arXiv:2403.15586*. https://arxiv.org/abs/2403.15586

Gotterbarn, D. Miller, K. & Impagliazzo, J. (2006). Plagiarism and scholarly publications: An ethical analysis. *Proceedings Frontiers in Education 36th Annual Conference*, San Diego, CA, USA, 2006, 22–27, doi: 10.1109/FIE.2006.322365.

Gustilo, L., Ong, E. & Lapinid, M.R. (2024). Algorithmically-driven writing and academic integrity: Exploring educators' practices, perceptions, and policies in AI era. *Int. J. Educ. Integr.*, *20*, 3. https://doi.org/10.1007/s40979-024-00153-8

Harris, R. (2001). *The plagiarism handbook: Strategies for preventing, detecting, and dealing with plagiarism*. Pyrczak Publishing.

Khalifa, M. & Albadawy, M. (2024). Using artificial intelligence in academic writing and research: An essential productivity tool. *Comput. Methods Prog. Biomed. Update*, *5*, 100145. ISSN 2666-9900, https://doi.org/10.1016/j.cmpbup.2024.100145

Koedinger, K. R., McLaughlin, E. A., & Stamper, J. C. (2015). A new approach to studying the impact of intelligent tutoring systems on academic performance. *Educ. Psychol.*, *50*(3), 144–155. https://doi.org/10.1080/00461520.2015.1060366

Macfarlane, B. (2021). Why choice of teaching method is essential to academic freedom: A dialogue with Finn. *Teach. High. Educ.*, *29*(2), 536–548. https://doi.org/10.1080/13562517.2021.2007473

Mennella, C., Maniscalco, U., De Pietro, G., & Esposito, M. (2024, Feb 15). Ethical and regulatory challenges of AI technologies in healthcare: A narrative review. *Heliyon*. 10(4), e26297. doi: 10.1016/j.heliyon.2024.e26297. PMID: 38384518; PMCID: PMC10879008.

Mouta, A., Torrecilla-Sánchez, E. M. & Pinto-Llorente, A. M. (2024). Design of a future scenarios toolkit for an ethical implementation of artificial intelligence

in education. *Educ. Inf. Technol. 29*, 10473–10498. https://doi.org/10.1007/s10
639-023-12229-y

Perkins, M. (2024). Academic integrity considerations of AI large language models in
the post-pandemic era: ChatGPT and beyond. *J. Univ. Teach. Learn. Pract.*, 20(2),
Article 7. https://doi.org/10.53761/1.20.02.07

Redrup Hill, E., Mitchell, C., Brigden, T. & Hall, A. (2023). Ethical and legal considerations influencing human involvement in the implementation of artificial intelligence in a clinical pathway: A multi-stakeholder perspective. *Front. Digit. Health*,
5, 1139210. DOI: https://doi.org/10.3389/fdgth.2023.1139210

Roe, J., Renandya, W. A. & Jacobs, G. M. (2023). A review of AI-powered writing
tools and their implications for academic integrity in the language classroom. *J. Eng.
Appl. Linguist.*, 2(1), Article 3. DOI: https://doi.org/10.59588/2961-3094.1035

Southworth, J., Migliaccio, K., Glover, J., Glover, J., Reed, D., McCarty, C.,
Brendemuhl, J. & Thomas, A. (2023). Developing a model for AI across the curriculum: Transforming the higher education landscape via innovation in AI literacy.
Comput. Educ. Artif. Intell., 4, 100127. ISSN 2666-920X, https://doi.org/10.1016/
j.caeai.2023.100127

Sutherland-Smith, W., & Bansal, S. (2015). Turnitin and the prevention of plagiarism: An evaluation of its efficacy in promoting academic integrity. *J. Acad.
Integrity*, 11(2), 85–98. https://doi.org/10.1007/s40979-015-0010-3

Xian, J., Yuan, J., Zheng, P. & Chen, D. (2024). BERT-enhanced retrieval tool for
homework plagiarism detection system. *arXiv preprint arXiv:2404.01582*

Xiong, J., Yang, J., Yan, L., Awais, M., Ayub Khan, A., Alizadehsani, R., & Rajendra
Acharya, U. (2024). Efficient reinforcement learning-based method for plagiarism
detection boosted by a population-based algorithm for pretraining weights. *Expert
Syst. Appl.*, 238(Part E), 122088. ISSN 0957-4174, https://doi.org/10.1016/
j.eswa.2023.122088

Zhang, H., Lee, I., Ali, S. DiPaola, D., Cheng, Y., & Breazeal, C. (2023). Integrating
ethics and career futures with technical learning to promote AI literacy for middle
school students: An exploratory study. *Int. J. Artif. Intell. Educ.*, 33, 290–324.
https://doi.org/10.1007/s40593-022-00293-3

10 Unlocking Potential

Personalizing Learning and Assessment with Cutting-Edge Technologies

R. Renugadevi, Maridu Bhargavi,
G. Kalaiarasi, P. Ranjith Kumar,
A. Arul Edwin Raj, and B. Saritha

10.1 Introduction

The educational landscape is undergoing a profound transformation due to the increasing integration of technology in teaching and learning. One of the most promising developments is the use of cutting-edge technologies to personalize learning and assessment, enabling educators to unlock the full potential of each student. Personalization offers tailored educational experiences that meet individual learning needs, styles, and paces, while advanced assessment tools provide more accurate and adaptive evaluation methods (Holmes et al., 2019). This chapter explores how emerging technologies are revolutionizing personalized learning and assessment, with a focus on artificial intelligence (AI), machine learning (ML), big data analytics, and adaptive learning platforms.

10.2 Contributions of the Work

This chapter offers several key contributions to the understanding of personalized learning and assessment through the use of cutting-edge technologies. These contributions are vital for educators, researchers, and policymakers aiming to improve educational outcomes by integrating advanced technological tools. The primary contributions include

Comprehensive Overview of Technological Innovations: This chapter provides an in-depth exploration of how AI, ML, big data analytics, and adaptive learning platforms are transforming personalized learning and assessment. It highlights real-world examples, such as AI-powered tutoring systems and adaptive assessments, illustrating how these technologies tailor educational experiences to individual students' needs.

Identification of Personalized Learning Benefits: By synthesizing existing research, the chapter underscores the advantages of personalized learning, including increased student engagement, improved academic performance, and the promotion of self-directed learning. These insights demonstrate the potential for technology to make education more effective,

DOI: 10.1201/9781003470304-10

equitable, and accessible, benefiting diverse learners across various educational settings.

Analysis of AI and Data-Driven Personalization: The chapter delves into how AI and ML are being used to analyze student behavior, performance, and engagement in real time. This analysis enables a more responsive and individualized approach to learning and assessment. The chapter outlines how AI-powered systems adjust content and instruction dynamically, contributing to a richer and more supportive learning environment.

Examination of Adaptive Assessment Technologies: The work contributes to the growing body of knowledge on adaptive assessments, detailing how AI-driven platforms modify question difficulty in real time to match student ability levels. By offering immediate feedback, these systems provide a more accurate and efficient evaluation of students' skills and knowledge, which is a significant advancement over traditional testing methods.

Incorporation of Gamification for Personalized Learning: The chapter highlights the role of gamification in enhancing personalized learning, showing how game-based elements motivate and engage students. By customizing challenges and providing real-time rewards, gamification platforms help learners stay engaged, while also offering personalized feedback that supports learning progression.

Insights into Future Directions and Challenges: Finally, the chapter outlines both the potential and the challenges associated with implementing personalized learning technologies. It addresses critical issues such as data privacy, equity in access, and the ethical use of student data. These insights guide future research and policy initiatives aimed at improving the safe and equitable use of educational technologies. In summary, this chapter contributes to the understanding of how cutting-edge technologies can be effectively harnessed to personalize learning and assessment. It emphasizes the importance of adopting innovative approaches to meet the diverse needs of students, while also recognizing the challenges and ethical considerations involved in leveraging these technologies as mentioned in Table 10.1.

10.3 The Need for Personalization in Education

Traditional education systems, often designed to cater to the average learner, have long struggled to address the diverse needs of individual students. Standardized curricula and assessments may fail to engage students with different learning preferences, backgrounds, and abilities. Personalized learning, in contrast, adapts content, instruction, and pace to the unique characteristics of each learner, making education more effective and equitable.

Research shows that personalized learning can improve student outcomes by increasing engagement, fostering deeper understanding, and encouraging self-directed learning (McCarthy et al., 2020). However, scaling personalized learning has historically been a challenge due to limited resources, large class

Table 10.1 Comparison table that incorporates the different technologies discussed in the context of personalized learning

Technology	Description	Key features	Challenges	Examples
Artificial intelligence (AI)	AI systems analyze data to tailor learning experiences and provide real-time feedback	Real-time feedback, personalized learning pathways, predictive analytics	Data privacy concerns, bias in algorithms	AI-powered tutoring systems (e.g., Carnegie Learning's MATHia)
Machine learning (ML)	ML algorithms continuously improve the system's ability to adapt based on data inputs.	Dynamic content adaptation, performance analysis	Requires large datasets, potential biases in decision-making	DreamBox Learning, Knewton
Big data analytics	Analyzes large volumes of data to understand learning behaviors and outcomes	Learning analytics dashboards, predictive modeling	Data overload, privacy, and security concerns	BrightBytes, Classcraft
Adaptive learning platforms	Systems that adjust instructional content based on real-time student performance	Customizes pace and difficulty, real-time adjustments	Scalability issues, requires substantial tech infrastructure	DreamBox, ALEKS
Gamification	Uses game-based elements like rewards and challenges to engage students in learning	Increases engagement, offers personalized challenges and feedback	Over-reliance on extrinsic motivation, balancing educational content and game mechanics	Kahoot, Classcraft

sizes, and a reliance on standardized testing. Emerging technologies offer potential solutions to these challenges.

10.3.1 Challenges in Personalization

Scalability and Resource Constraints: One of the primary challenges of implementing personalized learning is scaling it to accommodate a large number of students, especially in resource-constrained environments. Traditional models of personalized instruction often require one-on-one attention or small group settings, which are difficult to scale in schools with large class sizes and limited teaching staff (Pane et al., 2017). Teachers may lack the time or tools needed to implement individualized learning plans for each student.

Solution: The use of adaptive learning platforms and AI-powered tools can help address scalability issues. These technologies allow for real-time data collection on student progress and can automatically adjust instruction based on individual needs, reducing the manual workload for educators. AI tutors, for example, can simulate one-on-one instruction, making personalized learning scalable across diverse educational settings.

Data Privacy and Security: As personalized learning relies heavily on the collection and analysis of student data, privacy concerns are a significant challenge. Schools and educational institutions often gather sensitive information, including academic performance, behavior patterns, and learning preferences, which can be vulnerable to breaches or misuse (Williamson, 2020). Ensuring the secure handling and protection of student data is critical to the ethical implementation of personalized education.

Solution: Data encryption, anonymization, and robust data governance policies are essential to protecting student privacy. Furthermore, transparent communication with students and parents about what data is being collected and how it will be used helps build trust (West, 2019). Additionally, educators should advocate for policies that ensure data security and comply with international standards such as the General Data Protection Regulation (GDPR).

Equity and Access to Technology: Personalization often depends on access to digital tools and high-speed internet, which can be a barrier for students in low-income or rural areas. This digital divide can exacerbate educational inequalities, with students from under-resourced schools missing out on the benefits of personalized learning technologies (Pane et al., 2017).

Solution: To bridge this gap, governments and educational institutions must invest in infrastructure that ensures equitable access to technology. Public–private partnerships can play a role in providing affordable devices and internet access to underserved communities. In addition, schools can implement hybrid learning models that blend low-tech and high-tech approaches to accommodate students with varying levels of access.

Teacher Training and Preparedness: Many teachers may lack the necessary training and skills to effectively implement personalized learning approaches. Personalized education requires a shift from traditional teaching methods to more flexible, student-centered practices, and teachers need to be equipped with both the pedagogical and technical knowledge to do this.

Solution: Ongoing professional development is crucial to ensure that educators are prepared to utilize personalized learning technologies. Training programs should focus not only on how to use digital tools but also on how to interpret data and adapt instruction to meet individual needs. Peer collaboration and support networks can further enhance teachers' ability to transition to personalized learning (Siemens, 2018). The challenges of implementing personalized learning in education, such as scalability, data privacy, equity, and teacher preparedness, are significant but solvable. By leveraging adaptive technologies, strengthening data governance, promoting equitable access to digital tools, and providing comprehensive teacher training, educational systems can create more personalized and effective learning environments. These solutions are crucial to unlocking the potential of personalized learning and ensuring that it benefits all students, regardless of their background or location.

10.4 Artificial Intelligence and Machine Learning in Personalized Learning

AI and ML are at the forefront of personalized learning as shown in Figure 10.1. These technologies enable the analysis of vast amounts of data to identify patterns in student performance, learning behaviors, and engagement levels. By understanding these patterns, AI-powered platforms can provide customized recommendations for learning materials, instructional approaches, and assessments tailored to individual students.

AI-powered tutoring systems, such as Carnegie Learning's MATHia, use algorithms to offer real-time feedback, helping students strengthen areas of weakness while progressing at their own pace. Similarly, intelligent virtual assistants can monitor students' progress, answer questions, and provide hints, making learning more interactive and adaptive (Chen et al., 2020).

One notable AI application is adaptive learning platforms. These platforms continuously adjust the learning experience based on a student's performance. For example, DreamBox Learning, an adaptive math platform, analyzes over 48,000 data points per hour per student to create personalized learning pathways. Such systems not only adapt the difficulty of questions but also modify the presentation of information to match a student's preferred

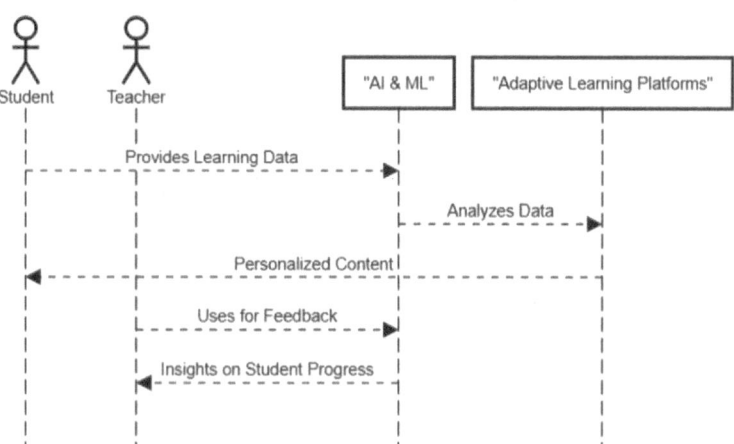

Figure 10.1 Artificial Intelligence and Machine Learning in Personalized Learning.

learning style. Adaptive learning systems use ML algorithms to personalize the learning experience by adjusting the content, pace, and assessments according to individual student performance. These systems dynamically respond to a student's strengths and weaknesses by offering customized learning pathways, which can include varied instructional strategies and assessments (Chaudhry & Kazim, 2021).

10.4.1 Challenges in AI and ML for Personalized Learning

Data Quality and Availability: AI and ML systems for personalized learning rely heavily on large datasets to train algorithms. However, many educational institutions struggle with poor data quality or insufficient data. Inaccurate or incomplete data can lead to ineffective learning models that fail to personalize effectively (Siemens, 2018). Furthermore, there may be a lack of standardized data formats across schools and platforms, complicating data sharing and use.

Solution: To address this challenge, educational institutions must invest in better data collection and management practices. Implementing standardized data formats and ensuring consistent data entry can enhance data quality. Additionally, partnerships between institutions and tech providers can facilitate access to larger datasets, improving the performance of AI/ML models. Regular audits and cleaning of data will further improve the effectiveness of personalized learning systems (West, 2019).

Bias in AI Algorithms: AI algorithms are only as unbiased as the data they are trained on. If the data used to train AI models contains historical biases, these biases may be reflected in the personalized learning outcomes, potentially disadvantaging certain student groups (Holmes et al., 2019). For example, if AI models are trained on data that underrepresents students from low-income backgrounds, these students may receive less accurate recommendations and support.

Solution: Mitigating bias requires careful attention to the data used for training AI models. AI developers must conduct bias audits to identify and correct any imbalances in the dataset. Additionally, using fairness algorithms to ensure that the recommendations and assessments generated by AI are equitable can help reduce the impact of bias (Chen et al., 2020). Diversifying the data sources used to train AI models is another crucial step to promote fairness in personalized learning.

Teacher Training and AI Integration: The integration of AI and ML into personalized learning presents a challenge for teachers who may not be familiar with these technologies. Many educators lack the technical skills to understand how AI systems function, and they may not be trained to effectively interpret the data produced by these systems to inform their instruction (McCarthy et al., 2020). Without proper training, teachers may struggle to integrate AI tools into their teaching practice.

Solution: Providing teachers with professional development opportunities focused on AI and data literacy is essential. Training programs should not only cover the technical aspects of AI tools but also focus on how to use data from AI systems to personalize learning for students. Collaborative training environments, where teachers can work with data scientists and AI experts, can further enhance their ability to use AI tools effectively in the classroom (Swargiary, 2023).

Ethical Concerns in AI Use: The use of AI in personalized learning raises several ethical concerns, including data privacy, transparency, and the potential for over-reliance on AI systems. AI systems often operate as "black boxes," where their decision-making processes are not transparent to users, which can be problematic in educational contexts (Williamson, 2020). Moreover, the use of AI to make decisions about student progress may raise concerns about the role of human judgment in education.

Solution: Ethical AI use in education requires transparency in how AI models make decisions and the implementation of robust data protection measures. Educational institutions must adopt clear policies regarding AI use, including data governance frameworks that ensure the protection of student information (Gikandi, 2019). Additionally, AI should be used as a tool to support, rather than replace, human decision-making in education. Teachers should remain at the center of the learning process, using AI as a supplement to their expertise. The integration of AI and ML into personalized learning faces challenges such as data quality, bias in algorithms, teacher preparedness, and ethical concerns. However, solutions like improving data management practices, conducting bias audits, providing teacher training, and establishing ethical guidelines can help address these issues. By tackling these challenges, AI and ML can play a pivotal role in enhancing personalized learning, leading to more effective and equitable educational outcomes for students.

10.5 Big Data and Analytics in Personalized Learning

Big data analytics is revolutionizing the way educators understand and address students' learning needs. By collecting and analyzing data on student interactions, assignments, quizzes, and even engagement metrics such as time spent on tasks, educators can gain insights into each student's learning journey. These insights can inform decisions about curriculum adjustments, interventions, and individualized instruction (Siemens, 2018).

Learning analytics dashboards offer teachers real-time visualizations of student progress, enabling more timely and effective interventions. For example, platforms like BrightBytes and Classcraft provide teachers with data-driven insights into student performance and engagement. Teachers can use this data to modify instruction, assign additional resources, or schedule one-on-one meetings with students who may need extra support.

Predictive analytics takes data-driven education a step further. By analyzing historical data, predictive models can identify students at risk of falling behind or dropping out. This allows for early intervention, improving student retention and success rates. For example, Georgia State University implemented an AI-driven advising system that uses predictive analytics to increase student retention by offering targeted support to at-risk students (Renugadevi et al., 2024).

10.5.1 Adaptive Assessments

Assessments play a critical role in education, but traditional tests often fall short in providing a full picture of a student's abilities. Adaptive assessments, powered by AI and ML, are designed to dynamically adjust the difficulty of questions based on the student's performance. This ensures that each student is challenged at an appropriate level, providing a more accurate measure of their knowledge and skills (Gikandi, 2019).

Computerized adaptive testing (CAT) system is one such innovation. Instead of presenting a fixed set of questions, CAT selects questions in real time based on the student's previous answers. If a student answers a question correctly, the system offers a more challenging one. Conversely, incorrect answers result in easier questions. This type of assessment allows for more precise measurement of a student's abilities in less time than traditional tests (Desmarais & Baker, 2012).

Adaptive assessments also offer the advantage of immediate feedback, which is essential for personalized learning. Instant feedback allows students to reflect on their mistakes and correct their misunderstandings in real time, rather than waiting for test results days later (Gikandi, 2019). Tools like Knewton and ALEKS offer these adaptive assessment features, enabling continuous learning and improvement. Learning analytics refers to the measurement, collection, analysis, and reporting of data about learners and their contexts, to understand and optimize learning and the environments in which it occurs. In personalized learning, learning analytics plays a crucial role in providing real-time insights into student progress, identifying at-risk students, and enabling data-driven decision-making for tailored instruction.

10.5.2 *Challenges in Big Data and Analytics for Personalized Learning*

Data Overload and Interpretation: Big data in education generates vast amounts of information, but one of the major challenges is managing and interpreting this data effectively. Educators may struggle to make sense of the sheer volume of data, leading to difficulties in using the insights for personalized learning (Siemens, 2018). Unstructured and heterogeneous data from multiple sources such as learning management systems (LMSs), student assessments, and behavior tracking further complicate the process.

Solution: The use of advanced analytics tools and AI can help process large datasets and identify key patterns. Educational data mining and learning analytics platforms can be leveraged to automate the analysis process, turning raw data into actionable insights. Training educators and administrators in data literacy is also essential to ensure they can interpret analytics correctly and apply them in the learning environment (West, 2019).

Privacy and Data Security: The collection and use of big data in personalized learning raise significant privacy and security concerns. Educational institutions often collect sensitive student data, including personal identifiers, academic performance, and behavioral records. Ensuring the protection of this data from breaches, unauthorized access, and misuse is a critical challenge (Williamson, 2020). Moreover, students and parents may be apprehensive about how their data is being collected, stored, and used.

Solution: To address privacy and security concerns, schools and educational institutions must implement stringent data governance frameworks. This includes anonymizing student data, using secure storage systems, and adhering to data protection regulations like GDPR. Transparency in data usage policies and obtaining informed consent from students and parents can further enhance trust and compliance (West, 2019).

Data Integration Across Systems: Big data often comes from multiple sources—LMSs, classroom sensors, student assessments, and online platforms—leading to issues with data integration. Different systems may store data in incompatible formats, making it difficult to aggregate and analyze effectively (Siemens, 2018). A lack of interoperability among educational tools can limit the ability to create a unified view of student learning and hinder personalization efforts.

Solution: Implementing standards for data interoperability and encouraging the use of open educational resources (OER) can help resolve integration challenges. Schools and educational institutions should adopt systems that are compatible with common data formats and protocols such as Learning Tools Interoperability (LTI). Integrating data from different sources into a centralized data management system or learning analytics dashboard will enable educators to gain a holistic understanding of student progress (Holmes et al., 2019).

Ethical Concerns and Bias in Data Use: The use of big data in personalized learning brings ethical concerns related to algorithmic decision-making and bias. If data analytics are used to guide instructional decisions, there is a risk that biases in the data could reinforce existing inequities. For example, predictive models might disproportionately favor certain student demographics, while underestimating the potential of others. Additionally, the opaque nature of some algorithms can make it difficult for educators and students to understand how decisions are made.

Solution: Educational institutions need to implement fairness checks in their data analytics systems. Auditing algorithms for bias and ensuring diverse representation in the datasets used for training ML models are essential steps to address these issues. Additionally, involving educators and students in the design and review of analytics systems can promote transparency and trust in data-driven decision-making (Gikandi, 2019).

Lack of Data Literacy Among Educators: Many educators are not fully equipped to interpret and use the insights generated from big data analytics. The gap in data literacy can lead to underutilization of personalized learning tools, as teachers may find it difficult to translate data insights into effective instructional strategies (McCarthy et al., 2020). Without adequate support, educators may feel overwhelmed by the complexity of data analytics, limiting the potential impact of these tools on student outcomes.

Solution: Professional development programs focused on data literacy and analytics are essential to empower educators. These programs should help teachers understand how to interpret data, use learning analytics tools, and apply insights to tailor instruction to individual student needs. Collaborative approaches, where teachers can work alongside data scientists or learning specialists, can further enhance their ability to integrate analytics into their teaching (Holmes et al., 2019).

The integration of big data and analytics into personalized learning presents challenges such as data overload, privacy concerns, system integration, bias, and a lack of data literacy among educators. However, these challenges can be addressed through the implementation of advanced analytics tools, the promotion of data governance and interoperability standards, the auditing of algorithms for bias, and professional development programs that enhance educators' data literacy. By overcoming these challenges, big data and analytics can play a transformative role in enabling personalized learning that meets the needs of all students.

10.6 Gamification and Engagement in Personalized Learning

Gamification is another technological approach that enhances personalized learning. By integrating game elements such as rewards, challenges, and levels into educational content, gamification makes learning more engaging and motivating for students. Gamified platforms like Classcraft and Kahoot offer personalized learning experiences by adjusting challenges to match individual students' skill levels and preferences. Additionally, game-based assessments can provide insights into students' problem-solving skills, creativity, and critical thinking, which are often difficult to measure through traditional testing. These platforms use in-game data to adjust the difficulty of tasks and provide real-time feedback, creating a seamless integration of learning and assessment.

10.6.1 Challenges in Gamification and Engagement for Personalized Learning

Overemphasis on Extrinsic Motivation: One of the major challenges with gamification in personalized learning is the over-reliance on extrinsic motivators, such as rewards, badges, and leaderboards. While these elements can drive short-term engagement, they may fail to cultivate intrinsic motivation for learning. Students might become more focused on earning rewards than on the learning itself, which can undermine long-term engagement and knowledge retention.

Solution: To address this challenge, a balanced approach to gamification is necessary. Integrating elements that foster intrinsic motivation, such as meaningful choices, self-paced learning, and opportunities for mastery, can help sustain engagement beyond external rewards. The key is to design gamified experiences that connect the learning content with the students' personal goals and interests, thereby making the learning process itself rewarding (Dichev & Dicheva, 2017). Gamification involves applying game design elements such as points, badges, challenges, and leaderboards to non-game contexts, like education, to increase engagement and motivation. In personalized learning, gamification enhances student engagement by offering a more interactive and rewarding learning experience. Personalized gamification adapts the game mechanics to individual learners' preferences, providing them with a tailored learning path that aligns with their progress and interests (Zhao & Deterding, 2023).

One-Size-Fits-All Gamification: Gamification strategies are often implemented in a generalized manner, without considering individual differences in students' learning styles, preferences, and motivations. A one-size-fits-all gamified experience may engage some students while alienating others, especially those who are not naturally competitive or who do not respond well to certain types of rewards. This can result in disengagement for a subset of learners who feel disconnected from the gamified learning process.

Solution: Personalized gamification can address this issue by tailoring game elements to individual students. For example, adaptive systems can customize challenges, rewards, and game dynamics based on the learner's progress, preferences, and needs. Incorporating flexibility in how students interact with the gamified environment allows them to choose the type of rewards they want to earn and the pace at which they wish to progress.

Difficulty in Balancing Educational Content and Game Mechanics: One of the significant challenges in gamification is finding the right balance between engaging game mechanics and meaningful educational content. Too much emphasis on game-like elements can distract from the learning objectives, while a lack of engaging mechanics can make the gamified experience feel superficial and unmotivating. Striking a balance between learning and engagement is particularly challenging when trying to maintain students' focus on academic achievement.

Solution: The solution lies in careful instructional design, where educational content is seamlessly integrated into game mechanics. Game-based learning frameworks such as "serious games" or "educational games" can be used to ensure that the learning objectives remain central to the experience. By making the game mechanics and learning outcomes interdependent—where progress in the game reflects mastery of the subject matter—educators can ensure that gamification enhances, rather than detracts from, the learning process (Plass et al., 2015).

Sustainability of Engagement: Another challenge with gamification is maintaining long-term engagement. While gamified systems may initially capture students' attention, the novelty of game elements such as points and badges can wear off over time, leading to reduced motivation and participation (Rapp et al., 2019). If students no longer find the game mechanics rewarding, their engagement with the learning material may decrease.

Solution: Sustaining engagement in gamified learning environments requires regularly updating and evolving the game elements. By introducing new challenges, increasing levels of difficulty, and offering personalized pathways based on student performance, educators can keep the experience fresh and engaging. Additionally, incorporating social elements, such as collaborative learning and peer competition, can help maintain motivation over the long term (González et al., 2014).

Technical and Resource Constraints: Implementing gamification in personalized learning often requires sophisticated technological infrastructure and resources that many educational institutions may not have. Developing custom gamified learning environments, integrating them with LMSs, and ensuring they work seamlessly across different platforms and devices can be resource-intensive. Budget constraints, lack of expertise, and limited access to technology can hinder the successful adoption of gamification in education.

Solution: A potential solution to technical and resource constraints is to use readily available gamification platforms and tools that can be easily integrated into existing learning systems. Open-source gamification plugins for popular LMSs like Moodle or Canvas can offer cost-effective solutions for schools and educators. Additionally, partnering with educational technology providers or leveraging government grants for educational innovation can help institutions access the necessary resources.

Gamification has the potential to enhance engagement and personalize learning, but challenges such as overemphasis on extrinsic motivation, one-size-fits-all approaches, balancing game mechanics with educational content, sustaining engagement, and technical constraints need to be addressed. Solutions like personalized gamification, careful instructional design, evolving game elements, and leveraging existing technological tools can help maximize the benefits of gamification in personalized learning, creating more engaging and effective educational experiences for students.

10.7 Future Directions and Challenges

While the benefits of personalized learning and assessment technologies are evident, several challenges remain. Data privacy and security are critical concerns, as the collection of large volumes of student data can potentially be misused if not handled properly. Ensuring equity in access to these technologies is also essential, as students from under-resourced schools may not have the same opportunities to benefit from personalized learning tools.

Nevertheless, the future of education is undoubtedly moving toward greater personalization. As AI, big data, and adaptive technologies continue to evolve, educators will have even more powerful tools to tailor learning and assessment to meet the diverse needs of all students.

10.8 Future Directions

Adaptive Learning Systems: One of the most promising future directions in personalized learning is the development and integration of more sophisticated adaptive learning systems. These systems use ML algorithms to dynamically adjust the learning content, pace, and assessment based on the real-time performance of each student. As adaptive technologies evolve, they will become more precise in predicting student needs and offering personalized pathways that optimize learning outcomes.

Future iterations of adaptive learning platforms may leverage AI to continuously learn from student data and make decisions about the best instructional strategies. This could lead to even more personalized learning experiences that are tailored not only to academic performance but also to the emotional and cognitive states of learners.

AI-Powered Assessment: In addition to adaptive learning, AI-powered assessment systems are becoming a major focus for future research and development. These systems have the potential to move beyond traditional exams and quizzes by offering more personalized assessments that align with the learner's individual progress and needs. They can provide real-time feedback and insights, allowing students to learn from their mistakes immediately and adjust their learning strategies (Holmes et al., 2019). AI-based assessment can also reduce bias in grading, ensure consistency, and assess complex skills like critical thinking and creativity through advanced data analysis methods. As AI assessment tools improve, they will become more integral to personalized learning environments.

Gamification with Advanced Data Analytics: The combination of gamification with advanced data analytics will likely shape the future of personalized learning. Gamification, when personalized through AI and data-driven insights, can create highly engaging learning environments that adapt to student preferences and learning styles. By analyzing real-time data on student interactions with the gamified system, educators can fine-tune game elements to maximize engagement and learning outcomes (Deterding, 2019). In the future, gamification could evolve to include more immersive elements such as virtual reality (VR) and augmented reality (AR), creating even more interactive and personalized learning experiences. These environments can simulate real-world challenges, offering students opportunities for practical application and personalized feedback in a virtual space (Williamson, 2020).

Data-Driven Personalization: Big data analytics will continue to play a crucial role in personalizing both learning and assessment. As the collection of educational data becomes more sophisticated, educators and institutions will be able to make data-driven decisions that personalize learning at scale. Future systems will use predictive analytics to identify students who are at risk of falling behind and offer timely interventions (Siemens, 2018). Moreover, learning analytics will help educators better understand the learning behaviors of individual students, enabling them to offer more personalized feedback and design instructional strategies that cater to the diverse needs of learners. This data-driven approach will transform how assessments are structured, providing students with more personalized and formative feedback.

Equitable Access to Personalized Learning Technologies: As personalized learning technologies advance, a major future direction will be ensuring equitable access to these tools. Currently, access to cutting-edge personalized learning technologies is often limited by geographical, economic, and technological factors. In the future, efforts must focus on addressing these disparities to ensure that all students, regardless of their background, can benefit from personalized learning opportunities. Developing low-cost, scalable solutions for adaptive learning and AI-powered assessment, particularly in underserved regions, will be a priority. Policy interventions, funding initiatives, and partnerships with technology providers can help close the digital divide, making personalized learning technologies more accessible to all students.

10.8.1 Challenges

Ethical Concerns and Data Privacy: One of the biggest challenges in implementing personalized learning technologies is ensuring the privacy and security of student data. As AI, big data, and adaptive learning systems collect and analyze more personal information about students, there are growing concerns about how this data is used, stored, and protected (Williamson, 2020). Ensuring compliance with privacy laws such as the General Data Protection Regulation (GDPR) and the Family Educational Rights and Privacy Act (FERPA) is essential, but balancing personalization with privacy remains a challenge.

Solution: Implementing strict data governance policies and utilizing secure, anonymized data can mitigate privacy risks. Additionally, transparency in data collection and giving students and parents control over their data will be critical for maintaining trust in these technologies.

Teacher Training and Resistance to Change: While personalized learning technologies offer significant advantages, a major challenge is ensuring that educators are properly trained to use these tools effectively. Teachers may resist adopting new technologies due to a lack of training or fear that they will lose control over the teaching process (McCarthy et al., 2020). Personalized learning requires a shift in pedagogy, and educators need support to integrate these technologies into their teaching practices.

Solution: Professional development programs focused on personalized learning technologies are essential. Providing ongoing training and creating collaborative communities where teachers can share best practices will help ease the transition to tech-enhanced personalized learning.

Ensuring Inclusivity in AI Algorithms: AI algorithms used in personalized learning have the potential to perpetuate bias if they are not carefully designed and tested. For example, if an algorithm is trained on a biased dataset, it may reinforce inequities in learning by favoring certain groups of students over others. This challenge is particularly pressing as more personalized learning tools rely on AI to tailor educational experiences.

Solution: To ensure inclusivity, it is crucial to audit AI algorithms for bias and ensure that datasets are diverse and representative of all student populations. Moreover, involving educators, ethicists, and policymakers in the design and implementation of these technologies will help prevent biases from being encoded into the systems.

Scalability of Personalized Learning Solutions: Personalized learning technologies, particularly adaptive learning systems and AI-based assessment tools, require substantial investments in infrastructure, software, and support services. Scaling these solutions to reach all students across different educational contexts presents a significant challenge, especially in regions with limited resources (West, 2019).

Solution: Open-source platforms and cloud-based solutions can help scale personalized learning technologies more efficiently. Partnerships between educational institutions, governments, and technology-providers will be key to ensuring that personalized learning tools are scalable, affordable, and sustainable in the long term. The future of personalized learning and assessment lies in the development of adaptive learning systems, AI-powered assessments, gamification, and data-driven personalization. However, challenges such as ethical concerns, teacher training, inclusivity in AI algorithms, and scalability must be addressed to unlock the full potential of these technologies. By overcoming these hurdles, personalized learning can transform education, providing more equitable and engaging learning experiences for all students.

10.9 Conclusion

Unlocking students' potential through personalized learning and assessment with cutting-edge technologies represents a significant shift in education. AI, ML, big data analytics, and adaptive platforms enable a more individualized approach to education, ensuring that every learner receives the support, content, and assessments that are most beneficial for their development. These technologies provide real-time feedback, adapt to learners' needs, and offer tailored resources that address specific areas of improvement. Moreover, the integration of sophisticated algorithms helps in identifying learning patterns and predicting future challenges, allowing educators to intervene proactively. Personalized learning environments foster a deeper engagement by aligning educational materials with each student's unique interests and strengths. The use of data-driven insights further enhances instructional strategies, making learning experiences more relevant and impactful. While challenges remain, such as ensuring data privacy and addressing the digital divide, the ongoing advancements in technology offer exciting possibilities for a more personalized, engaging, and effective educational experience. The future of education holds the promise of a more inclusive and equitable system where technology bridges gaps and supports every learner's journey. As these technologies evolve, they will continue to transform how we approach teaching and learning, making education more adaptable and responsive to the needs of each individual student.

References

Chaudhry, M. A., & Kazim, E. (2021). Artificial intelligence in education (AIEd): Opportunities and challenges. In K. Watanabe & C. Holmes (Eds.), *Artificial Intelligence and Emerging Technologies in Education* (pp. 105–128). Springer. 10.1016/j.caeai.2020.100002.

Chen, X., Xie, H., Zou, D., & Hwang, G.-J. (2020). Application and theory gaps during the rise of artificial intelligence in education. *Computers and Education: Artificial Intelligence*, 1, 100002. DOI: 10.1016/j.caeai.2020.100002

Desmarais, M. C., & Baker, R. S. (2012). A review of recent advances in learner and skill modeling in intelligent learning environments. *User Modeling and User-Adapted Interaction*, 22(1), 9–38. DOI: 10.1007/s11257-011-9106-8

Deterding, S. (2019). Gamification in education: 21st-century learning or 21st-century corporate-colonialism?. In T. Reiners & L. C. Wood (Eds.), *Gamification in education and business* (pp. 101–121). Springer. DOI: 10.1007/978-3-319-10208-5_5

Dichev, C., & Dicheva, D. (2017). Gamifying education: What is known, what is believed, and what remains uncertain: A critical review. *International Journal of Educational Technology in Higher Education*, 14(9), 1–36. DOI: 10.1186/s41239-017-0042-5

Gikandi, J. W. (2019). Effective use of formative assessment and adaptive learning in higher education. *Journal of Learning Analytics*, 6(2), 1–15. DOI: 10.18608/jla.2019.62.1

González, C., Mora, A., & Toledo, P. (2014). Gamification in intelligent tutoring systems. In *Proceedings of the Second International Conference on Technological Ecosystems for Enhancing Multiculturality (TEEM'14)*. Association for Computing Machinery, New York, NY, 221–225. https://doi.org/10.1145/2669711.2669903

Holmes, W., Bialik, M., & Fadel, C. (2019). *Artificial intelligence in education: Promises and implications for teaching and learning*. Center for Curriculum Redesign. DOI: 10.13140/RG.2.2.15765.68324

McCarthy, K. S., Watanabe, M., Dai, J., & McNamara, D. S. (2020). Personalized learning in iSTART: Past modifications and future design. *Journal of Research on Technology in Education*, 52(3), 301–321. https://doi.org/10.1080/15391523.2020.1716201

Pane, J. F., Steiner, E. D., Baird, M. D., Hamilton, L. S., & Pane, J. D. (2017). *Informing progress: Insights on personalized learning implementation and effects*. RAND Corporation. DOI: 10.7249/RR2042

Plass, J. L., Homer, B. D., & Kinzer, C. K. (2015). Foundations of game-based learning. *Educational Psychologist*, 50(4), 258–283. DOI: 10.1080/00461520.2015.1122533

Rapp, A., Hopfgartner, F., Hamari, J., Linehan, C., & Cena, F. (2019). Strengthening gamification studies: Current trends and future opportunities of gamification research. *International Journal of Human-Computer Studies*, 127, 1–6. DOI: 10.1016/j.ijhcs.2018.11.007

Renugadevi, R., Ranjith Kumar P, Kalaiarasi, G, Sivabalan S, Ruthravarshini, R. (2024). *Enhancing healthcare decision support systems with advanced analytics and machine learning techniques, cybersecurity and data management innovations for revolutionizing healthcare advances in healthcare information systems and administration*, pp. 51–80, https://doi.org/10.4018/979-8-3693-7457-3.ch003

Siemens, G. (2018). Big data in education: Analytics and its implications. *Journal of Educational Data Mining*, 10(2), 15–28. DOI: 10.5281/zenodo.3554694

Swargiary, K. (2023). *Artificial intelligence in education*. Scholar's Press. ISBN: 978-620-5-52474-9. DOI: 10.5281/zenodo.8191257

West, D. M. (2019). *The role of technology in personalized learning in K-12 education*. Brookings Institution. DOI: 10.13140/RG.2.2.15182.61767

Williamson, B. (2020). Datafication and automation in education: Critical perspectives on emerging ed-tech policies and practices. *Learning, Media and Technology*, 45(3), 264–278. DOI: 10.1080/17439884.2020.1811641

Zhao, Y., & Deterding, S. (2023). The role of gamification in personalized learning environments: Motivating and engaging learners. In C. Lang & R. Baker (Eds.), *Innovations in Educational Technology* (pp. 150–178). Routledge.

Index